1295

Exhibi

EXHIBITIONS

A Key to Effective Marketing

ALFRED ALLES
DIC, Dipl Ing, CEng, MIMechE

CASSELL

Cassell Educational Limited
Artillery House,
Artillery Row,
London, SW1P 1RT

First published 1973 as *Exhibitions: Universal Marketing Tools*
This edition published 1989

British Library Cataloguing in Publication Data
Alles, Alfred
   Exhibitions: a key to effective marketing.—2nd ed.
   1. Trade exhibitions—Manuals
   I. Title
   659.1'52

ISBN 0–304–31640–7 (paperback)
     0–304–31865–5 (hardback)

Typeset by Fakenham Photosetting Limited, Fakenham, Norfolk

Printed and bound by The Camelot Press, Southampton.

To Lala

CONTENTS

Contents

FOREWORD

Almost two decades have passed since the late Franklin Colborn, then Director of the Institute of Marketing, and I set about creating what was then a unique library of books on industrial marketing to be written by practising marketing men and women. In reviewing the subjects for inclusion we quickly alighted on one area of marketing that was badly served with appropriate literature but was perhaps one of the most critical of all marketing tools—exhibitions.

There was no shortage of books of the 'how to design an exhibition stand' variety but there was nothing on the use of exhibitions within the total marketing activity. Indeed there appeared to be very little knowledge of the value of this vastly important tool and exhibitions were seen by many managers as either a 'jolly' or an unfortunate necessity because the competition was present. Moreover, such commentary as there was, was written almost entirely from the exhibitor's viewpoint. There was no guidance for visitors seeking information on goods and services on how to maximize the time invested in attending an exhibition profitably.

In deciding that this unfortunate gap in marketing literature must be filled, we turned to Alfred Alles, whose knowledge of and engagement in international exhibitions have always been an important part of his work for many major industrial firms. We wanted a wholly practical book and a wholly comprehensive one; we wanted checklists, formats, guidelines; we wanted problem identification and solutions because it was obvious that there was much to be learned both by those who claimed a knowledge of exhibitions and by those who, despite an admitted lack of knowledge, were nevertheless involved in them. We asked for a book that began with help on deciding whether to participate in or visit an exhibition at all and ended with a methodology for checking effectiveness. We got it. *Exhibitions: Universal Marketing Tools* appeared in 1973 and has remained both the seminal and the standard work on the subject. Indeed when it went out of print it became the objective of many a second-hand book 'trawl'—not as a collector's item, because that implies it was purchased for its rarity value, but for its implementive merit.

Thus the decision by Cassell to commission an update from Alfred Alles is a most welcome one. Some 20 years of further experience and the impact of new technologies have given it an added value, while the original material still remains wholly valid.

The value of exhibitions properly used is now far more widely appreciated. Nevertheless the new book is timely in every respect and makes a considerable contribution to the sum total of marketing knowledge and skill. It will be welcomed by everyone involved in marketing and particularly in exhibiting and, as importantly, by those visiting exhibitions to review products and services for their own use.

Aubrey Wilson

PREFACE

Plus ça change, plus c'est la même chose

The invitation to revise and update the author's *Exhibitions: Universal Marketing Tools* prompted a review of the changes which have occurred since its publication in 1973, both in the industrial scene generally and in the international exhibition scene particularly.

In the ominously turbulent environment of the industrial market place we observe rapid advances in international telecommunications and transportation; at the same time the issues of ecology, safety and conservation generally and of the quality of industrial products and product liability particularly are gaining more importance and sensitivity.

New sciences and technologies emerge from their theoretical and experimental stage and develop into fully fledged industries. Increasingly information is being regarded as one of the most important corporate resources. The demand for more information is growing but its quality and the skills required to make purposeful and profitable use of it present problems. Discussion of these is beyond the scope of this book, but exhibitions are excellent sources of information and the sections dealing with the now enhanced means of gathering and disseminating information, with exhibition intelligence and with visiting exhibitions remain relevant and valid.

In December 1987 the president of the Confederation of British Industry was reported to have stated, *inter alia*, that it was wrong to view 1992 from behind national blinkers for if the country was to realize many of the benefits, the British must think and act as Europeans. In 1888, 100 years ago almost to the day, Mr Gladstone stated: 'We are part of the community of Europe and we must do our duty as such.'

The prospects of an integrated European market, and of the channel tunnel, have serious implications for participating in and visiting exhibitions. The importance of exhibitions in the context of European markets, European customers and European competitors means that the most pertinent issue for British industry is the recognition by top management of the role of exhibitions in the marketing mix.

The numerical and qualitative variety of European exhibitions means that only a systematic approach to this rich source of information and opportunities can yield valuable and cost-effective results. Changes in the international exhibition scene are mostly those of proliferation and specialization and of defined market sector and even market niche orientation. In the UK the advent of new exhibition halls of varying size and quality is also accompanied by proliferation and specialization and occasionally by unjustified duplication. Exhibitors' efforts have improved both in organization and display techniques but there are still too many exhibitors who violate even the most liberally interpreted tenets of good marketing and effective exhibiting practice. It is sometimes amusing to observe exhibitors displaying the latest achievements of sophisticated communication technology but doing so on badly designed stands using primitive, obsolete and ineffective information and display methods.

Some readers of the earlier book criticized the 'excessive emphasis on language problems and translations'. However, the extensive treatment of languages and translations gains poignancy when seen in the light of perennial exhortations (even as long ago as 1906 in a *Business Blue Book*) and a more recent report* which found 'language deficiencies applying to firms all over Britain' and a correlation between effective communication in foreign languages and export performance.

Users of the book—the book was meant to be not only read but also used—remarked on the utility of the checklists, which were variously used for action, seminars, instruction courses, briefing sessions, performance analysis and as more mundane reminders of details, personal equipment and similar items.

For one user exhibitions provided the best means to demonstrate and promote the non-price competitiveness of his industrial products, and to lessen the drawbacks of adverse currency fluctuations.

The fundamental problems of education, training, responsibility and professionalism were, and still are, the subject of continuous debate and discussion. Some negative attitudes persist and rational and systematic marketing motivation for exhibiting still seems far from being the rule.

The selection and treatment of material for a book of this type inevitably reflect the background, experience, preferences and prejudices of the author. The emphasis on industrial products and industrial exhibitions is thus explained but it is also justified by the importance to the economy of the manufacturing industries and of their successful mastering of all marketing techniques.

In this new edition appearing under a new title some sections have been placed in a better functional sequence and concise sections on an exhibition audit, on the application of project management concepts to exhibiting and on training programmes have been added to the text.

---

* Hagen, S. (1988) *Languages in British Business: an Analysis of Current Needs*. Newcastle upon Tyne Polytechnic.

INTRODUCTION

Throughout the centuries markets, fairs, trade fairs and exhibitions have been the places for exchange of goods offered by a multiplicity of sellers and appraised, acquired or rejected by a multitude of buyers.

If marketing started in the market-place and exhibitions claim to be directly descended from the great markets which became great trade fairs, then it is only appropriate that exhibitions should be studied for what they are—marketing tools. According to Ezekiel, Chapter 23, at the international fair regularly held at Tyre, the following goods were offered by suppliers from twelve different countries:

    Silver, iron, bright iron, tin, lead, brass vessels.
    Coral, agate, precious stones, ivory, ebony.
    Wheat, honey, wine, cassia, calamus, spices.
    Fine linen, white wool, purple, embroidery.
    Blue clothes, precious clothes for chariots, chests of apparel.
    Slaves, horses, mules, lambs, rams, goats.

In the Middle Ages great fairs were held in towns, usually once or twice a year, and were attended by merchants from all parts of Europe. These were in fact international market-places, as distinct from local markets attended mostly by craftsmen offering their own products. Wine from the Rhine, silks and spices from the East, woollens from Flanders and armour from Lombardy were carried across Europe on trade routes crossing frontiers and connecting towns and cities.

Market laws dealing with fairs and markets came into being in the ninth century and were applied by special courts—heavy penalties were imposed for transgressions.

The markets and great fairs which in the eleventh and twelfth centuries reflected the revival of trade proliferated in the thirteenth century to such an extent that legal restrictions were imposed on their activities. The Leipzig Fair claims a foundation date of 1165 and its subsequent development from market-place to samples fair to general and industrial exhibition became a model for many followers. Frankfurt was enfranchised to become a centre of trade fairs under a royal decree of 1240.

Industrial exhibitions made their debut in the sixteenth century, when an exhibition which is regarded as the first of this kind was held in the town hall of Nuremberg in 1569.

Exhibitions of industrial arts were held in Paris in 1683 and 1763, and in Britain the Society of Arts exhibited prize-winning designs, models and machines in 1761.

In France, recovering from the aftermath of the Revolution, the commissioners of the formerly royal factories of Sèvres porcelain, Gobelin tapestries and Savonneries carpets in 1797 mounted an exhibition of these products to stimulate sales of accumulated stocks and to alleviate unemployment. During the following fifty years of the Napoleonic regime and the restoration, there was a series of industrial exhibitions, most of which showed unmistakable signs of a campaign aimed against British industry.

In other parts of Europe and in America similar industrial exhibitions were held during this period, while Britain remained somewhat aloof, although a number of local exhibitions connected with the Mechanics Institute movement took place.

Then came the Great Exhibition of 1851. It displayed to the world the achievements of British manufacturers, but it also revealed that newcomers to the international industrial scene were developing their skills with considerable speed. The International Exhibition held in Paris in 1867 and what was seen there prompted the setting up of a Commons Select Committee to enquire into the shortcomings of technical education in Britain and indirectly led to the foundation of Whitworth Scholarships.

The Crystal Palace exhibition of 1851 initiated the era of great international exhibitions and world fairs, an era which is still with us. The displays of engineering achievements seen at industrial exhibitions have contributed as much as the engineers who created them to changes in our environment, have brought about direct changes in urban developments and have influenced styles and fashions of buildings, furniture and articles of everyday use.

Following the display of Japanese buildings at the Philadelphia 1876 and San Francisco 1894 fairs, Japanese design elements made their appearance in interior house decorations and furniture. The classic-style façades of the Chicago Columbian exposition in 1893 are held responsible for generating in America the taste for pseudo-classical architecture and columned buildings.

Exhibition buildings transformed town centres and stimulated the creation of new districts. The Crystal Palace, first erected in Hyde Park, was later moved to Sydenham; the 1862 exhibition buildings erected in South Kensington were moved and re-erected at Alexandra Palace. In Paris the Trocadero of the 1878 exhibition, the Eiffel Tower (central feature of the 1889 exhibition), the Grand Palais, Petit Palais and Alexander III bridge of the 1900 exhibition are all still in use. Permanent buildings erected for the Brussels 1953 exhibition were later used for the annual Brussels Trade Fair.

The 1951 Festival of Britain and the Brussels 1958, Montreal 1967 and Osaka 1970 world fairs all made their mark and left behind some of their buildings and their influences. The motorways serving the Hanover Fair and its complex of exhibition buildings and those of Düsseldorf, Frankfurt, Paris, Turin and many others are all witness to the exhibition activities which continue unabated all over the world.

The Essence and Substance of Industrial Exhibitions

Industrial exhibitions, or rather exhibitions serving industrial markets, suffered for a long time, and still do, from a misunderstanding and misinterpretation of their purpose and of their capability.

A great many of these misconceptions, both pronounced *ex cathedra* and published in textbooks, stray down one common line of thought: they confuse activities with objectives. They deal in great detail with exhibition stand functions or activities but fail to embrace the concept of a total exhibition effort. Thus, according to one definition, exhibitions are 'just another form of sales promotion' and another definition states that exhibitions are 'three-dimensional advertisements'.

It is true that for industrial products one could hardly find a better sales promotion medium. As for the latter definition, it will be asserted later in this study that ineffective use of an exhibition effort reduces it to being no more than a three-dimensional advertisement, which is an irresponsible and wasteful misuse of resources and opportunities. However, one could argue that even as a three-dimensional advertisement an exhibition can do more than any other medium.

Most industrial objects can be shown in their actual size and shape, if they make a noise it can be heard, they can be touched and, if not too heavy, lifted, they can move under their own power, they can be taken to pieces and re-assembled, they can be operated, demonstrated, tested to destruction, they can have almost anything done with and to them. In offering all that the exhibition must be a good advertising medium.

No definitions of general concepts have ever been proposed without generating modifications, additions, paraphrases, shortened and expanded versions, dogmatic distinctions and occasional accusations of being irrelevant or even absurd.

Many definitions of marketing have been made by economists, academics, industrialists, sociologists and marketing practitioners. They range from the narrow, product-oriented and somewhat disparaging definition that 'marketing is a sort of sophisticated selling' concerned solely with stimulating demand, through the broader definition that 'marketing is the management process responsible for identifying, anticipating and satisfying customer requirements profitably', to the pontifical one that 'marketing is an all-embracing system with technical and social functions aiming at ensuring a profitable life and growth of businesses'. The most convincing is the invocation that 'marketing should be a dynamic, creative activity aiming at satisfying the needs and expectations of customers'.

Whatever its definition, the aim and ultimate purpose of the marketing function establishes it legitimately as a top management responsibility. If it is accepted that economic viability and development are a cardinal corporate goal, then the effective mastering of marketing is not only a prerequisite to achieving that goal but also a measure of management performance. The effective mastering of marketing requires the use of the best available techniques and tools. It is the aim of this study to demonstrate that:

> for the overwhelming majority of industrial markets, exhibitions are excellent, versatile and essential marketing tools;

> the systematic and disciplined use of exhibitions can bring very high marketing benefits and rewards.

One of the assertions of this study is that, despite perennial exhortations, reports and critical appraisals, many exhibition activities are planned and/or carried out without an effective application of marketing precepts. Exhibition organizers, exhibitors and visitors alike can be found in the ranks of sometimes inveterate sinners.

Many years of experience and the continuous observation of ineffectual exhibition efforts and of indifferent and negative attitudes to exhibitions lead one to the conclusion that there can be only two reasons for such a state of affairs. Either a very large number of firms engaged in the marketing of industrial goods misunderstand or fail to appreciate the value and use of *exhibitions as marketing tools*, or it is not the tool which is misunderstood but the *concept of marketing*. This study suggests that for all exhibition activities marketing motives should be the moving spirit and the basis for decisions.

We live in an era of substantial changes in the concepts and structures of sciences, technologies, industries and markets and of concomitant openings and closures of marketing opportunities. Depending on who you are and what you do, these changes can be auspicious or threatening, modest or radical, but in any case they require a fast response by dynamic and creative market initiatives. In this context international exhibitions play an important role: they provide an eminently suitable marketing platform for entry into changed or new markets and a rich source of crucial information about the pattern of changes, innovations and new concepts.

At exhibitions, apart from orthodox marketing functions such as sales operations, sales promotions, all forms of publicity and public relations, market and product intelligence can be gathered, sources of supply can be located and the efforts of the competition can be surveyed. You can display new or improved capabilities and services or you can observe your competitors doing just that. Invitations to apply for agency and distributorship arrangements can be displayed. A competent and impressive exhibition effort can act as an oblique, perhaps even unintended, personnel recruitment drive. A fairly recent development is the mounting of special personnel-recruiting exhibitions.

An exhibition can be used as a laboratory for the observation of marketing behaviour, of manifestations of talents, of techniques, of establishment of rapport, of conflict-creating behaviour. These observations can be made on your stand and on other stands, and valuable insights can be gained into conditions and situations which cannot be expected to be observed in the field and are rarely reported on.

Exhibitions are also very good observation posts for the study of more abstruse phenomena: group behaviour in special situations, reactions to extraneous conditions of rain, sleet, cold or heat and their influence on changing intentions to visit indoor stands or outdoor areas and vice versa; different types of stance adopted by stand personnel towards different types of visitors; the influence of the time of day on length of visits to stands.

This study examines the range of opportunities that all exhibitions should, and many do, offer to prospective exhibitors and visitors and reviews the miscellany of ordinary, and some not so ordinary, marketing activities which can be carried out at exhibitions.

The Proliferation of Exhibitions

The proliferation of exhibitions is an international phenomenon noticeable particularly at the two ends of the size range of exhibitions. At one end many small, often short-lived, exhibitions appear on the scene, indistinguishable from each other except by their location and slight differences in their small-minded ambitions. At the other end large exhibition enterprises erect bigger, better and more magnificent exhibition halls and compete fiercely for top place in the international exhibition world and for the patronage of long-contract exhibitors.

The proliferation of exhibitions puts a great premium on any systematic approach to selection and participation. Exhibitions have become very big business, graduating from being a marketing medium for other industries to being an important industry providing a marketable service. Some exhibition enterprises clearly display their acceptance and practice of marketing concepts, others sell their exhibitions as patent medicines were once sold, wrapped in alluring promises of colossal success if partaken of and dire results if rejected.

In fact the reverse often occurs and dire results come from taking the medicine. This surfeit of exhibitions creates a general aura of perplexity before the event and of disillusionment after it which unfortunately affects attitudes to other excellent and important exhibitions, both large and small, which serve a specific marketing purpose and serve it well. Some new small and medium-sized specialist exhibitions are carefully aimed at selected market sectors, perhaps even specific niche markets. Others only duplicate an already existing event which proved to be successful and the marketing myopia of such ventures is usually shown up by postponements and cancellations.

The trends towards decentralization and deurbanization of production made possible by new technologies and the emergence of regional industrial clusters have also contributed to the proliferation of exhibitions serving specific product groupings or market segments or geographical areas.

The Internationalization of Industrial Exhibitions

The conceptual separation of home and export markets based on selling as an end function and on a geographical territory as a market area, when applied to industrial markets was a misconception even before the advent of marketing as a management philosophy.

It emphasized the differences between the two markets as if each domestic national market was one homogenous unit which must be compared with another, foreign, homogenous national unit. Analysts who took great pains to examine, dissect and classify the various sectors of the domestic market retreated into generalizations and summary treatment of foreign markets. It is only recently that the similarities of market sectors at home and in foreign countries have been recognized as more significant, from a marketing point of view, than the differences which they obviously show by being located in different national environments. Inevitably the same home—export discrimination was applied to exhibitions. The difficulties to be overcome when exhibiting abroad were mostly explained in terms of deviations from established home practice with an implied assumption of the supremacy of that home practice.

When marketing became recognized as a concept with selling as one of its functions and when, in parallel, exporting became a function of international marketing, exhibitors and visitors looked up and noticed that international exhibitions in their domestic market showed marked affinities to similar exhibitions in other countries. The standards of stand design, types of visitors and methods of display were similar in their general aspects, although there were differences in approach as a result of national characteristics and marked differences in favour of exhibitions abroad in such aspects as quality of exhibitors and visitors, organization and administration, and facilities for exhibitors, visitors and the media.

Many British manufacturers participate in exhibitions abroad, but a very large number of medium and small companies do not. It is immaterial for the end result whether the abstention from international exhibitions is based on rational arguments of lack of material or human resources, is a matter of vague feelings that not much would be gained by participation and visits or is based simply on inertia and a 'we know best' attitude. The fact is that the competitors of these firms can visit such international exhibitions in their own countries and in great numbers do so. The fact that arrangements for a visit to Paris, Brussels or Amsterdam can be made as simply and quickly as for a visit within the United Kingdom is not always appreciated by those who still consider exports as a 'foreign' activity.

It is a matter for speculation (and it could be a subject for a research study) to what extent the absence of truly international industrial exhibitions in Britain during the pre-war and immediate post-war years deprived British technicians of the impact and stimulus of competitive designs and technical developments and to what extent the

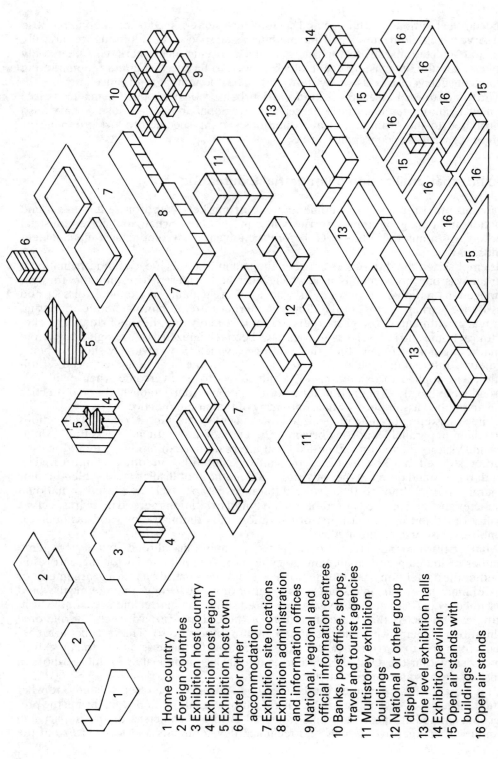

1 Home country
2 Foreign countries
3 Exhibition host country
4 Exhibition host region
5 Exhibition host town
6 Hotel or other
  accommodation
7 Exhibition site locations
8 Exhibition administration
  and information offices
9 National, regional and
  official information centres
10 Banks, post office, shops,
  travel and tourist agencies
11 Multistorey exhibition
  buildings
12 National or other group
  display
13 One level exhibition halls
14 Exhibition pavilion
15 Open air stands with
  buildings
16 Open air stands

FIGURE 1. TOPOGRAPHY OF AN EXHIBITION

prolific growth of the main European exhibitions contributed to the more successful performance of many European industrial products.

The development of international communications and transportation has led to an increase in cultural and social exchanges, has made many markets more accessible and has increased competition in these more accessible markets. Many industrial products now move through several industrial markets and national frontiers before emerging incorporated in a complete industrial product. Changes in the structure of national markets, such as the dismantling of barriers between members of the European Community and the harmonization of European standards, have important implications for the formation of European marketing strategies. The closeness of exhibitions to markets, customers and competitors makes them a prime source of information and an excellent platform for marketing initiatives, both so vital in the context of these changes.

The complexity of international or multi-market activities and the difficulty of reconciling the variety of available exhibitions with marketing strategies often baffle those charged with the task. Some managements allot computer programs and time to the solution of problems with a claim for attention subsequently justified more by the sheer volume of the print-out than by the solutions generated. The same managements react with surprised disbelief when requests are made for computer help in the solution of problems of exhibitions, of selection, of participation.

The Marketing Mission of Industrial Exhibitions

This study is concerned with industrial exhibitions, and therefore by inference with the marketing of industrial products, both terms, i.e. 'industrial' and 'products', being used in their widest senses. If we look at the vast array of relevant industries we invariably find that some form of engineering is involved in their activities. In most industries several kinds of engineering operate in active partnership, such as mechanical and

GLOSSARY TO FIGURE 1

1. *Home country* is the country of residence of the exhibitor or visitor to the exhibition or the country in which the headquarters of an exhibitor's or visitor's organization is located. The distance of the home country from the exhibition host country and the available travel and transport facilities will influence the time and cost factors involved in exhibiting or visiting.
2. *Foreign country* is any country outside the exhibitor's or visitor's home country and outside the exhibition host country. The location of a foreign country in relation to the home country and to the exhibition host country and its marketing merits for the exhibitor or visitor may influence the decision to combine exhibition activities with visits to a foreign country.
3. *Exhibition host country* is the country in which the exhibition is held.
4. *Exhibition host region* is a region of the exhibition host country in which the exhibition is held and with identifiable market characteristics or marketing merits.
5. *Exhibition host town* is the town or city in which the exhibition is held. The town or city may have its own general marketing merits, e.g. a capital city, a commercial centre or an industrial centre; on the other hand it may have no other marketing merit than being a host to the exhibition.
6. *Hotel* or other accommodation is the location of available hotel or other accommodation in relation to the exhibition site. The quality of the available facilities can be an important time, transport and fatigue factor as well as a cost factor, particularly where such accommodation is only available at a distance from the exhibition site.
7. *Exhibition site locations* are exhibition halls or display areas which can be dispersed over more than one location; the distances between these locations and the available transport and travel facilities can be a serious time and fatigue factor.
8–16. *Exhibition halls and display areas*: these can vary in scope, size and quality and can only be assessed individually for each exhibition.

electrical, chemical and civil, electronic and pneumatic, or in other more complex and involved interrelations. Engineering enters industries in their embryonic stage when they emerge from the phase of scientific or inventive concepts, it then has an all-pervading presence in the manufacturing stage and is still with them in the shape of operational, maintenance and service activities when the products of industries are in the hands of customers and users.

Engineering is therefore deeply involved in the industrial marketing system and so are engineers, irrespective of whether they are aware of the involvement in a marketing sense or not. If industrial marketing is to succeed in its task, if its efforts are to produce the right response in the market, it is just as important for those practising marketing to know about engineering and engineers as it is for engineers to understand marketing and those practising it, and for both parties it is imperative that they should continue to enlarge their mutual understanding with open minds.

The marketing capabilities of industrial exhibitions serve the great range of industrial products, from miniature components to giant structures and machines; they also serve scientific disciplines and technologies. They were and still are the showrooms for new developments, new services and new concepts. They enable, develop and on occasions restore contacts between people with different national, social, educational or professional backgrounds.

At an exhibition the exhibitor is the host, the visitor is the guest; this is a sufficient first qualification. One may become a seller and the other a buyer; that is why most of them came to the exhibition. Exhibitions serve small firms and large ones and it is not always the large ones that secure the best results. These are the opportunities. There are also problems, mostly of uncertainty. But uncertainty need not inhibit initiative and planning. If you exhibit you aim at exposure; if you exhibit efficiently you can achieve maximum exposure. Under certain circumstances you may prefer optimum exposure instead.

This book aims to contribute to a better understanding of the marketing missions of exhibitions, of the opportunities offered and of the motivation and decision-making process which should govern participation in and visiting of exhibitions. It is an appeal to marketing executives to apply to exhibition activities the professionalism applied to any other essential marketing activity.

The mastering of exhibition efforts is neither a science nor an art but rather a practice, which to be effective must be a disciplined practice in which both science and art can, and should, play their part. Nevertheless, the practice of exhibiting, while using the best techniques available, should be neither a dogmatic application of a set of rules nor a surrender of decision-making to the tyranny of a computer print-out. Reliable information, logic, experience and intuition all have their place in the decision-making process and perhaps the most difficult problem is deciding how to decide.

Exhibitions are, above all else, meeting places for people, be they buyers, sellers, observers or seekers of information. People and their attitudes, their training, their experience but also their prejudices, preconceived ideas and social behaviour will decide the success or failure of an exhibition effort.

Summaries of Parts

Part One deals with the structure of exhibitions and provides a basis for the review, in following sections, of exhibition activities. Any prospective exhibitor or visitor of exhibitions has to consider most of the structure elements of an exhibition before deciding on participating in it or visiting it.

The different categories of exhibitions, their aims and titles are reviewed. The importance of the location of exhibitions, the implications of the time elements and the significance of the historical progress of exhibitions are reviewed.

The roles of exhibition organizers, promoters and sponsors are examined and the importance of the exhibition administration and of the services and facilities provided is discussed.

Finally the role of the exhibition catalogue as a guide to the exhibition and as a reference book or directory is examined, and the question of entries in catalogues of international exhibitions is discussed. The implications of computer information and stand location devices are probed.

Part Two deals with the issues and problems encountered between the pillar of the intention to exhibit and the post of participating in an exhibition. Observed attitudes to exhibitions, which seem to persist over the years, are reviewed. Principal and subsidiary, ordinary and not so ordinary marketing motives are examined as a guide to selecting exhibitions for participation. However, before selection can be effected the general and specific marketing merits of exhibitions must be surveyed and the merits and demerits of the different exhibition environments appraised in detail.

A method of merit rating of exhibitions and a selection procedure are suggested and illustrated by a case study. Finally, budgeting for exhibitions generally and the issue of returns and costs are discussed. An example of time budgeting is presented in a case study.

Preparations for exhibiting are included in Part Four to enable their discussion in the full knowledge of all activities involved. Preparations for visiting exhibitions are dealt with in Part Five.

Part Three deals with actual exhibition activities. The preceding sections provided the material background and investigated the issues, problems and activities leading to the decision to participate in an exhibition. This part deals with the implementation of that decision. The stand, its design, exhibits and facilities are discussed and aesthetics and art patronage are briefly mentioned.

Exhibition stand personnel are extensively scrutinized. Stand management qualifications, stand personnel duties and manners, foreign languages and gathering of information are reviewed. The transposition of buyer and seller roles at industrial exhibitions and the issue of peripheral influences are examined and supplemented by illustrations. Three case studies illustrate the issues raised.

Preparations should logically precede actual exhibition activities, as can be seen in the chain of activities in Figure 2. They are discussed at the end of Part Three so that they can be considered against the background of the full range of exhibition activities and the relevant checklists.

Part Four deals with two groups of activities. One group consists of analysis and audit, follow-up and preparations, and is concerned only with actual exhibition efforts. The second group consists of publicity and public relations, intelligence, training and projects, which in their own right have a place in the marketing mix and can also be actively involved in exhibition activities.

Exhibition performance analysis and the exhibition effort audit are not only natural sequels to an exhibition effort but also vital tools of marketing management. They provide guidelines for follow-up actions and validate the motives and objectives of exhibiting or suggest modifications. Stand design, stand team performance and attainment of objectives are all critically scrutinized.

Follow-up actions and techniques are discussed, the role of the follow-up function as

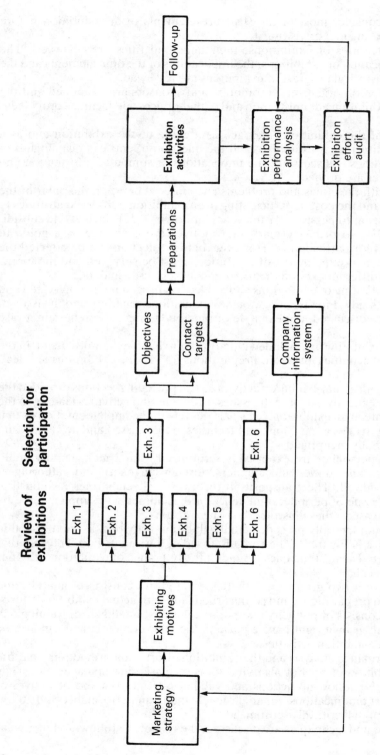

FIGURE 2. THE CHAIN OF ACTIVITIES OF AN EXHIBITION EFFORT

a productive part of the exhibition effort and the importance of a speedy and well-prepared reaction to exhibition contacts are emphasized.

In addition to general preparations for exhibiting, such issues as preparation of the material structure, of personnel and of information aids are dealt with in detail. If the 'project team and project management' concepts, discussed later, are accepted as operational techniques, preparations naturally fall within their orbit.

Publicity and public relations are reviewed mainly in their relation to exhibition efforts, but many of the points raised are also valid beyond the boundaries of exhibitions. The attitudes of technicians to publicity and of engineers to publicity practitioners are observed from an industrial marketing standpoint. The need for cooperation between stand design and publicity functions is stressed and exhibition organizers' publicity is commented on.

Sales and technical literature is dealt with from the point of view of international marketing of industrial products. The case for the use of the universally understandable language of drawings, sketches and photographs is pleaded and developments in reprographic techniques and electronic translation systems are briefly mentioned. The suitability of house journals and technical bulletins for exhibition purposes is considered and exhibition organizers' publicity and the need to exploit publicity facilities available at exhibitions are dealt with.

Exhibition intelligence is a component of general marketing intelligence, but distinguished by the fact that it can be carried out in an exceptionally favourable environment. The tasks of exhibition intelligence are discussed in detail and the preparations required for these tasks are described. Intelligence vigilance is advocated. The conduct of intelligence interviews, language problems and the subjects of different intelligence interests, including technological, product and exhibition merit interests, are fully dealt with.

The importance of training for exhibition activities is discussed and the benefits of good training programmes are stressed. It is suggested that this book, and particularly its checklists, can make a substantial contribution to training initiatives concerned with participating in and visiting of exhibitions.

General observations are made on the relevance of the concepts of project teams and project management to the whole range, or to selected elements, of an exhibition effort. Although a comprehensive treatment is beyond the scope of the study the techniques involved are recommended for consideration.

Part Five deals with visiting exhibitions.

Textbooks on marketing subjects usually deal with exhibitions in a few paragraphs, at the most in a few pages and in at least one notable case not at all. An extensive literature is available on the subject of exhibitions but the texts deal mainly with techniques of exhibiting from the viewpoint of the exhibitor. The subjects discussed, often with great expertise and on the basis of long experience, are stand design, display, presentation, graphics and lighting. The interests of visitors are hardly considered, except in brief remarks about their comfort.

Some texts emphasize the best ways and means of attracting visitors and some mention visitors' needs, but only as customers or potential customers of the exhibitor. That visitors are in their own right customers of the exhibition enterprise, without whom it could not exist, is seldom mentioned.

The attendance figures of visitors to individual exhibitions are counted in thousands, tens of thousands and even hundreds of thousands and it must be in the marketing interest of exhibition venue owners, exhibition organizers and exhibitors to afford these customers and potential customers proper attention.

Motives for visiting are discussed, visiting tasks are categorized and the authority of visitors is defined. The types of contacts and contact times are reviewed. A range of different visiting interests is dealt with at length and the time elements, planning and preparation of an exhibition visit are illustrated by a case study.

Checklists

A systematic approach to exhibiting and visiting exhibitions involves the participants in *motivation*, *discrimination* and *selection* processes which must be completed before actual exhibition activities can be initiated and implemented. Very often these processes have to be applied in areas of insufficient information, complexity or perhaps unfamiliarity.

To assist in these processes, the elements of the subjects discussed in this study are arranged in checklists placed at the end of relevant parts. These checklists can be used for *monitoring* of activities and materials by means of simple item checking, for *yes–no decisions* and where appropriate for *rating*, *ranking* or *weighting* procedures. The lists have *individual* validity but they can also be used *sequentially* and several can be arranged in *matrix* formation and used for *optimum selection* or *optimum solution* purposes. In practice the addition of auxiliary checklists with suitable ranges of monetary values, real time periods and actual dates would enable the use of checklist matrices for *expenditure budgeting* and *function cost analysis*. In view of the great variety of exhibitions, exhibitors and visitors and of the diversity of their needs, the checklists are intentionally designed to be no more than a guide to a possible method of procedure which can be adapted to individual requirements.

PART ONE

The Structure of Exhibitions

Categories of Exhibitions

The classification of exhibitions into two broad categories of consumer and industrial goods events, although frequently encountered, is a simplistic division of these events, which serve a vast assortment of markets, sub-markets, market sectors and niche markets.

The division is unambiguous for such goods as turbines and cosmetics but loses validity for trade fairs combining the two kinds of goods, for goods on the border line of the division or straddling it and for goods changing from one sector to another depending on application. Many general trade fairs of half-yearly frequency devote the spring fair to consumer goods and the autumn fair to industrial products, or vice versa. However, at the so-called consumer durables end of the range the dividing lines between consumer and industrial goods become somewhat blurred and some products make their way from one category to another. The high technical content and service requirements of some consumer durables bring them very near to the family of industrial products. On the other hand many industrial products, like fasteners, hand tools or consumable tools, are by their nature more consumable than industrial. The crossing and re-crossing of the imaginary consumer–industrial frontier by such products as do-it-yourself equipment or packaging containers further clouds the issue. Apart from organizational and structural differences of the industrial and consumer environment, buyers in both sectors seem to be motivated as much by emotions as by cold assessments and in the final, person-to-person, encounter show more similarities than differences in their purchasing behaviour.

The pursuit of exhibition activities by exhibitors and visitors would be greatly assisted by an internationally agreed classification system with an orderly arrangement of data of interest to exhibition organizers, exhibitors and visitors. To be workable such a classification system must have a clearly stated practical purpose and to be effective its objectives must be limited to that purpose.

It is surely in the marketing interests of exhibition organizers to publish about their events basic, preferably independently audited, data attractive enough to tempt potential exhibitors and visitors to probe more deeply into the merits of such events and to consider them for inclusion in their programme of exhibition activities. To assist exhibitors and/or visitors in their search, 'exhibition data' should enable those interested to locate exhibitions which, in the first instance, are at least nominally suitable for their particular purpose.

On first thought it would seem that the suitability of an exhibition could be ascertained from its published title and programme of activities and that the importance of an exhibition could be measured by its capacity to attract an optimum attendance of exhibitors and visitors of the right calibre. Here we encounter the first difficulty, in the form of the duality of the basic interests of exhibitors and visitors in their roles as buyers and sellers and of the interaction of these two interests. However, the motives of exhibitors and visitors are by no means all of a simple buying or selling character, nor are the merits of exhibitions merely a matter of counting exhibitors and visitors.

The growing interdependence of national economies is reflected in the growing internationalization of many exhibitions which traditionally had a regional or national character. Exhibits seen at truly international exhibitions bear witness both to the decline of frontiers as economic and political obstacles to the manufacturing and marketing activities of one firm in several countries, and to the increasing number of products including components and accessories made in different countries. Mergers, conglomerates, horizontal and vertical integration activities on an international scale also become evident, either obliquely by virtue of the displayed range of goods, or manifestly by means of a deliberate display of the international capabilities of a new combination of enterprises.

In the wake of this internationalization many minor ventures delude exhibitors, visitors and mostly themselves by placing the 'international' tag in front of whatever title their effort has. Their reputation and future business would be much better served if they declared what they really are, that is usually small exhibitions of specialized interest, and if they exploited a well-defined market segment on sound marketing principles. They could then plan for steady growth, instead of suffering a painful descent on the sharp edges of a sawtooth diagram of regression.

General trade fairs and exhibitions usually combine industrial and consumer goods and, in some cases, agricultural equipment and produce. The great majority are known by the town or region in which they are held, while their scope and aim as declared in the prospectus may change from time to time.

The majority of general trade fairs and exhibitions are international events but there are also fairs with a declared national, regional or even local character. Many of these are held twice a year, mostly in spring and autumn. Many general fairs originated as samples fairs and some still retain that title while some, like the Leipzig Fair, retain only the symbol.

The *combination of industrial and consumer goods* in one trade fair has many critics, but seems justified for small or compact markets, which are perhaps remote from the mainstream of trade and commerce. From a buying point of view such a general fair enables buyers who may be dealing in both types of goods to survey the offering. From a selling point of view, the country or region can display all it has to offer in a better and more effective manner than it could do for separate sectors of its capacity.

In sophisticated markets general trade fairs develop into a conglomeration of specialized sections catering for industrial, consumer durables and consumer goods. They become in effect a number of separate specialized exhibitions sharing the same exhibition grounds and the same date and time.

The arguments for and against such general ventures are many and varied. Local pride and organizers' ambitions, trade associations' and other interests enter into the controversy. The existence of exhibition halls or plans to build new ones and the granting or threat of withdrawal of municipal subsidies play their role. The merits of alternative solutions from the point of view of the marketing interests of the customers, i.e. exhibitors and visitors, seem to remain somewhere in the background instead of being the primary consideration. *Local exhibitions* are mostly organized by trade associations with specialized interests or by trading or manufacturing groups with common interests within a defined geographical area. Often the emphasis is not so much on actual products as on a display of manufacturing, sub-contracting or servicing facilities. Such local exhibitions are also used by firms from outside the area to display their local distribution, spares depot and service facilities. In highly industrialized areas, firms of national or even international standing participate in local exhibitions to display their capacity to supply auxiliary products, particularly of consumable character, such as lubricants, cleaning materials, abrasives, small tools, etc., and occasionally they use the occasion for recruiting local agents and representatives. Contacts made during such exhibitions are usually in the area of medium-level buying decisions and decision influences and of a small-to-medium bracket of expenditure budgets.

Agricultural fairs and exhibitions are one of the oldest manifestations of marketing techniques and even today they occupy a numerically leading position in the multitude of all types of exhibitions. They range in importance from nothing more than glorified local cattle markets to *great international exhibitions* covering livestock, produce and equipment. They have also produced a number of *specialized* offshoots and divisions into separate livestock, produce and machinery exhibitions. Even the most international of them retain a strong regional or local flavour and there is little doubt that their natural propensity to seasonal timing has influenced the not always rational following of other exhibitions into the same crowded seasons.

As the industrialization of agriculture has grown over the years, so have the entries of equipment, implements and, lately, aids to administration and management. The potential marketing scope of agricultural, horticultural and forestry fairs and exhibitions as marketing targets reaches into a great variety of sectors of the economy. At one end of the spectrum there are buckets, brushes, gifts and toys; at the other bulldozers and silos. Biological, environmental and soil sciences are involved, and so are aspects of human and animal health and comfort. The interrelations with forestry and horticulture are natural, the affinity to food production obvious. A schematic representation of these relations is shown in Figures 3 and 4.

Economic activity exhibitions deal with such subjects as export or import trade, insurance, banking, finance, credit, leasing and investment, and any other specialized activities which can be interpreted as coming under that heading. These exhibitions have become more numerous in recent times and many adopt an international stance. Some exhibitors participating in such exhibitions find that their marketing interests would be better served by participating in major international industrial exhibitions, where there are ready-made gatherings of potential customers.

Touring exhibitions are itinerant events and their main characteristics are that they come to their customers' doorstep, or as near as possible, and their life span can extend over weeks and months. They can be private ventures organized by one firm or can serve a group of exhibitors of related interests. The dissemination of knowledge of manufacturing techniques and of concepts such as industrial waste recovery, safety, hygiene and welfare are often the subjects of travelling exhibitions organized by official or semi-official bodies. Aircraft, ships, trains, vans, caravans, trailers, portable buildings and plastic domes which can be blown up are used as exhibition halls by touring exhibitions. The effectiveness of touring exhibitions should be assessed on the basis of their subjective aims. Touring exhibitions often serve as a vehicle for a single or special campaign and their cost effectiveness is then assessed by special criteria.

15

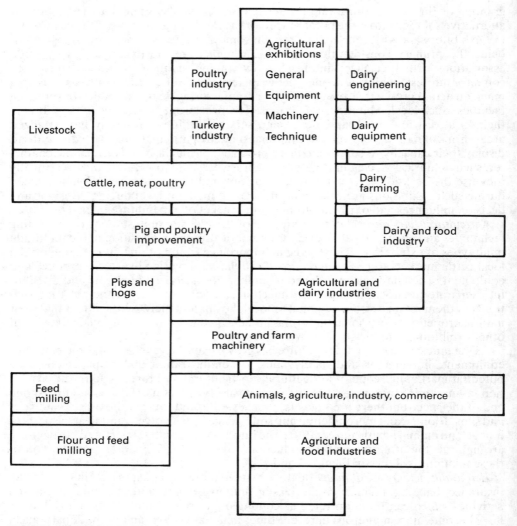

FIGURE 3. AGRICULTURAL AND AGRICULTURE AFFINITY EXHIBITIONS

This figure shows exhibitions directly linked to the main body of general agricultural exhibitions, with definite affinity to agriculture and including the term agriculture in their title.

Figure 4 shows exhibitions of a secondary affinity resulting from a direct connection of food to agriculture.

Mobile exhibition structures can be also incorporated in conventional exhibitions, particularly as outdoor stands in open air areas or as demonstration facilities supplementing indoor exhibition stands.

Congresses, conferences, conventions and symposia are in many cases organized as events complementing established exhibitions. In others these meetings of people are the main events and exhibitions are an appendage to them. The relative importance of the two elements in such combined activities varies widely. A gathering of scientists of great eminence is taken by suppliers of relevant instruments or equipment as an opportunity to show their wares and to offer lavish hospitality. An exhibition displaying

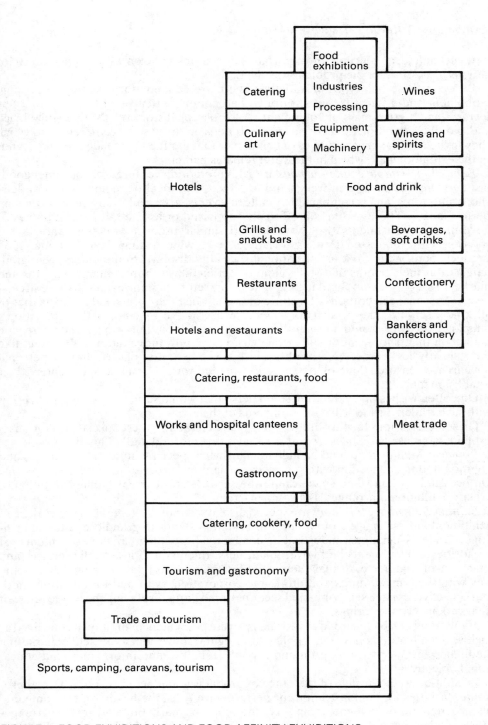

FIGURE 4. FOOD EXHIBITIONS AND FOOD AFFINITY EXHIBITIONS

This figure shows exhibitions directly linked with the main body of general food exhibitions and with more or less close affinities to food as an industrial concept. Food exhibitions have a primary affinity to agricultural exhibitions, thus providing the link between the two groups.

new technological concepts or important innovations is taken as an opportunity for serious discussions of the problems involved.

Between these two types of initiatives there are combinations ranging from some equipment and a lot of lectures, through half equipment and half lectures, to a few lectures and a great mass of equipment. An apocryphal story relates that some black sheep of the exhibition fauna organize exhibitions on the basis of conferences to which they invite as speakers executives of companies that are then persuaded to take stands in the exhibition hall, which in the event remains half empty.

Exhibitions without exhibition halls are sales promotion ventures for consumer goods lasting from one to several weeks and arranged with local or regional sales outlets, shops and stores, and accompanied by cultural events, arts exhibitions, theatre and film performances. These ventures are usually supported or assisted by official bodies or government departments. Book weeks and similar product oriented ventures are sponsored by interested trade associations, e.g. wine testing days, national food product sponsorship, folk-art or national speciality displays. Stall holders, who graduated from their booths and stalls mounted in medieval thoroughfares, squares and market places to lock-up shops in later times, now return to some extent to these streets. Festive seasons, celebrations of historic or pseudo-historic events and anniversaries of all kinds, serve as the pretext for elaborate decorative schemes and illuminations. Shopkeepers who would normally remain behind their imposing façades, relying mainly on their shop-windows to attract customers, now move out into the street like their slightly less respectable brethren in less sophisticated places, and by personal appearance ensure that by-passers are invited and persuaded to enter their establishments.

One often wishes that exhibition stand personnel would serve a short apprenticeship with such traders just to learn the rudiments of the art.

On some occasions the favourable atmosphere created by these special promotions is exploited and used as a background for a sales drive for 'related' industrial products.

Private exhibitions are held by individual firms in specially hired halls or hotels and are mounted in connection with special campaigns, sales drives or service campaigns. On occasions, when stand space cannot be secured at a current public exhibition, a private exhibition is arranged as a compensation.

Exhibitions within exhibitions are special displays within the general framework of an exhibition and can range from modest information stands to grandiose national pavilions. Trade associations, industrial or commercial groupings, regional or municipal authorities, governments and government departments, utilities, public services and chambers of commerce, display their activities and services that are connected in some way with the aims of an exhibition. Large corporations with multi-product or multi-market activities have self-contained sections or pavilions displaying the whole range of their products and offerings.

Showrooms can be regarded as a form of private permanent exhibition if conceived as such as a deliberate policy, i.e. a policy of using the showroom as an active marketing medium, which serves sales promotion, public relations and information and educational objectives.

In addition to the display of the range of products manufactured and, where appropriate, facilities for demonstrations or performance tests, the history of the company, its research and development capacity, the scope of marketing and service arrangements, and perhaps also important achievements and awards can be displayed.

Works visits by customers and potential customers can be encouraged. Professional institutes, schools, colleges and university faculties are invited to visit the works. Some firms have specially trained personnel in attendance at such visits and, depending on the standing and qualifications of the visitors, appropriately qualified members of the staff assist at conducted tours. Open days are extensions of random visit arrangements and on such occasions the whole establishment becomes an exhibition for specially invited or selectively admitted guests.

Firms with training schools for operators of their products can make very good use of showrooms with ingenious displays, sectionalized equipment, models of operating principles, slides, films and other audio-visual aids. It can be argued that such arrangements cannot be classed as exhibitions, but it is a fact that the displays and exhibits provide an excellent inspiration, if not the actual items for, what might be called true exhibitions.

The effectiveness of showrooms depends to some extent on the location of the main establishment and on whether they are directly connected with the main establishment or are separate from it. Works in regions remote from centres of commerce or difficult to reach may require separate showrooms in cities of national or regional importance, while works easy to reach from main business centres can have showrooms attached to their headquarters. The main difference between public exhibitions and these private quasi-exhibitions is the absence of competitors, of uninvited visitors and of restraints on location and time. The choice of exhibits, the manner of displaying and the choice of visitors are all matters for internal decision.

A showroom will be an excellent private exhibition only if the space allocated is suitable for effective presentation of exhibits and if information elements such as films, transparencies, multilingual audio-visual aids, etc., are in working order and are up-to-date. Most important of all, competent personnel must be available to show, demonstrate, explain and conduct visitors, all this without being a burden on normal day-to-day activities.

Occasionally one encounters showrooms which by their decor and showpieces proclaim past glories instead of current activities, and which somehow manage to produce an aura of obsolescence. Highly polished brass doorknobs bear witness that cleaners are probably the only visitors. When there is a sudden influx of visitors and the showroom has to be used as a waiting room, there are apologetic remarks by executive-hosts and mental notes to do something about it. Perhaps.

Views on the merits, demerits, costs and nuisance value of these quasi-exhibition activities vary considerably. However, if the objectives of the exercise are clearly defined in terms of aims, means and resources and if they are then effectively pursued on that basis, it soon becomes apparent whether the purpose is being achieved.

National trade centres are usually organized by official, semi-official or other promotional bodies in domestic or foreign markets. These centres have permanent exhibition facilities which are also utilized for periodically mounted special exhibitions. In foreign locations official sponsorship can add prestige and importance to the displays and special promotions, and is particularly helpful in issuing invitations and supporting them by receptions and other forms of hospitality. To executives of potential customer firms a personal invitation issued by a commercial attaché or, perhaps, even by an ambassador usually makes a strong enough impression to secure a good response.

World trade centres are complexes of buildings occupied by rent-paying firms of international provenance, by government agencies, purchasing missions and other official or semi-official bodies concerned with international marketing activities. Although essentially designed as information exchange centres, these complexes usually include exhibition facilities of a permanent or temporary character.

World fairs are perhaps the unintentional expression of an ultimate marketing concept attitude as they serve a universe of exhibitors, users and consumers, combining the display of the fulfilment of current needs with a sometimes optimistic look into a brighter future. Their futuramas have an air of technological forecasting. They have the potential power to influence the market place in matters of taste, fashion and awareness of technologies. Their remoteness from direct or immediate purchasing possibilities perhaps adds some credibility to the participating exhibitors who profess to serve no one but the future customer.

The titles of world fairs, such as 'Man and his world' or 'Harmony for mankind', disclose their ambitious aims, if not always their actual achievements. The influence of great world fairs as an international sociological and economo-political phenomenon deserves a full scale study quite beyond the framework of this book. Due to their gigantic size and scope only treasurers of very large corporations and of national coffers can provide the resources required to meet the expense of participating.

Exhibition Titles

The title is a distinctive character feature of an exhibition, particularly if it is an expression of its objectives and scope. The manner in which the title's objectives are achieved and the continuity of that achievement determine the character of an exhibition. Long-established general trade fairs and exhibitions usually carry in their title the name of their host town or region and some venerable institutions still retain their medieval invocation of patron saints. Their aims and scope are defined by tradition and usage: some have changed their character in keeping with modern trends, some mix trade and popular amusement as of old.

A change in an exhibition title can reflect a real change in marketing objectives, a superficial following of current fashion or an artificial attempt to elevate the descriptive title from a humble trade level to the lofty heights of science. The emergence of new technologies, products and processes creates a bandwagon effect which encourages several new exhibition ventures to sprout on the same patch, when one would be sufficient. After one or two appearances they wither to nothing or link with others in what is claimed to be a logical combination. Maintenance becomes terotechnology, lubrication becomes tribology and what was once waste disposal graduates through materials reclamation to pollution and environmental control.

Some children of sedate parents become fully fledged and bouncing offspring in their own right, e.g. cryogenics from refrigeration, fluidics from hydraulics and pneumatics. There are exhibition titles, mostly of a 'new' or 'first of its kind' variety, which on closer inspection reveal that the change of title is no more than a semantic attempt to be just a little different from an established competitor. However, there are also titles which are so definite and expressive that no doubt can be entertained as to the aim of an exhibition, even if at some of them marketing eyebrows may be raised in wonder. Some examples are: biotechnology, copiers, infra-red technology, military microwaves, international trenchless construction for utilities. On the other hand a prospective exhibitor of a computer application product of, in his opinion, international appeal would have to review entries in an exhibition directory under the heading 'computers and software' amounting to a total of 97 events, of which 36 are located in the UK, 30 in the rest of Europe and 31 in the rest of the world.

Objective information about exhibitions is not easily obtained without a special effort on the part of the information seeker. The scarcity and ambiguity of the information readily accessible in directories is surprising for products so widely sold at such high prices. Detailed information can only be obtained by approaching promoters, organizers or representatives of exhibitions, but that procedure in itself requires considerable effort. Thus, the ground is laid for hasty decisions, cancellations or simply giving up in despair.

Most lists of exhibitions that are generally available are compiled in a way which suggests that those compiling them assume that the user knows enough about exhibitions to find what he needs even if the presentation is not very effective. Group headings taken from traditional industrial classifications compiled for entirely different purposes often lead to misunderstandings or even absurd arrangements. When new titles appear they are included in a product group formally justified, but closer scrutiny often reveals that the basis for such an inclusion is a misunderstanding of the technological meaning of an exhibition title or perhaps a bad translation of that title from a foreign language.

The arrangement under product group headings also has the disadvantage that the titles of exhibitions include items which could legitimately appear under several other headings, so that several entries would be required. The appearance of new titles leads to the need for creating new group titles, or to the inclusion of the new exhibition title in groups so remote that only the compiler understands the connection. There is no doubt that the variety and complexity of exhibition titles contributes to the difficulty of arranging them under meaningful group headings, but the obvious remedy for such a difficulty, namely the provision of an exhaustive index including subtitles, seems to escape the great majority of compilers of exhibition lists.

There are many reasons for such a state of affairs; one of them could well be that the process of classifying information is left to clerical staff without sufficient discriminatory abilities, so that incoming information is interpreted on the basis of direct dictionary translations. These sometimes produce curious titles, such as an exhibition of 'blind and revolving shutter products' and the classifying of 'alimentary equipment' under 'other engineering' instead of under 'food machinery'. These are complaints of minor importance; the problem becomes more serious when an attempt is made to assess the scope of general titles like 'engineering', technical and industrial', 'trade and commerce', 'world wares' or 'crafts and industries'. The vagueness of these titles is only matched by the vagueness of the decision-making process which uninitiated newcomers to the exhibition scene are advised to adopt in making a choice on the basis of 'excellent attendances from many different countries'. Assuming that the data currently available would allow us to classify if not all then at least a great number of exhibitions in accordance with a system built on the requirements of exhibitors and visitors, there remains the aspect of the quality of the classified exhibitions.

An exhibition may claim by its title, by its programme and by the number of domestic and foreign exhibitors and visitors to exert an international influence; in the formal numerical sense that may be true. Whether the quality of these visitors is of interest to the prospective exhibitor or vice versa is another matter.

There are many exhibition organizers and advisory organizations who can assist but to an outside observer it is a matter of surprise that the exhibition industry, which provides as a product such an excellent medium of marketing communications, should be satisfied to use in its own marketing effort a standard of communications so far below the best available.

Location of Exhibitions

The *geographic location* can be a significant factor of importance to the exhibitor. The distance of the location from the exhibitor's base determines the cost of resources in terms of time, travel and transport for stand personnel, exhibits and equipment. Climatic conditions can affect the selection of the stand personnel and may impose restrictions from a health and endurance point of view. The preparation and selection of exhibits may also be affected. The geographic location is important in relation to competing exhibitions and other marketing activities. These can take place in times before and after the exhibition, and in places en route to and further afield than the exhibition.

For an exhibitor participating in one or two exhibitions, the geographic location is a technical detail. For exhibitors with widespread market interests, the geographic location of all the events in the programme and the incidence of marketing visits to several countries pose serious problems of co-ordination. A distant geographic location can become a decisive factor which can endanger participation in an otherwise attractive exhibition. In such cases this participation can be combined with sales promotion visits to the host country of the exhibition and to neighbouring territories. A logistic approach to such multiple marketing activities can make an impressive contribution to operation and cost effectiveness.

The actual location site of an exhibition can be *permanent*, i.e. at the established frequency cycle the exhibition returns to the same exhibition site or locality. The location can be *mobile-peripatetic*, i.e. the locations are changed within a defined choice of different locations in an established sequence. Finally the location can be *mobile-free*, i.e. the location is changed without any predetermined rules. All types of mobility can apply to exhibitions within one country as well as to international changes of location. The mobility aspect of exhibitions is important from the point of view of long range planning of participation and requires careful scrutiny of venues and their sequences in case there are significant differences in facilities, organizational skill and environmental factors between one venue and another.

For visitors the geographic location of an exhibition is not so critical because they can combine their visit to an exhibition with other activities in or near its location, and perhaps improve the cost-effectiveness of visits to distant territories.

The internal and external environments of exhibitions are discussed at length on pages 45–54.

Time Elements of Exhibitions

Three basic event-time elements of exhibitions are critical from the point of view of exhibitors and visitors who are required to make decisions about selecting, participating or visiting exhibitions. They are:

event frequency (semi-annual, annual, biennial, regular, irregular)
event date (position in week, month, year)
event duration (number of days)

The *event frequency of the exhibition* is significant for the long-term planning of exhibition activities and also when related to the time characteristics of the marketing strategy of an exhibitor.

Some general trade fairs are staged twice each year, mostly in spring and autumn, and some exhibitions combining industrial and consumer goods are staged annually and rarely biennially. The effectiveness of industrial exhibitions staged at annual intervals for industrial activities with longer periods of gestation of new ideas or of significant improvements is constantly discussed by participating exhibitors. One of the conflicts of ideas is caused because, although a gestation period of three years may apply to a particular type of industrial equipment, not all firms start the development at the same time. The question of showing your new development too early, of giving your competitors a chance to evaluate, copy and perhaps even improve on your concept, must be weighed against the advantages of being the first in the field and related to the copying time and effort which your competitors would have to devote to following your lead.

The advocates of longer time interval events maintain that such intervals would contribute to a better maturing chance for new developments; these could then be geared to the exhibition events. Firms with projects not sufficiently advanced would, according to these theorists, be deterred from a premature display. Others reply that there always will be firms inclined to steal a march on competitors, no matter what state of development their project is at. The most persuasive argument is one of cost. The attendance at biennial events permits a better application of resources and a better preparation of display and manning. Biennial or longer frequency events may require some other form of display activity between main events. If the marketing objectives require more frequent exposure than a specialized exhibition can provide, private exhibitions or works exhibitions can be used to fill the gap. Participation as the 'odd man out' in other related exhibitions is occasionally used and the display of new products can be harmonized with the rarer exhibitions of sufficiently high marketing merit. From a visitor's point of view the event frequency is not so important, as he can mostly substitute other means of achieving his objectives.

The *date of an exhibition* has to be related to the time scale of marketing activities, particularly if they are of seasonal character. A badly timed exhibition participation is not only costly in terms of the expenditure of human and material resources, but can also harm other activities by untimely demands on production schedules, delivery times and development programmes. The concentrated incidence of events in spring and autumn is probably due to an inheritance from the time when fairs held for trade purposes were combined with religious festivals and also to the influence of agricultural fairs held after the harvest was gathered or early in spring.

During the crowded spring and autumn seasons, the proliferation of exhibitions competing with each other for exhibitors and visitors is the source of conflict and sometimes of despair for prospective exhibitors. Even the most experienced, seasoned and convinced supporters of exhibitions wince at the prospect of making a rational selection of suitable venues during these two seasons.

The position of the exhibition time in the week can influence travel arrangements and activities before and after the exhibition. Exhibitions ending on a Friday allow a reasonable return home or perhaps travel to a distant location. Some exhibitions have duration periods extended to include Saturday or Sunday or both and are open on these days to the public, reserving weekdays for trade and professional visitors. Some exhibitions, although not many, are scheduled near or during traditional holiday or personnel leave times and this can create stand staffing problems.

If several exhibitions serve your market sector in a close time proximity, the marketing merit factors will play an important part in your decision. If the competing exhibitions serve related market sectors, or non-related sectors which are of interest to your customers, you have to assess the relative merits of these competing exhibitions and their ability to attract some, most or all of your customers.

Personnel availability is probably already considered in your marketing programme and activities, and so are the additional factors of holiday schedules, training programmes, special functions and perhaps the seasonal incidence of illness.

Attendance at an exhibition can be affected by non-commercial events taking place at the same time, either in the location of the exhibition or in a location of important customers. Political events, elections, state visits, congresses, both in the host country of the exhibition and in neighbouring and other countries, can also influence the number of visitors to an exhibition.

The *duration of the exhibition* is significant for the exhibitor because the number of days and the opening hours of the exhibition determine the exhibition time available and thus influence the choice and number of stand personnel and the stand design strategy. Events of three to four days' duration with high marketing merits may require provisions for receiving large numbers of visitors in a short space of time. At such events it is easy to lose visitors who are under pressure to accomplish their tasks in a short time and cannot afford to wait for attention or discuss problems in overcrowded conditions. The total number of days of the duration of an exhibition indicates the inclusion of Saturdays and Sundays, which can be important when travel arrangements and visits before and after the exhibition are taken into account.

Variations in the duration of exhibitions are influenced by national, commercial and social customs and traditions. These variations can be quite disconcerting to exhibitors and visitors entering the international exhibition scene and assuming that the customs and usage of their home ground will apply elsewhere as well.

The advantages and disadvantages of short *versus* long periods are very difficult to evaluate. For exhibitors, duration periods of more than five to six days are certainly very tiring and for medium and small firms they present a serious personnel problem. The quality of stand personnel performance suffers during long duration exhibitions either because the same personnel find it difficult to maintain enthusiasm throughout the period or because there are changes in quality when relief arrangements are made. An advantage of short duration periods of three to four days is that arrangements for the attendance of chief executives can be made with more certainty, so visitors can rely on meeting them.

Events of more than five days' duration would have to claim a very high marketing merit to justify attendance for the whole time of the exhibition. An exhibition lasting three days calls for a short but very intensive effort on the part of exhibitors, but limits the choice of days for visitors, who can have conflicting engagements. An exhibition lasting ten days calls for an untiring and sustained effort by the exhibitor, but gives visitors a much better chance of selecting the most convenient time for their visit. The implications of the 'total exhibition time' factor are discussed further in the sections dealing with the tasks of stand personnel and visitors in Parts Three and Five.

A visitor benefits from events of long duration as he has a wider choice of days on which to visit an exhibition, can sometimes combine two or three events in one trip, or can utilize the time between two events for other activities if they lie in the path leading to or from the exhibition.

Historical Progress of Exhibitions

The history, life span and development of an exhibition are features of its character and just as old age does not necessarily mean decay, youth does not guarantee progress either. What matters most is the maturity of an exhibition as a marketing medium. If a certain exuberance, not quite matched by organizational skill, can be excused in a well-conceived new venture, one must also make allowances for some measure of organizational stiffness in old-established events which have been on the scene for a long time.

Exhibitions can be old, established, recently established and new ventures, but these terms are of necessity of relative significance. The Leipzig Fair celebrated its 800th anniversary in 1965 and industrial exhibitions have been in existence for 200 years. The

Hanover Fair rose from small, almost reluctant, beginnings in 1947 to its present international eminence. New, highly specialized events need no tradition if they fill a real marketing need; long-established exhibitions can show clear signs of stagnation or decline if they are of the 'we have always done it that way' school.

A well-documented review of the development of an exhibition supported by factual proof can assist in long-term planning considerations, as it eliminates doubts about its future viability. The historical progress of an exhibition provides valuable background information for the assessment of its general and special marketing merits.

Exhibition Organizers, Promoters and Sponsors

An exhibition can be promoted and organized by the same body or it can be promoted by one organization, supported or sponsored by another, organized by a third and mounted in the exhibition hall of a fourth. It can of course be initiated, promoted, organized and mounted by the same organization in its own exhibition facilities. The opportunities for an exemplary display of co-operation, high organizational skill and diplomacy are many. And so are the pitfalls of misunderstandings, crossed lines of communication, local or national idiosyncrasies, plain inefficiency and helpless muddle.

There is no general remedy except to apply the best management criteria and techniques in assessing the quality of the exhibition organization, to exert control from the highest level in the matter of final choice and to institute a method of reporting and assessment which will at least prevent repetitions of past failures and at best ensure the success of future efforts.

The *sponsorship and support of exhibitions* can range from a formal eulogy on the first pages of the exhibition catalogue followed by a speech at the opening ceremony, to full active and organizational assistance. It can also imply the protection of specialized interests.

Sponsorship by a trade or other association may have a considerable influence on the number and quality of exhibitors, depending in turn on the strength and character of the membership of the association. Such sponsorship can also have a negative influence, e.g. preferential treatment of association members and restriction or exclusion of non-members, discrimination in stand allocation, etc. Sponsorship by a trade journal has the advantages of wider than usual publicity, for both the exhibition and the exhibitors, and opportunities for well-directed mail shots.

The reputation, standing and organizational skill of an *exhibition organizer* are contributory merit rating factors, but their influence is mainly felt when it reaches negative values. The business of exhibitions, a very big business, is subject to the same marketing criteria which apply to other goods or services. In this case the product offered is a medium of communications between exhibitors and visitors. Both exhibitors and visitors are customers and constitute the market. The most beautiful exhibition hall without exhibitors would attract no visitors, the most impressive collection of exhibits would have no purpose unless it was seen by visitors. Successful exhibitions are the result of a good marketing concept, of good management and of an understanding for the business needs and human comforts of all customers.

Badly conceived exhibitions have the unfortunate propensity to distribute loss and disappointment impartially to both exhibitors and visitors. An exhibition with badly conceived aims or objectives will not become a good marketing medium only by virtue of being excellently organized in the technical sense. But the effects of inadequate preparation and organization can seriously lower the marketing merit of the best conception. The operating capacity of exhibitors and the absorption capacity of visitors are affected, and the reputation of the exhibition suffers despite its inherent marketing virtues.

Some exhibition organizers see their aim only as selling as much floor space as possible at as high a price as the market will stand and at as low a rate of investment in facilities as they can get away with. They are no doubt confirming their historical fairground and side-show lineage by being very good short-term showmen, providing primitive services in not very congenial surroundings, but accompanying the effort by much self-satisfied, self-advertising and self-congratulating noise.

There are of course many well-organized and well-attended exhibitions, which is as it should be, but even so, strange and paradoxical contrasts can occasionally be observed between the main theme of an exhibition and its services and facilities. Some examples are:

- A shortage of exhibition catalogues on the second day of an Information Fair, in which the latest achievements in data processing were shown.
- You were invited at the entrance to another exhibition to have a plastic visiting card embossed 'to help you make the most of your time at this exhibition. . . . a quick, simple and sure way of obtaining the information you require'. In effect you had to queue for 10 minutes to obtain the card.
- At a waste disposal exhibition, the floor was littered with empty plastic cups and papers and refuse bins were overflowing.
- At a food industry exhibition there was bad restaurant service, stale sandwiches, appalling litter of used serviettes and of empty sample containers, etc.

The fortuitous corollary of this situation is that bad organizers often seem reluctant to learn from their mistakes, while good ones tend to improve their successful ventures all the time.

Part of the problem is caused by the fact that of the two kinds of exhibition customers, i.e. visitors and exhibitors, only exhibitors have direct access to exhibition organizers and even that access varies considerably in the degree of influence it exerts, but visitors have no way to express their views except by being absent or complaining after the fact.

The elements affecting the organization merit of an exhibition are usually listed in the prospectus of organizers with varying amounts of detailed description. It must also be said that there are occasions when the provision of services is more an expression of optimistic intentions than of actual arrangements. Many a disappointment caused by delayed completion of the stand, its unsatisfactory furnishing and other shortages results not so much from lack of preparation on the part of the exhibitor as from too much faith in the promises of the exhibition prospectus.

The checklists of the organizational and administrative elements are intended as an indication of the points to watch. They may prove too elaborate for one event or not detailed enough for another. Their purpose is not to say that every time you participate in an exhibition or visit an exhibition your task is to check all the points. An established and well-organized exhibition will provide most of the data on its own initiative or on request. If you had the opportunity to verify their claims of services on one or more previous occasions you will have already established a merit rating for that exhibition. The checklists are as much for your preparation as for an assessment of that aspect of the structure of an exhibition. But what to the experienced exhibitor is clear at a glance is not so apparent to a newcomer or to stand personnel atending for the first time.

As a result of superficial impressions during a short visit, visitors from your own or other organizations may blame you for shortcomings which should be laid at the door of the exhibition organizers. Conversely, a lack of knowledge of all exhibition facilities may result in opportunities for valuable contacts and openings being neglected, thus reducing the effectiveness of a costly exercise.

The 'quality' of the technical and personal comfort facilities of an exhibition affects the capacity of stand personnel to perform their tasks and the capacity of visitors to absorb the offerings.

The checklists are also important aids for re-assessing your original exhibiting aims and objectives in the light of the reality of a selected exhibition. It may be that you can expand your aims because a particular exhibition offers more scope for your activities than originally required, or perhaps you have to restrict your objectives because to try to achieve them in an exhibition of low quality would put too much strain on your staff.

The realization of the facilities for potential contacts will also indicate preparatory actions such as the issue of invitations to visit your stand and, most important, it may affect the selection and numbers of stand personnel.

Exhibition Administration and Services

The quality of an exhibition and its effectiveness as a marketing tool for the declared area of interest depend not only on the soundness of its conception, but also on the services, facilities and amenities which it offers to the exhibitor and to the visitor. The organization of an international exhibition demands the application of varied administrative skills of a high standard, combined with a knowledge and understanding similar to that required for a complex business undertaking dealing with customers (i.e. exhibitors and visitors) from all walks of industrial and commercial life.

The *administrative and organizational structure* of an exhibition in most cases reflects the organizational standards of the promoters or sponsors of the exhibition. There are occasions when the administrative skill of an exhibition organizer is superior to that of the promoters or sponsors. In that case exhibitors and visitors are offered a marketing tool of greater effectiveness than they normally employ—providing they take full advantage of it. There are other occasions when the organizer of an exhibition does not, for one reason or another, achieve the standards which would be in keeping with the importance of the subject matter of the exhibition.

In that case customers are offered a marketing tool inferior to their usual standards of effectiveness. Exhibitors and visitors are disappointed and the blame is laid at the door of the easiest target—the exhibition. Scrutiny of the available *facilities*, *services* and *amenities* of an exhibition is a basic preliminary assessment of its suitability for the purposes of exhibiting and of visiting. For an exhibitor this scrutiny should be not only a formal check of the facilities and services listed in the exhibition promotion literature, but also a thorough investigation before the final decision by a visit or by a review of available reliable reports and interviews with participants. A visitor takes less risks than an exhibitor and in this case discrepancies between promises and reality usually result in no more than personal discomfort and some loss of time.

Exhibition Catalogues

The exhibition catalogue is a vital element of the exhibition effort and the actions concerned with it should be governed by the objectives motivating participation in a selected exhibition and by general corporate image precepts. The exhibition catalogue is not only a guide for visitors to a particular exhibition, but in the case of important exhibitions also a reference book with an effective life span of one or more years.

Exhibition catalogue elements which concern an exhibitor are listed in Checklist 6. The list makes no claim to be complete and some readers will find omissions, others a surfeit of items. The intention is to draw attention to a number of elements which can be overlooked under the pressure of tight time schedules, because of decisions delayed too long or simply lack of experience. The primary aim of your entries and advertisements in an exhibition catalogue is to attract visitors to come to your stand and to establish personal contact with your stand personnel. The term visitors, and not customers, is used advisedly for reasons argued in the discussion of exhibiting motives and objectives. It embraces customers as well as other persons with direct or indirect buying influences, or persons for whose needs you claim to cater, or whom you want to convince of your standing and capabilities.

A reader of the catalogue entry should be informed of what you exhibit, of what, if anything, you do in addition to that, and whether there are any special reasons why that particular reader should visit your particular stand. When composing entries for catalogues of international exhibitions you must consider that some readers of the catalogue may not be familiar with your name and activities, even if it is a household name on your home ground. This could be because these readers are new to your market or too young to have heard your name or possibly because your publicity and public relations efforts are not widespread enough to ensure an international awareness of your corporate mission. What you exhibit and what you offer must be clearly defined and simply stated, so that this can be easily pinpointed by an interested visitor, by a minor clerk in an information centre or by a glamorous, allegedly multilingual, but not very bright receptionist at the exhibition entrance or foreign visitors' reception desk. The advent of computer print-out information services suggests that descriptions of your exhibits and other capabilities should be concise yet sufficiently generic to ensure easy location.

The outlines, formal details and restraints of editorial catalogue entries are usually suggested or insisted on by the organizers; last year's catalogue is a good guide to these details. The lay-outs and arrangements of catalogues of different exhibitions vary greatly and no generally valid recommendations can be made. The description of your exhibits is the most important entry and the arrangement of the catalogue in question will determine the most effective way of presenting it. Next in importance are the address and style of your company and the names and addresses of your local representation and other outposts that are relevant to the influence sphere of the exhibition.

The entry should also provide, as far as its limitations permit, an indication of your compass of business and capability. Some catalogues provide special sections for exhibitors' business entries, in addition to the section listing only the exhibitor's name and exhibits. When editorial limitations prevent comprehensive entries, and if the marketing merit of the exhibition and its catalogue justifies it, an advertisement may provide the required space. New products, new offerings or new benefits should be emphasized and invitations to demonstrations should be included. Special capabilities such as design or consultancy should be mentioned.

If your interests are spread over more than one section of the exhibition you should explore the opportunities for multi-entries, but then inclusion of all products in the product index requires special attention. It is always advisable not to rely on the compilers of the catalogue to extract all relevant headings from your entry text, but to ensure inclusion and ease their job by providing a separate list of relevant headings.

For some industries, such as chemicals and plastics, an index of trade marks and trade names is of considerable importance. When last year's catalogue had no such index, it may be worthwhile to use your influence to ensure that it should be included in future. Attending personnel can be listed in the entry, the stand executive or manager by name, attending specialists by function only or by function and name. The languages spoken on the stand should be indicated.

Special exhibiting objectives, e.g. a search for agents or an invitation to discuss franchise or licence arrangements, should be included in the entry, as this may attract visitors who normally would not visit your stand.

Entries in foreign language catalogues should be checked by people competent to assess both the quality of the translation and the expressions used and their relevance to your business and products.

If you are new to the exhibition host country or if you are introducing new trade marks, trade names, brand names or slogans, check whether they conflict with regulations or offend local susceptibilities of custom, taste or even religion. Designs, shapes, colours, artificial word formations and slogans can be separate or cumulative offenders. An additional pitfall is ridicule or a distortion of meaning in relation to the product, and evocative brand name formations are particularly vulnerable. To offer 'strutting cranes' may not be too bad, but 'laughing sewage pumps' seems slightly inappropriate.

The effectiveness of the exhibition catalogue as a reference book and as an advertising medium depends to a large extent on the marketing merit of the exhibition and in some cases on the catalogue make-up and arrangement. A catalogue without a product index is useless as a reference book. Some exhibition catalogues are compiled in a manner which makes the locating of a product of interest such a laborious procedure that it is easier to go through all the advertisement pages than to follow the different product, stand, name, number, letter, section and page references in a tiresome sequence. In such cases an advertisement serves partly the interest of the exhibitor and partly the dubious purpose of compensating for the shortcomings of the catalogue.

The remarks made earlier concerning foreign language entries and translations apply to advertisements as well. In advertisements the language content can be reduced to a minimum by the use of drawings, sketches and photographs but these must be vetted to avoid conflicts. The preparation and timing of all elements involved in exhibition catalogue entries and publicity should be scheduled to reach the exhibition organizers in time for the issue of their advance catalogue or similar advance publication. These are usually abridged versions of the catalogue, and it may be sufficient to supply provisional entry details and to amend or revise the full entries for inclusion in the final version of the exhibition catalogue at a later date.

The following entry in the catalogue of an international instruments and electronics exhibition is an example of a complete misunderstanding of the purpose of an exhibition catalogue:

> All instruments on display are grouped by function and each group has secondary illumination in addition to the normal stand lighting. The groups of instruments, e.g. pressure flow, temperature, etc., are coupled symbolically by a central motif consisting of several large transparent edge-lit sheets, one for each function, each sheet carrying legends describing the function and any variant—the sheets are lit in sequence and in synchronism with the secondary illumination groups referred to above—the centre of the motif depicts a new product, symbolizing its data collection and interface function.

Let us examine this entry from the point of view of one particularly interested foreign visitor. All he can learn about the exhibits is that among them will be 'pressure, flow, temperature, etc.' instruments. He obviously wonders why the 'etc.' are exhibited if they deserve no better description. He is mystified by 'legend-carrying sheets' and wonders whether he will be able to understand these legends 'lit in sequence'. He concludes that the main purpose of the stand is to display edge-lit transparent sheets in which he is not really interested.

Considered more seriously, the entry is an antithesis of any marketing purpose of exhibiting, unless it is a sales plug for the stand designer. The entry does not inform a visitor to the exhibition of *what* is displayed, but only of *how* it is done. It has no post-exhibition value at all.

Another entry in the same catalogue is an example of how it should be done. After enumerating the range of instruments displayed and their applications, the entry concludes:

> Our capability to assume total responsibility in the food and brewing, oil and gas, pulp and paper, and marine industries is emphasized.

In the technical press pleas are often made for earlier publication of exhibition catalogues to enable visitors to plan their visits and use their time economically. There are exhibitions, mostly abroad, which provide catalogues one or two months before the event. There are other exhibitions at which catalogues are only obtainable on entry and on occasions the stock is exhausted after about five hours, the next batch becoming available next day.

Some exhibition organizers show a strange disregard for visitors—who after all are also their customers—because they seem to imply that most visitors know all there is to know about exhibitors, and need no further help from an exhibition catalogue. The omission of a product index from an exhibition catalogue is a manifestation not only of such disregard, but also of a most 'non-marketing' behaviour.

Checklists 1–6

	CATEGORIES OF EXHIBITIONS	
	World fairs–great international exhibitions	
	Great national fairs and exhibitions	
	General trade fairs and exhibitions:	
	international	
	national	
	regional	
	samples fairs	
	local	
	Agricultural fairs and exhibitions:	
	international	
	national	
	regional	
	specialized:	
	forestry	
	horticulture	
	fisheries	
	Consumer goods exhibitions	
	Industrial goods exhibitions	
	Combined consumer and industrial goods exhibitions	
	Combined agricultural and industrial goods exhibitions	
	General industrial exhibitions	
	Specialized industrial exhibitions:	
	exhibitions within exhibitions	
	Congresses, conferences, conventions, symposia	
	Special type exhibitions:	
	world trade centres	
	national trade centres	
	economic activity exhibitions	
	touring exhibitions	
	private exhibitions	
	showrooms	
	exhibitions without exhibition halls	

Checklist 1   CATEGORIES OF EXHIBITIONS

Whether you are an exhibitor with an established exhibition programme or a newcomer to exhibitions, you will be interested in the categories of events of particular interest to you, as in most media information about them will appear under one or more classification headings. You may be interested in new ventures in your sphere of activities or you may find that general headings are not specific enough for your purpose or that some general trade fairs contain specialized sections which are much larger than some exhibitions devoted entirely to that speciality. When you have established your classification interest you can turn to Checklist 2 to see whether the titles of the class of interest to you really cover your requirement or whether you have to consider more than one classification or more than one title, as relevant.

	EXHIBITION TITLES	
	General	
	Group:	
	industries, technologies	
	Specific:	
	product, product group	
	discipline, technique, service	
	LOCATION OF EXHIBITION	
	Geographic location:	
	permanent, mobile	
	home town, home country	
	EEC	
	Western Europe	
	Eastern Europe	
	Near East	
	Africa	
	Asia	
	Australasia	
	North America	
	South America	
	TIME ELEMENTS OF EXHIBITIONS	
	Event frequency of exhibition:	
	single	
	seasonal	
	annual	
	biennial	
	other frequency	
	Date of exhibition:	
	fixed	
	movable	
	Duration of exhibition:	
	1 day	
	2–3 days	
	4–5 days	
	other	
	Time competing events:	
	other exhibitions	
	non-commercial events	

Checklist 2   TITLES, LOCATIONS AND TIME ELEMENTS OF EXHIBITIONS

Following the review of the categories of exhibitions of interest to you (Checklist 1) you proceed to a scrutiny of their titles and their relevance to the widest definition of your interests. Their locations have a decisive bearing on their marketing merit and on the cost of participating. Their dates and duration times will indicate their compatibility with your internal time schedules.

	HISTORY OF EXHIBITION	
	History and progress of exhibition	
	Character, tradition, reputation	
	Statistical survey data	
	EXHIBITION ORGANIZERS, PROMOTERS AND SPONSORS	
	Government or other authority	
	Independent, commercial	
	Industrial or trade associations	
	Professional institutions, societies	
	Chambers of commerce	
	Press or publishers	
	ADMINISTRATION	
	Executive, secretariat	
	Foreign relations	
	Halls, buildings, open areas	
	Technical services	
	Inland and foreign exhibitors' reception	
	Inland and foreign visitors' reception	
	Information bureaux, kiosks, desks	
	EXHIBITION PUBLICITY	
	Pre-exhibition publicity, in host country or in other countries	
	During exhibition (important in metropolitan locations)	
	Press information office, regular press conferences	
	Publicity material for media	
	Live radio, television, newsreel facilities	
	New products publicity	
	Posters, leaflets, stickers, printing blocks, badges	
	Invitation cards, complimentary tickets	
	RESTRAINTS AND RESTRICTIONS	
	Limitations on stand design or exhibits	
	Publicity, sound, light, moving elements	
	Limitations and discrimination in allocation of stands	
	Formal difficulties and delays, e.g. visas, permits	
	Restrictions on personnel (nationality, political)	
	High cost of local labour and/or materials	
	Lack of skilled local labour and/or materials	
	Strikes, delays, postponements, cancellations	
	Inadequate security, pilfering, damage	

Checklist 3 HISTORY, ORGANIZERS, ADMINISTRATION AND PUBLICITY OF EXHIBITIONS

Continuing the search for suitable exhibitions you review the past and current record of exhibitions which could be of interest. The administrative features of an exhibition and the implications of their strictness, liberality or laxity are examined as they affect your own exhibiting efforts, stand design, selection of exhibits, publicity and perhaps even selection of personnel. The quality and character of the administration may be directly influenced by promoters or sponsors in some cases, only to some extent in others or not at all.

EXHIBITION HALLS AND DISPLAY AREAS	
Exhibition grounds	
Exhibition halls	
Open exhibition areas	
Test and demonstration areas	
New products section	
SPECIAL FACILITIES FOR:	
Congresses, conferences, symposia, lectures, film shows	
Separate offices, hospitality suites	
EXHIBITION HALLS AND DISPLAY AREAS SERVICES	
Security	
Lighting	
Heating, ventilation, air conditioning	
Public address system	
Storage facilities	
WC and washing facilities	
First aid facilities	
STAND SERVICES	
Electricity, gas, water	
Telephones	
Compressed air, vacuum, steam	
Waste disposal, stand cleaning	
Stand erection and dismantling	
Stand decoration and repairs	
Fire protection	
HIRE FACILITIES	
Furniture, typewriters, calculating machines, office equipment	
Refrigerators, cookers, percolators, electric kettles	
Crockery, tableware, glassware	
Fire extinguishers	

Checklist 4 EXHIBITION FACILITIES, SERVICES AND AMENITIES

The physical facilities, services and amenities of exhibitions can vary considerably from venue to venue and are best assessed on the basis of personal experience. If your exhibiting programme includes regular participation in an exhibition, this checklist can be used as a questionnaire for stand personnel or visitors, so that changes in quality or services or improvements can be noted. A dossier of services and facilities will also assist in assessing the merits of the exhibition environments and of the exhibition complex. (Continued on Checklist 5.)

	SPECIAL SERVICES	
	Customs clearance arrangements	
	Patents protection	
	Exhibitors' club	
	Interpreters, guides	
	Travel and airline bureaux	
	Hotel and accommodation reservation office	
	Theatre and entertainment booking office	
	COMMUNICATIONS	
	Post office, telex, international telephone service	
	Public address system	
	Messengers	
	AMENITIES	
	Restaurants, snack bars, refreshment trolleys	
	Cloak rooms, left luggage rooms, lost property office	
	Baths, showers, hairdressers, massage, swimming pool	
	Rest rooms, meeting rooms, shelters	
	First aid, chemists	
	Shops, newspapers and magazine kiosks	
	TRANSPORT	
	Parking arrangements	
	Car hire facilities	
	Taxi stand	
	Public transport arrangements (frequency, season tickets)	
	Internal exhibition transport	

Checklist 5   EXHIBITION FACILITIES, SERVICES AND AMENITIES

This checklist is a continuation of Checklist 4.

	EXHIBITION CATALOGUE	
	Exhibitor's individual entry:	
	name, address, telephone, cable, telex:	
	branches, agencies, connections	
	exhibition stand:	
	exhibits	
	other products and capabilities	
	new products, new benefits	
	special items, star features	
	demonstrations, tests, lectures	
	stand executive, specialists, languages	
	invitation to discuss:	
	agencies, representations	
	licensing	
	franchises	
	joint venture arrangements	
	subject index entries ⎫ computer index	
	trade name/mark entries ⎭	
	advertisements:	
	in text	
	in special section	
	covers, section dividers	
	spine	
	inserts, markers	
	translations:	
	entries	
	advertisements	
	slogans	
	timing:	
	provisional entry	
	final full entry	
	Exhibition catalogue quality and utility:	
	exhibitors' interest utility	
	visitors' interest utility	
	directory value	
	pre-exhibition availability	

Checklist 6   EXHIBITION CATALOGUE

The exhibition catalogue checklist serves two purposes. One is to provide a guide to the benefits which can be obtained from an exhibitor's entry; the other is to assist in the evaluation of the merits of the exhibition and its administration. The failings or shortcomings of an exhibition catalogue are usually pointers to a weak administration or to a lack of co-ordination between sponsors and organizers.

PART TWO

Motives, Merits, Environments, Selection and Budgeting

Attitudes to Exhibitions

A rational decision whether to participate in exhibitions and, if so, in which exhibitions must be based on a definition of your marketing motives, on an assessment of the merits of suitable exhibitions and on a selection of exhibitions compatible with your motives and your resources. Experience and continuous observation lead to the conclusion that in many cases such a rational approach to an exhibition effort is, if not completely lacking, only seldom consciously applied.

A summary of 110 interviews conducted over a period of two years will best illustrate attitudes to exhibitions. The interviews were conducted with executives of firms regularly participating in national and international exhibitions. The spectrum of attitudes to exhibitions expressed by interviewed decision-making executives ranged from one extreme of absolute rejection, through indifference, passive acceptance of the inevitable and reasoned approval, to the other extreme of uncritical enthusiasm.

A disconcerting absence of rationale was noted in a majority of the strong negative statements. Persons professing to 'hate' or even 'loathe' exhibitions, or to find them 'corrosive' and 'repulsive', regarded their position and rank as sufficient proof of competence to make such pronouncements, without having to justify them. The statements made in relation to exhibitions generally were further probed to establish the degree of discrimination between 'participating' and 'visiting' activities.

Most of the shallow negative attitudes were supported by generalizing statements that 'it's all the same', i.e. participating and visiting activities are equally unpleasant. Executives who passively accepted the need to exhibit 'because our competitors do' did not see the need to visit exhibitions in which they did not participate. 'It would be a waste of time' or 'our salesmen are better employed in the field' and similar pronouncements disposed of the question. Positive attitudes to exhibitions were found to apply to participation as much as to visiting, with perhaps some reservations which are best characterized by one statement: 'we visit as many exhibitions as we can, but we participate in as few as we can get away with'. Decisions to participate were attributed to a combination of pressures exerted by trade associations, official bodies, persuasive exhibition organizers and sponsors, who provided proof of 'all the important firms in our sector taking part'. Ever-increasing demands placed on human and material resources led to decisions based on doubtful motives. In some large organizations with elaborate publicity and exhibition departments, the instinct of departmental self-preservation acted as an encouraging selection factor and the criteria applied were very far removed from sober marketing considerations.

Familiarity with an exhibition in which 'we have always taken part', the availability of elaborately prepared exhibits and stand fixtures, the preservation of a budget allocation and similar arguments decided the participation in an exhibition for one company. Conversely, in times of tight budgets it appeared easier and safer to another company to curtail exhibition activities summarily on the grounds of their excessive budgetary and personnel demands, than to undertake an elaborate and tiresome selection of the few exhibitions which deserved participation from the many which clamoured for it.

Negative attitudes to visiting exhibitions were traced to: disappointments with obtained results, high cost for meagre returns, lack of suitable personnel and depletion of base office personnel. The sources of the disappointments proved to be: inadequate definition of aims, assignment of unsuitable personnel, selection of wrong exhibitions, poor preparation of visits, lack of visiting strategy, or a combination of some or all of these avoidable shortcomings.

Badly organized exhibitions deepened these self-inflicted disappointments. Only in three of 110 cases investigated were disappointing results turned later into positive benefits by a systematic assessment of what was in fact achieved in relation to what could have been achieved, and what therefore should be done next time.

Participating in Exhibitions

In greatly simplified terms the intention to participate in an exhibition requires answers to the following questions:

> Why do we want to exhibit?
> What do we want to exhibit?
> Where do we want to exhibit?

In terms of the marketing concept the reply to the first question requires definitions of your business, of your markets, of your position in them, of your marketing mix and of the range of marketing media you employ. The reply to the second question requires a selection of offerings (products, services, etc.) which you have chosen in the context of the objectives defined in the reply to the first question. The reply to the third question requires a review of exhibitions serving your markets and your objectives as defined in the replies to the first two questions.

Organizations with a full awareness of their corporate marketing aims and position in the markets in which they operate will find no difficulty in replying to the first and second questions. This may apply equally well to medium and small companies as to large corporations, even if the former do not always express their marketing orientation in a currently fashionable jargon. But there are exceptions in both camps. It may seem presumptuous to demand a corporate heart searching exercise before embarking on such a simple undertaking as participating in an exhibition, but the demand becomes fully justified if only some thought is given to the potential marketing impact of exhibitions, to the great rewards which can be gained, to the danger of substantial losses which can be sustained and most of all to the opportunities which are offered but could be missed.

Marketing Motives for Exhibiting

Motives for exhibiting take their inspiration and guidance from the mission of the company and its marketing strategy and they are thus true marketing motives. When the selection process is completed these motives may require re-appraisal when confronted with the realities of the selected exhibition and its merits and limitations. When concerned with different forms of conduct they can be reduced to the three principal motives of increasing, maintaining or recovering a share of the market.

They suffer to some extent from the width of their definitions and unless we also define subordinate motives of a fundamental nature and establish for them a system of ranking, or priorities, the object of the exercise, that is a systematic and rational approach to exhibiting, will be defeated. The ranking of subordinate motives must be flexible enough to allow any of them, in certain circumstances, to be elevated to principal motives or at least to top rank subordinates.

While the desire to increase your market share provides an obvious progressive motive for exhibiting, merely *maintaining a market share* may appear at first sight to be a regressive motive, but there are situations in which such a policy seems appropriate. The example of imports of motor cars being restricted to a 'safe percentage of the market' so as not to upset indigenous manufacturers is well-known. Another example is given in more detail in Case Study 1 on page 43.

Market penetration motives are frequently generated by acquisitions and mergers, by diversification activities, as protective measures to counteract shrinking markets or competitive threats to market sectors, or more constructively by an energetic and outward looking marketing policy. If the market penetration target is a planned economy market the most favourable timing for participation in an exhibition could be determined by the incidence and length of the official planning period and the ordering and negotiating periods applicable to the particular goods. You can aim at maximum impact and prepare to apply that impact before the next full planning period. Alternatively, and if justified by the situation, you can attempt a market penetration exercise in the middle of the planning period, your aim being to fill gaps created by the unfulfilled promises of other suppliers or, more rarely, by supplementary budget allocations.

Market development motives are more suitably evolved for new products, equipment, processes and concepts. The character of a new market sector may require a probing exercise because marketing research investigations, while establishing the existence of a substantial potential, also find that reactions to the exhibitor's attack on that sector cannot be predicted with sufficient certainty to justify the cost of a full scale launch. Participation in an exhibition of known impact is considered as the best means of probing into the market at reasonable expense.

Market exploration can be a valid motive for exhibiting if market research investigations indicate that an exhibition is the only viable marketing medium or the best practical means of exploring the potential of that market.

Infiltration into a new market can be greatly assisted by participating in exhibitions if such participation is planned and executed as an integral part of the overall marketing strategy and is co-ordinated with other media and activities. It can be just as costly and damaging to rely on an exhibition to take the whole burden of a marketing campaign as to neglect that most versatile of marketing tools.

Sales promotion is the most frequently quoted motive for exhibiting. More than that, people who still regard marketing as no more than a fanciful name for selling also define exhibitions as sales promotion functions. If the difference in interpretation were confined to semantics no great harm would result. The fact that more often than not the same people interpret sales promotion as sending out three sales representatives where

39

previously two operated and consider the staffing of an exhibition stand as tantamount to suspending operations in the field temporarily. They also naively proclaim that the best way to obtain good results from an exhibition is to secure a stand near an entrance or on a main gangway.

If sales promotion is an exhibiting motive, it must be assumed that the exhibition effort is one of the elements of a planned sales campaign. It is therefore no more than sound logic that the selection of exhibitions suitable for participation and the manner in which to participate should be based on and be in harmony with the intended exhibitor's general marketing and sales promotion strategy. The elements of that strategy which will most decisively affect the initiative and decision to participate in an exhibition are:

> The promotion planning period
> Sales objectives
> Market penetration targets
> Promotion budget
> Promotion continuity and flexibility

The time element of the promotion planning period is important, because exhibitions, by their nature, require long-term planning. Most exhibitions with a high marketing merit are heavily booked. Some may be biennial events, several may overlap or have very close event dates. This means that new entrants to the exhibition scene would require advance planning periods of at least two to three years before they could participate. Companies already participating in exhibitions have an easier task, unless of course the campaign is a venture into a new market sector so that the company becomes a newcomer to the relevant exhibitions.

The definition of *market penetration targets* will determine the title and timing of exhibitions suitable for the declared sales objectives. An overall promotion budget which includes a provision for exhibitions will enable the selection of exhibitions with the highest merit within the limitations of the budget. Promotion continuity plans and provisions for flexibility will indicate long-term sales promotion objectives, targets for the next planning period and possibly the widening of market penetration targets and thus of the exhibition effort.

For some products the effects of exhibiting may not become apparent for several months after the exhibition; for others only the second or third appearance at a particular exhibition will produce a significant response. This means that planned exhibition activities must have a built-in flexibility to meet foreseen variations of response as well as totally unexpected reactions. A negative response to a new development requires prepared counteraction, while an overwhelming response can be embarrassing if no provisions are in hand to cope with it.

When *marketing of innovations and improvements* is an exhibiting motive, the inevitable exposure to the strong and penetrating light of an exhibition requires a frank critical questioning of the elements of newness:

- Is the improvement the result of progress or is it only an improvement of a hitherto inadequate feature?
- Is a new development just catching up with competitors or is it overtaking the field?
- Is there an improvement in design or only a cosmetic change in appearance?
- Is it an innovation or merely a novelty?
- Does it offer new benefits or does it only remove existing shortcomings?

Genuine newness deserves maximum exposure; spurious newness requires muted treatment lest it draw attention to a previous failure or deficiency.

Some exhibitions provide special *facilities for new products*, such as separate display areas, competitions, awards and separate catalogue entries. Where these facilities are not available it is up to the exhibitor to emphasize the subject by display signs, posters and special entries in catalogues.

Some improvements for which exhibitions are good marketing media are of the kind which might be called *'anodyne' improvements*. These are concerned with noise reduction, elimination of vibration, reduction of toxicity, stress and strain reduction, waste prevention, reduction and elimination and similar efforts. Although socially and economically very laudable, such improvements often encounter the resistance of customers-manufacturers, the inertia of intermediary customers and the lack of knowledge of ultimate users.

An exhibition provides the opportunity to demonstrate the improvements to a cross-section of the market, to encourage the more progressive manufacturers, to enlighten the end users and to put pressure on intermediary customers. A good, even if somewhat dated, example is the case of a tractor engine with a considerably reduced noise level. The majority of first equipment manufacturers showed little interest in paying extra for this improvement and environmental considerations were not fashionable at the time. Only one tractor manufacturer could be persuaded, with the incentive of cost sharing, to incorporate this 'noiseless' engine in one of his tractors to be demonstrated at a forthcoming agricultural exhibition in Switzerland. A very wealthy farmer witnessed the demonstration and immediately ordered several more expensive tractors with these 'noiseless' engines. This, for a Swiss farmer very rash, procedure naturally puzzled the exhibitor, as the robust customer and his even more robust farmworkers were not particularly known for their sensitivity to engine noise. As can be guessed, the motive when disclosed was a commercial one. The excellently situated farm had a great number of tourists staying in many of its chalets, and they did not like to be wakened at 6 o'clock in the morning. Noisy tractors meant losing either valuable working hours, or not less valuable tourists.

The *marketing of pioneering concepts* or products as a motive for exhibiting goes one step further than the motive for innovations and improvements. It is fraught with pitfalls and dangers, the gravest of which is that pioneering concepts often induce a product orientation into the decision-making process of organizations which are normally market-oriented. Publicity executives and stand designers find pioneering products much more interesting than existing ones and are fascinated by the opportunity to extol their virtues in a new idiom of display and superlatives. Only companies practising management-by-objectives techniques will have no difficulty in applying them to motives of marketing a pioneer concept or product.

Before a truly pioneering concept is to be exhibited, the most important question to be asked is what can be achieved as a result of showing this pioneering effort at a particular exhibition and at a particular time. Complex and speculative time-acceptance factors need to be evaluated—a procedure difficult enough for a new exhibit, let alone a pioneering one. Technological, market and possibly even social and economic repercussions must be foreseen and reactions of competition anticipated. It is not enough to extrapolate from past experience and to hope that events will follow the established pattern.

If the display of the pioneering exhibit involves functional or operational elements reliance on a single prototype can be fatal. The single prototype syndrome is critical enough in the development state when rogue components, accidents, failures or freak conditions of a single unit can cause long and costly delays. In the environment of an exhibition such failures have as devastatingly negative an effect as badly finished or inadequately functioning units requiring constant adjustments and demonstrated to the accompaniment of profuse apologies and explanations, particularly if they are a central element of the exhibition effort. A pioneering exhibit presented in a form and method as near to its future normal use as possible, functioning properly and finished to a reasonable standard, will demonstrate the feasibility of the concept and its reliability.

'Ahead of time' exhibits, which are even more advanced than pioneering ones, require special consideration. Paradoxically their utopian character imposes less restraints on their exhibition treatment than that of merely new or pioneering exhibits. The display of 'ahead of time' exhibits usually benefits from a certain duality of purpose. The underlying conceptual and functional principles should be explained in scientifically valid, but simplified, terms and also in generally understandable popular terms. The actual exhibits should demonstrate an area of immediate practical applications and also the scope for future, perhaps even visionary, developments and possibilities.

The remarks concerning the display aspects of exhibiting pioneering and 'ahead of time' exhibits are to some extent anticipating the discussion of stand design and of exhibits dealt with in detail in the following chapter, but in the case of these exceptional exhibits it is important to subject the motives for exhibiting to a critical feasibility test of the necessary display techniques.

Marketing strategy. Opportunities for making otherwise *elusive contacts* can be a strong subsidiary motive for exhibiting and are best illustrated by a few quotations from press reports of exhibitors' statements:

> We make chemical processing equipment consisting of a combination of semi- and fully automatic units. The nature of some products processed by our equipment is of a nature discouraging free access to the plant in which it is installed. The result is that in such applications we are only called in when serious trouble develops. The equipment is almost completely trouble free when we can instruct and keep up to date process engineers, maintenance men, electrical engineers and instrument setters.

> By participating in suitable exhibitions in markets with critical applications, we invariably find that our stand is visited by otherwise elusive technicians. We find that we can solve many worrying but, from our point of view, easily corrected malfunctions and that we collect extremely valuable fault locating information.

> Our customers can talk freely to our management.

> Customers with production problems can talk to our engineers.

> The people operating our equipment are usually so far removed from us that misuse and underexploitation of potential performance is a disturbing occurrence. We participate in strategically located public exhibitions and also stage private and mobile exhibitions to overcome this problem.

A marketing strategy of *challenging entrenched positions of competitors* deserves, in abstract marketing terms, a better position than that of a subordinate function, but in the environment of the exhibition the challenging exhibits must be assured of a high marketing impact before they can serve such a strategy. Irrespective of whether the challenge is fought as a test of strength between rival giants, as a David–Goliath contest or as an exercise to eliminate small fry, the motives for exhibiting should be subjected to a scrutiny of their validity on the basis both of the absolute marketing impact of the exhibits and of the special impact required for a successful challenge.

Marketing techniques. Participation in an exhibition as a means of initiating, imple-

menting or sustaining marketing techniques and functions is usually motivated by special conditions in the exhibition host country, or in the case of large international companies by their marketing policies. The motives for such participation are seldom strong enough in their own right and are more likely to share their influence on the final decision with public relations motives and external activity motives.

Public relations. Conventional public relation activities of presenting the corporate image of an exhibitor are a natural subsidiary motive for exhibiting. In exceptional situations an exhibition can provide the only acceptable means for an expression of gratitude or for extending hospitality to special customers or influential bodies.

Special market opportunities, such as the advent of or changes in the political and economic grouping of markets, the conclusion of trade agreements and the granting of development and reconstruction aid and loans, provide valid motives for participating in exhibitions, particularly if encouraged by official bodies and perhaps supported by cost participation.

The previously discussed intention to participate in exhibitions and the definition of motives for exhibiting provide the background for a speculative search of exhibitions seemingly compatible with these motives and your exhibition strategy. The selection of exhibitions in which participation can be implemented may require a re-appraisal of the motives for exhibiting and a review of the available material, human and time resources.

It may be argued that marketing motives rationally established on the basis of valid aims should not require any further review. Theoretically this may be true, even if inadvisable; in practice it sometimes is so because strong departmental or executive influences, or in smaller firms personal convictions or prejudices, preclude a revision of declared motives. But neither the data generally available about exhibitions, nor the practice of a realistic and flexible marketing strategy, warrant a headstrong attitude. Having made this apology to formalists, we can proceed to review and probe the initiative for participation and the thinking which led to the definition of the marketing motives for exhibiting. The depth and extent of that probing will depend on the role and hierarchical position of the person wielding the probe. A simple scrutiny of the marketing rationale of the motives may suffice in one case, a dismissal of motives based on parochial or vested interests could be necessary in another. The approval and reinforcement of strong functional motives and their evaluation to a higher rank of importance can contrast with an enquiry into the omission of valid motives because of ignorance or fictional obstacles.

The formulation of valid marketing motives and objectives also provides guidance for exhibition effort strategies and display techniques, for targets to be attained and, most importantly, for benchmarks to be used when evaluating results.

Marketing Motives—Case Study 1

A manufacturing company participating regularly in major exhibitions relevant to their international marketing of industrial catering equipment attained a position in the market which, from an overall strategy point of view, was quite satisfactory and which was gained against the very strong and sometimes vicious opposition of competitors. After the battle, all competitors settled down to an uneasy sharing of the market. Systematic and continuous observation of the market by the company's marketing researchers indicated that due to their superior marketing techniques, a further substantial increase of their market share would be quite feasible. But it was also established that such an expansion would provoke a very strong reaction from competitors. All the products competing for the market, although well-established in their current form, were in a declining phase of their technological life cycle. The company had at that time developed a new range of products, strongly protected by patents and due for launching two years hence. They were faced with the problem of the manner of exhibiting, i.e. with defining the objectives of the forthcoming series of participations in exhibitions which were scheduled in their long-term exhibition programme. The question of not exhibiting at all was broached theoretically, but rejected for a number of reasons, of which the decisive one was the almost certain loss of stand space in a number of very heavily booked exhibitions.

The main policy consideration was not to provoke a price cutting war which would affect the price policy of the new range, when it became available. The danger was seen in the mounting, in keeping with past practice, of an intensive exhibition effort which had made a substantial contribution to their success in the market in the past. Such an effort was bound to be interpreted by competitors as a further incursion into the settled pattern of market shares.

The marketing motives for exhibiting (Checklist 7, page 78) were defined as:

> principal activity motive:
>> maintaining existing market share
> subordinate functional motive:
>> sales promotion of established products.

The exhibiting activity techniques (Checklist 23, page 125) were defined as:

> appealing to:
>> customers
>> end users
> display and demonstration of features of exhibits
>> performance
>> economy
>> operation
> display of service and spares capabilities
>> service availability
>> spares availability

As can be seen from the definitions of motives, design and appearance features were not included as display elements. Normally at a biennial event at least a new colour scheme would have been introduced, together with improvements in shape and probably in performance.

The stand personnel were very thoroughly briefed about the policy on which the objectives were based and all executives visiting the exhibition were also explicitly informed about the policy and exhibiting technique. This briefing was particularly important as enthusiastic sales personnel and sales executives could easily have misunderstood the mild tone of the exhibition efforts and perhaps tried to compensate for it by unwittingly disclosing future plans.

Marketing Merits of Exhibitions

General and Specific Merits

The marketing merits of an exhibition are its fundamental *raison d'être*; they determine its development and sustained progress and its power of attracting exhibitors and visitors.

The general merits or demerits of an exhibition are circumscribed by the marketing validity of its aims and scope, by its physical structure and location, by the quality of its organization, by its exhibitors and visitors and by the advantage or shortcomings of its different environments. General marketing merits of an exhibition which are compatible with the motives for exhibiting and the aims and resources of intending exhibitors and potential visitors are transformed into specific marketing merits valid for individual exhibiting initiatives.

A critical examination of specific merits of an exhibition and of the measure and manner in which they support and advance the accomplishment of stated aims, and a comparison with other exhibitions seemingly serving the same market, will provide a basis for the merit rating or ranking and for the final selection of exhibitions suitable for participating.

An assessment of the general marketing merits of an exhibition can be made by a scrutiny of the following main features:

> The validity, from a marketing point of view, of the exhibition's title, its declared aims and its scope, when related to the structure of the target markets.

> The competence of the exhibition organizers and the relevance and effectiveness of their publicity, public relations and other promotion efforts.

> The date and duration time of the exhibition. The quality of the exhibition structure, its halls and other stand locations and the quality and efficiency of technical arrangements and facilities and services for exhibitors and visitors.

> The quality and quantity of visitors attracted to the exhibition related to the stated aims and scope of the exhibition and the potential of the target market.

> The quality and quantity of exhibitors and the historic frequency of their participation.

> The geographic location and geographic spheres of influence of the exhibition.

> The marketing relevance of the different exhibition environments when related to the main aims of the exhibition and to the interests of exhibitors and visitors.

The specific merits or demerits of an exhibition can only be established when general merits, about which reliable information is available, are confronted with the motives, aims and resources of an intending exhibitor. There are no absolute values of exhibition merits, only relative ones. Irrespective of their objective high value, the same features, i.e. the same merits, can be more or less attractive to two different prospective exhibitors.

Exhibition Environments

The general and specific merits of exhibitions are strongly influenced by their environments. The space–time characteristics of exhibitions place them in a unique position in these environments. They are of it, yet only for a short space of time. Their impact may or may not continue after they have closed down. Depending on the strength of that impact they can alter the environment, or at least substantially contribute to changes in it, or alternatively they may leave hardly any trace. Some exhibitions with long years of tradition behind them enhance their importance and influence as time goes on, others have not much more to offer than a slowly dying memory of past glories. However, the better defined their purpose, the more purposeful their aims, the more they become within their environment a microcosm with a separate identity.

Because of their insularity and short existence exhibitions have two environments: an internal one created by the exhibition as a self-contained unit and an external one, the environment of the venue in which the exhibition is held. The frontiers between the two environments are not always clearly defined and for exhibitors and visitors both can have their own specific merits and demerits.

A perceptive and imaginative marketing attitude will indicate to exhibition organizers how best to take advantage of a favourable external environment and how to overcome, counteract or compensate for an unfavourable one. Exhibition organizers with no such perception and no imagination manage to waste the opportunities which a cosmopolitan or metropolitan host environment offers them, by mounting catchpenny events of parochial unimportance.

In this section we will examine the nature of various environments, their merits and the influence they can exert on your decision to participate in an exhibition or to visit one.

Location Environment

The merit of the location of an exhibition's venue and of its geographic sphere of influence is determined by the characteristics of that location when related to your marketing motives, both in the narrow sense of the exhibition in which you participate and in the wider sense of your general marketing strategy.

The exhibition host country may be your primary target market, but it can also have ethnic, linguistic, economic or historical links with neighbouring or distant countries which extend its marketing influence beyond its own frontiers. Whatever the definition and character of a market is, all marketing operations have to be carried out in a definable location or territory. It is from this point of view that the geographic influence range of an exhibition is important. The definitions of spheres of influence are of necessity fairly open. Thus *local* may mean a sizeable town, an industrial or urban conglomeration or a market town and its agricultural hinterland. A *national* sphere of influence needs no comment, but an *international* sphere of influence can range from two small neighbouring countries to many large ones. A sphere of influence which due to special circumstances extends over the whole of the North American continent could be classed as *continental* and such a sphere extending to both Americas as *intercontinental*. For some marketing objectives the general economic structure of an area can be a decisive factor and for some world-wide operations the United Nations designations of Economic Class I, II and III areas could be significant.

From the point of view of Alpha Company, conventional geographic areas may be of no more than formal conceptual value and the company would have to construct its own categories strictly related to its marketing strategy. From the point of view of Beta Company, one or a combination of several geographic categories could provide the required basis for selection and decision.

The locale of the exhibition, i.e. the town, region, province or country in which it takes place, endows it with a sphere of influence created by the importance and demographic character of the location. Thus, for example, exhibitions held in or near London, Paris or New York will benefit from the metropolitan and cosmopolitan character of these cities, exerting a *centrifugal* outward dispersing *marketing force*, whereas local exhibitions held in Elda or Colmar will benefit from the *centripetal* inward saturation *marketing force* of these locations.

The centrifugal marketing force in metropolitan locations will extend the orbit of contacts to government offices, corporation headquarters, financial and investment institutions, foreign government and trade representations, trade missions and trade centres and to contacts with people visiting the metropolis on other than exhibition business.

The centripetal marketing force in enclave locations exerts its influence on a concentration of specialized industrial or commercial activities giving opportunities for a strong impact on a narrow sector. Large-scale exhibitions serving internationally significant industries will derive maximum benefits from cosmopolitan locations; highly specialized regional or single industry oriented exhibitions will benefit most from local exhibitions. However, there is no inherent advantage in the locale except in relation to the marketing merit of the exhibition taking place. The merit of a well-organized international exhibition with an established reputation is in no way affected by its location in a provincial town; a badly organized and badly housed exhibition will not redeem its failings by being held in a cosmopolitan capital city.

A critical assessment of the location environment of an exhibition will influence decisions concerning the manning of stands, the inclusion of special exhibits, the visits of executives not directly connected with the exhibition effort (financial, legal and patent specialists and licence negotiators) or the attendance of technicians expert in particular fields of the market.

Exhibition Hall Environment

The environment of the exhibition hall area in which your stand is located is important but not necessarily critical as long as the facilities are adequate. When this environment is exceptionally favourable, as it could be with airy, well-proportioned air-conditioned halls, or exceptionally unfavourable, as it would be with a crowded maze of upper floor galleries neither properly lit nor adequately ventilated, then the hall environment becomes a merit factor. In some exhibitions you may find some old halls and some new ones and from your point of view as an exhibitor it may be important in which of these your stand is located and in which the stands of your competitors. The quality of the hall environment is certainly perceived by visitors and they are influenced by it. Their inclination to linger just that much longer in a favourable environment has been frequently observed.

The range of moods created by exhibition halls, consciously or by default, is very wide indeed. You might have the busy atmosphere of the woodworking section of an exhibition, with the high-pitched whine of saws and the inviting aroma of sawn timber. You may witness the grotesque spectacle of giant plastic moulding machinery spewing out half-useless components with faults which would not even pass the eyes of an inspector looking the other way, and the sight of endless queues of visitors of assorted sexes and ages waiting for up to 10 minutes to secure the free gift of a plastic bucket of sickly yellow colour with a weak spot probably somewhere in its bottom.

You can enjoy the aesthetic pleasure of darkened stands with cunningly lit display cases of precision instruments or electronic components, vying for your attention as much as would jewels or crystalware. But you have also the spectacle of unbelievably crowded stands, which seem to have come straight from the street market, in which suppliers of motor car and boating accessories so lavishly indulge.

The general quality of the exhibition hall will also affect your stand position. Not all

47

exhibitors can have first-class positions, and the better the hall layout and design, the fewer chances of dead corners, obscured views, obstructing columns and draughty gangways.

There are exhibition halls which by their poor quality seem to belie their very purpose. An old building is usually blamed for all shortcomings, but this is not a very valid excuse. Promoters of exhibitions have by the nature of their business access to the best and most ingenious designers. Why they do not inspire them to take the same advantage of an existing structure as stage designers do within the limitations of an old theatre building is a matter of surprise or, perhaps more aptly, another example of the marketing myopia so well documented for other products.

In the case of multi-floor exhibition buildings, the environments of different floor locations assume added significance. If you can only secure a stand on an upper floor which in fact is no more than an overflow area, the potential flow of visitors may be seriously affected. You may have to compensate for such a disadvantage by issuing special invitations and additional publicity, in other words by incurring extra cost. If your exhibiting objective is to attract a great number of new contacts even such efforts may not produce the required result. A multi-floor building designed for exhibition purposes poses other problems. The efficiency of lifts and escalators, effective signposting and access and exit locations become important factors. You may be reluctant to accept a top floor location, because top floor attendances are reputed to be lower than average, but the availability of direct express lifts may counteract that assumption effectively. The top floor may contain a restaurant or other special feature and your stand will benefit from its proximity to the resulting flow of visitors. Regrettably, once more it is difficult to give a general ruling on the merits or demerits of such locations. An assessment of the situation can be made by judicious questioning of actual exhibitors and best of all by personal reconnaissance.

Stands, Exhibits and Personnel Environments

The aesthetic and functional qualities of exhibition stands and of displays of exhibits are usually a reflection of the exhibitors' attitudes to design.

Fashions in stand design and display techniques come and go as they do in other spheres of life. In an exhibition environment they will be mostly the reflection of styles prevailing in the exhibition host country, which will account for the majority of the exhibitors. A prospective foreign exhibitor needs to take note of that environment and relate it to his intended participation and to stand designs so far adopted by him. What appeared more than adequate in one location may prove disastrous in another. The bold and daring stand suitable for a cosmopolitan setting can appear pretentious and exaggerated in more modest provincial surroundings.

Your observations of stand design and the display techniques of exhibits should be related to the general standard of exhibition stands and to the standard of stands in your sector of industry, in your exhibition hall or in other relevant groupings, with particular attention paid to the stands of competitors. If previous experience is not available and if repeat participation is contemplated, a systematic survey conducted by your stand designer, accompanied by your stand manager, usually handsomely repays the trouble taken.

The problems of stand personnel are fully discussed later on, but the stand staffing environment of an exhibition deserves a note of its own. The expertise and professionalism of personnel staffing the stands at an exhibition has a high marketing merit content. Your own stand personnel will be subject to comparison with those of your competitors and the comparison will be made by very influential judges—your customers or potential customers.

At international exhibitions your neighbours may be international companies with multilingual experts. Conversely, at another exhibition and despite your more modest stand, you can be the exhibitor who paid the exhibition host country the compliment of stand personnel speaking the language of the country, even if it is a rare one, while your big neighbours did not bother.

The quality of the staffing of stands can set the 'tone' of an exhibition and contribute to its reputation. Assessment of the quality of stand staffing can be made on the basis of recent past experience and observation, of exhibition intelligence, press reports of interviews and, when conferences or technical discussions are part of the exhibition programme, on the basis of the linguistic aptitudes of participants.

Exhibitor Environment

The quality and numbers of exhibitors participating in an exhibition are cardinal merit factors and their correct assessment can, and should, influence your decision whether to participate in an exhibition and if so in what manner.

The exhibitor environment requires evaluation of three main groups of exhibitors: customers, competitors and suppliers. Not all three groups would necessarily be represented at the particular exhibition you are investigating but at another exhibition serving the same market this could be the case.

The customer environment can include current, new, potential and lapsed customers and an evaluation of potential purchasing power is one way of establishing the merit of that group of exhibitors. On the other hand your exhibiting objectives may aim at a different goal, such as the introduction of a new product or the demonstration of your service capabilities, in which case you will survey the group of customers from the point of view of their susceptibility as targets for your tasks. If your products are of the component, auxiliary or accessory type, the willingness of your customers to acknowledge their incorporation, or to display them on their stands, or both, has an important bearing on the merit rating of the exhibition.

The term exhibitors-customers extends also to indirect customers and users. Evaluation of their quality will be based on other criteria, but always related to your marketing strategy and exhibiting objectives. Assessment of their exhibition effort is interesting as background information and possibly from the point of view of an identification of your products in their exhibits if the case applies.

The importance of the competitor environment of the exhibition needs no special emphasis. The national and international standing of your competitors in relation to your position, their marketing skills and resources compared with yours, their importance in your particular market sector, perhaps the absence from the exhibition of market leaders or their attendance in strength—all these factors noted and evaluated by marketing research, will influence your decision, your budget allocation, your selection of exhibits, and your exhibition strategy. During the exhibition you will supplement your information with up-to-date observations. Particular attention should be paid to your competitors' exhibition efforts, and comparison made with your own effort.

The supplier environment is of secondary interest unless your exhibiting objectives include buying interests or changes of sources of supply. The merit of the suppliers' environment will then depend on the capacity of exhibitors as actual or potential suppliers.

An analytical review of the main groups of exhibitors will also enable you to form a picture of the corporate environment in which your own exhibition effort will operate and contribute to the assessment of the internal technological environment of the exhibition. It will reveal whether you will be in the company of leaders, improvers or followers in your particular market.

The national provenance of the exhibitors is significant for the assessment of geographical markets and of import–export patterns. Examination of the exhibition catalogues of two or three preceding exhibitions will disclose changes in participation, the development or decline of the exhibition and the relative importance of lapsed or new participants. Analysis can be carried out by methods ranging from simple ranking and weighting to sophisticated data processing, the criteria applied depending on the basic data available and on the complexity of the situation. The rank could indicate the objective importance of the exhibitor as an organization and the weight his subjective standing in the market. For well-established exhibitions the changes in participation of important exhibitors may be a sufficiently good indicator of the up-to-date merit of the exhibition.

Continuous systematic observation of the exhibitor environment is of particular value when you are participating in exhibitions in different countries serving the same market, or when you are participating in annual or other sequences of the same exhibition.

Exhibitions of high marketing merit are very good indicators of the mood of the market, but a deliberate and systematic effort must be made to read the signs. Supplementary merit factors of the exhibitor environment could be added by reviewing the participation of exhibitors outside the three main groups.

Participation by official bodies, government, local government, municipal and institutional can open opportunities for personal contacts which would normally be difficult to establish. An invitation to visit your stand is the most natural request at an exhibition but in other circumstances it may not be welcome or advisable. Exhibitors of products of indirect marketing interest but of direct plant or office interest, such as instrumentation, materials handling, safety or office equipment, can provide you with an opportunity to see new developments in these fields.

The presence of banks, investment institutions and insurance companies is a sign that serious business transactions are usually conducted during the exhibition. It must of course be established whether more than simple foreign currency exchange facilities are provided. Banks with offices at an exhibition usually issue reports, which may provide comments on your competitors and customers. International exhibitions of repute are often visited by official trade missions and, in the case of planned economy markets, contacts with such missions can be of important marketing value.

For some products or markets the indirect merit indicators can do no more than strengthen a decision taken on other merits but for others they could be factors of considerable importance.

Visitor Environment

In the environment of an international exhibition of high marketing and organizational merit, the exhibitors' stand personnel can encounter a vast range of visitor categories. These categories are listed in Figure 9 (page 109). The fact that they contain so many individual functions does not necessarily mean that all would appear as single and separate persons. In a large organization the 'buyer' may be a person delegated by a purchasing department which in turn is subject to the control or directives of technical or commercial decision influences. In a small organization a purchasing function involving complex technical and commercial decisions may be concentrated in one person. A visitor could combine several roles because the organization could not, or would not, delegate more than one person to visit the exhibition.

A well-selected, trained and prepared stand team will be able to cope with all technical and commercial problems, but it can exert only a small degree of influence over the incidence of occasions on which they are confronted by the different categories. The time factor becomes very important and the only way to control it is to discriminate in the time allocated to the different visitor categories and to use as many non-personal aids as are compatible with an effective exhibition performance. Such aids must be clearly used only in support of personal attention or as temporary expedients to relieve the visitor's tedium while waiting, but never as substitutes for person-to-person contact. Identification of the quality of visitors, their interests, status and buying influence becomes a vital, initial approach function as it will determine the character of the action to be taken. This identification is also an essential element of post-exhibition analysis and follow-up actions.

The influence categories affecting an industrial product, later discussed in more detail, are illustrated in Figure 7 (page 103). In normal trading conditions the inner-circle confrontation is the end-result of the peripheral influences exerted in both semi-circular sectors. An assessment of the influence category and of the proximity factor of the visitor's interest, during the opening stages of the interview, is important in any situation. For industrial products incorporated in one or more assemblies before they reach the final product and its user, the influence and proximity factors determine the approach to the visitor and the need, if any, to call in specialists, e.g. application engineers, designers, chemists, etc.

An important marketing merit is the number of new visitors, particularly if they can be identified as to their status and interest. The opinion that it is a great merit if an exhibition admits only trade buyers and trade visitors needs serious investigation. Some exhibition organizers boast about the exclusion of the general public from their events, and some exhibitors clamour for such exclusion. It is by no means certain that such exclusion generally contributes to the marketing quality of an exhibition. Many industrial products are so remote from the ultimate user that they could only benefit in the markets from a nearer acquaintance and better understanding among the general public. Separate days or special hours of attendance are a compromise arranged where too great an influx of the general public is anticipated, although this in itself should be a sign of interest. If so, the public should be not only admitted but invited.

In general trade fairs with sections covering a number of different industries, the total number of visitors is an indication of limited value to the exhibitor, unless his exhibits are represented in several sections. For exhibitors with one stand, the position of the hall in which the stand is located, the position of the stand in that hall and the influence of these positions on the likely flow of visitors are more important than the total number of visitors passing the entrance turnstiles.

It may be interesting to note that one exhibition was visited by 22 000 buyers from 22 countries and another by 110 000 buyers from 55 countries, but much more information would be required in order to relate these figures to the marketing strategy of an individual exhibitor.

Technological and Industrial Environment

A sober and dispassionate assessment of the technological position of your products in their markets is a basic requirement of marketing. It may have to be adjusted from the general to the particular market in which the products are exhibited. If such an assessment is not available, the advent of an exhibition effort provides a good opportunity to highlight the need for it.

The technical simplicity or complexity of the product, its up-to-date, advanced or perhaps obsolete design features, its pedestrian, sophisticated or exaggerated appearance, its adequate, excellent or poor performance—all these factors add up to its technological position in relation to a particular exhibition and to the market it is intended to serve. An evaluation of the technological position should be made in relation to the state of art in that market and against the background of competitive products exhibited and otherwise available in the market. This evaluation will show which product advantages can be emphasized and which shortcomings should be played down. In some situations the decision may be reached to postpone participation or not to participate at all.

The circumscribed markets for industrial components, elements and auxiliary equipment are particularly sensitive to technological position factors, whilst complete products operate in more open markets, where their overall marketability has a decisive influence. An exhibition held in a highly industrialized country or in a region specializing in the particular industry it serves is located in a technological environment of predominantly external character. It remains an environment of merit irrespective of the quality and quantity of exhibitors participating in the exhibition.

Let us for example assume that the exhibition is not very well-organized and that you are the only technologically prominent exhibitor among competitors of lesser quality. You could gain a considerable advantage from this exceptional status if you make sure that your presence is known to potential customers, particularly those who would not otherwise bother to visit an exhibition which, from their point of view, has a low marketing merit.

The exhibition can be located in an *external industrial environment* which is expanding, stagnating or regressing, be it because the industries are in one of these states of their life cycle or because external circumstances exert an encouraging, maintaining or restricting influence.

The exhibition can have an *internal industrial environment* which is in a state of stagnation while the external environment is expanding or vice versa. The evaluation of these factors will assist you in arriving at a merit rating of the exhibition from this technological and industrial point of view.

Symposia and conferences combined with an exhibition also contribute to the shaping of the internal technological environment of the exhibition. The merit rating of such events is not an easy matter and must be related with care to your exhibiting objectives. A symposium of high technological merit does not necessarily elevate a low merit exhibition to a higher level, nor does an exhibition of high marketing value ncessarily ensure the high technological merit of a symposium combined with it.

Usually there is a connection between the industrial and technological environment of the host country and the merit of an exhibition-symposium combination. Occasionally such combined events of high technological merit are held in what might be called an industrially incongruous environment. Exhibitions-symposia on automation, instrumentation and cybernetics held in Yugoslavia and Hungary are examples.

Scientific Environment

The presence or proximity of universities, technical colleges, scientific institutes and research laboratories can influence the marketing merit of an exhibition located within their radius of influence or access.

The buying expertise of customers can be augmented by calling on the services of members of faculties or specialists. Testing and experimental facilities of institutes can be used for assessment purposes, by both the customer and the exhibitor. The claims made for advanced designs or progressive concepts are subject to scrutiny by people with up-to-date knowledge—even if often only theoretical—of the latest achievements.

You have to assess how such an environment will affect your exhibits and how it will help or hinder your marketing strategy.

On the whole one can say that a sophisticated scientific environment will be favourable for progressive equipment or for products based on sound design and operational principles, and unfavourable to products with overt or hidden characteristics of design or operational obsolescence.

External Marketing Environment

The external marketing environment of the exhibition is particularly significant for territorially defined markets, as the majority of visitors to an exhibition will come from the exhibition host country. The actual percentage of inland to foreign visitors varies considerably but it is safe to assume that not less than about 70 per cent of visitors come from the host country and in most cases about the same proportion of inland exhibitors.

If your motive for exhibiting is market penetration or entry into the exhibition host country a careful scrutiny of the character of its marketing environments will influence your decision to participate and the manner of that participation. Sophisticated channels of distribution and promotion media in your target market may require an effort beyond your resources, while established competitors-exhibitors can back up their stand activities by an extensive marketing capability. A situation may arise in which a very good response to your exhibition effort would put a great strain on your, perhaps modest, resources. An investigation of the marketing environment may thus lead you to a different emphasis in your exhibition objectives. Your exhibits could be chosen with a view to attract the attention of potential agents rather than direct customers.

The availability in the market of container terminals, free ports, free trade zones or free transit zones are important marketing environment elements, particularly for market entering and market penetration objectives. Associations of import agents, consumer protection societies, government or official test and approval agencies must be considered as influencing the overall market environment.

National Environment

Despite the internationalization of markets and industries, each country has its own culture, traditions, preferences, foibles and idiosyncrasies—rational or irrational as the case may be. The following 'environments' are but a few pointers to what an exhibition effort, if it is to be effective, must take into account.

Economic environment factors have the most direct influence on the marketing environment, and generally they are also the best documented and most widely communicated. Information about changes in internal credit conditions, investment policies, politico-economic conditions, industrial groupings and similar factors is less readily available and in markets inclined to reticence in publishing such information deeper probing is required. Impending changes in import quotas, tariffs and custom duties are obvious factors requiring timely observation. The prevailing trading pattern in market sectors which are of particular interest, the ratio of private to public trading and the importance of government trading agencies should be reviewed. Existing or projected agricultural or industrial development schemes, investment subsidies or aid grants, tax concessions or international loans should be related to your marketing objectives.

Political environment factors can affect the decision to exhibit and the scope and mode of participation. An unfriendly political climate could indicate that it would be wise to use alternative means of marketing; an exceptionally friendly one could encourage a more sumptuous participation than would normally be considered. In an unstable situation a diplomatic absence may prove less embarrassing at a later date than participation during a time of impending change. Products of direct or indirect strategic character are particularly affected by this factor.

Discrimination by the public sector against suppliers on the basis of their national origin or prejudices in the private sector can adversely affect the marketing merit of an exhibition. A friendly political environment and the establishing or renewing of political associations can affect it favourably.

Legal environment. Legislation can affect the choice of exhibits and, under certain circumstances, the marketing techniques and price policies which have to be adopted, e.g. monopolies and anti-trust legislation, standards requirements, price regulation, distributors' and agents' legal protection, exclusive market arrangements, franchises, unfair competition legislation or advertising restraints.

Social environment factors may favour low-priced mass consumption goods in one situation or luxury and leisure goods in another. Changes in social habits, in incomes, in housing programmes or in health services, would indicate, depending on the direction of the change, a favourable or a discouraging situation for the products affected, e.g. building, hospital and public works equipment.

Aesthetic environment. Assessment of the esoteric values of aesthetics generally and of appearances and tastes particularly is full of pitfalls, but in the environment of international exhibitions it deserves serious consideration. The exhibition offers an opportunity for direct comparison at close quarters of the styles, shapes and colours of displayed exhibits, of the stand and of its elements. To disregard that aspect of your exhibition effort is as inadvisable as to disregard the now acknowledged emotional involvement of industrial buyers making purchases of industrial equipment.

The aesthetic environment of your exhibits and stand will be different in Denmark and Portugal, in Hong Kong and Rio de Janeiro, in Mexico and Bombay. Although a badly designed stand can spoil the effect of well-designed exhibits, exhibits not acceptable on aesthetic grounds will not be made more acceptable by the best stand design. The question of what is bad, acceptable or best design must be left to the beholder.

The cultural environment can have an indirect influence on the merit of an exhibition. It can enhance the understanding by visitors of sophisticated or science based products but it can also cause very critical attitudes to inadequate products or presentation. Theatres, concert halls, art collections and other cultural events can provide opportunities for extramural contacts and entertaining, which in carefully selected cases can be of great value.

Merit Rating of Exhibitions

The discussion of marketing motives for exhibiting and of the merits of exhibitions and the checklists enumerated the factors relevant to the selection of exhibitions suitable for participation. But decisions cannot be based on a list of factors. A measure of quality and quantity is required so that preferences can be expressed, the expression of preferences being the essence of any decision-making process.

Merit rating can be used for measuring quality or performance, but any such rating can be only as good as the judgement of those operating it. If merit rating is regarded merely as a tool and not as a means in itself, and if it is used with circumspection, reasonable results can be ultimately obtained. Even in situations where data and performance assessments are plentiful and reliable and the means of selection as sophisticated as modern science and technology can make them, there comes a point when merits have to be rated and weighted, when judgement has to be used.

In the exhibition situation, complexity, variety and interaction of all manner of factors abound, but often not enough reliable information is obtainable or, if it could eventually be obtained, the effort to do so in terms of cost and time would defeat the main object of the exercise, which is to make decisions about participating in exhibitions. We must therefore have recourse to *elliptical merit rating* by reducing the factors involved to those considered as key factors or as otherwise critical.

Elliptical merit rating can be used for its advantage of shortening a merit rating procedure but its disadvantage must be taken into account—it can obscure the presence of constraints and negative influences when the identification of critical factors is at fault. For the selection of exhibitions elliptical merit rating is not a palliative but a dire necessity.

The assessment of some of the merit elements must of necessity be based on past performance. Exhibitions of long standing can be relied upon to maintain or improve the standards of their technical organization. Long-term stand contracts enable an assessment within fairly safe limits of exhibitor participation and quality. Assessment of the quality and quantity of visitors is subject to some uncertainty, as in the event considerable variations can occur, particularly due to unforeseen circumstances. Even new exhibitors must declare their intention at least twelve months in advance, while visitors can decide at the very last moment not to attend. The merits of an exhibition can be distorted by a change in trading patterns in a particular market, by a decline of attendance or by overcrowding, by the emergence of competitive ventures, by labour difficulties and by changes in the political or economic climate. To some extent the merits can be assessed on the basis of information supplied by the organizers, providing it is supported by evidence of reliability and meaningful analysis.

The assessment can be supplemented and verified by a close scrutiny of exhibition catalogues from one or more previous years and by questioning relevant trade associations, customers, friendly competitors and consular posts in the case of foreign exhibitions.

Trade journals usually review important exhibitions in their field, but in many cases their reports are no more than summaries of press hand-outs with a few highlights of interest. On several occasions personal interviews which the author held with the reporter responsible for a review yielded very enlightening additional information. The merit rating of exhibitions for which participation is planned for several events ahead should be constantly reviewed and brought up to date. The exhibition's general rating and even more importantly its specific rating related to your own marketing objectives should be assessed for improvement and decline, and also in comparison with other existing or newly arrived competitive exhibitions. In short, you should treat an exhibition as a discriminating buyer would treat the acquisition of a highly priced product or service.

An exploratory visit is the best way to assess the marketing merits of an exhibition. Even after all the pertinent documentary information is obtained and analysed, there are always intangible impressions which cannot be conveyed by a report and which to an individual prospective exhibitor could be of considerable importance. Exhibitors participating in an exhibition have of course an excellent opportunity to assess its specific marketing merit, providing that their own marketing objectives and exhibiting motives are clearly defined and used as bench-marks and that the assessment procedure is made a subject of explicit instructions, as discussed in the chapters dealing with stand personnel and intelligence.

In some situations a systematic merit rating has to be supplemented by the consideration of market features which can be best described as *notional, condition* and *attitude* market characteristics. They are seldom susceptible to exact quantitative evaluation, but their qualitative assessment can add another dimension to the merit rating of an exhibition. The *risk elements* of an exhibition provide another set of factors which can affect the merit rating and therefore the decision to participate in or visit an exhibition. Examples of market features which can be used as aids for merit rating and selection are arranged in Checklist 15 (page 86). Notional market characteristics are based on territorial, population and economic activity concepts. Market density, freedom and progress constitute the market condition group of factors and attitudes factors are listed under market and official attitudes and market discrimination headings. The list could be extended almost indefinitely. You may find that none of the quoted examples fits your case, or that situations which are presented as risks are to you no more than routine procedures.

Notional market characteristics. The exhibitions in which you will participate or which you will be visiting will serve a market. The definition of that market may be sufficiently well-expressed in the exhibition title and its tradition, or its established reputation may be a reliable indication of that market. When selecting exhibitions you have to reconcile the target-market you expect to reach by exhibiting with the market offered by the exhibition. However, your target-market may have physical or conceptual boundaries far beyond the reach of the exhibition. Notional market characteristics attributed to your target-market can help in such cases in the final selection of exhibitions or in shaping your exhibition strategy for the events already selected.

A territorial market concept may indicate that your target-market is continental and you may have the choice between a number of smaller exhibitions covering the continent or one or two large ones attracting exhibitors and visitors from the whole continent. On the other hand your market can have a pronounced regional or local bias and in addition to its territorial aspect you may have to consider its linguistic elements or potential sociological obstacles to your products. At the same time you could encounter an overcrowded market with an antagonistic attitude or a spacious one with a receptive attitude.

The marketing concept of an exhibitor and the range of products involved may lead to a *technology definition* of the markets and it is important for you to be able to assess the marketing influence of an exhibition in relation to the technology or technologies it serves. It is equally important to ascertain that an exhibition in fact has no such concept or falls between two stools in that respect. On the other hand an exhibition may bridge two or more interacting technologies and so give exhibitors and visitors new market insights and opportunities. If the motives for exhibiting or visiting have a strong technological content the merits of the technological environment of the exhibition assume a dominant role. In locations of concentrated industrial activity the industrial environment can also contribute to the merit of an exhibition.

The linking of several subjects or concepts in one exhibition can be the result of a number of reasons or initiatives. General trade fairs are *linked subjects exhibitions* as a result of historic development and tradition in the case of old established events and as a result of deliberate policy in newer events. The organizational aspect of linked subjects exhibitions can range from a haphazard mixture of stands catering for the different interests to an effective division into different sectors, so that the end result is more in the nature of a series of specialized exhibitions linked only by the common site and organization. Exhibitions catering for specialized interests can link subjects in logical combinations of two or more items. There are natural affinities, e.g. maintenance and safety, hygiene and welfare. There are universal affinities when one activity, product range or concept is relevant to almost any other activity, e.g. materials handling, packaging and storage, measuring, inspection and testing, waste disposal and material recovery, leasing, contract hire and service contracts.

Different technological techniques combine in the solution of newly emerging problems and interaction between technologies and other disciplines results in linked activities, e.g. biomedical engineering, biomedical computing and bio-astronautics.

In some cases the linking of different subjects in one exhibition seems to be devoid of any logical or marketing justification. It is usually revealed as a blatant attempt to fill an exhibition hall which would otherwise remain partly empty of stands. To the visitor it is as transparent a device as the provision of lavish rest areas, which are, in effect, empty stand spaces filled by tables and chairs. To all, except perhaps to the most unobservant, such devices demonstrate clearly that had it not been for the failure to sell space, the organizers would not have provided the irrelevant added interest items, nor would they be so concerned with the seating comfort of visitors. Exhibitors usually have a cogent comment—'never again'.

In the selection for participating, the merits of linked subjects exhibitions should be related to the dominant marketing motives of the exhibitor and to his subjective merit requirements. In the selection of exhibitions for visiting, linked subjects exhibitions based on natural affinities can have a special attraction for visitors with *buying interests* or *intelligence interests*, as it is more than likely that most of the linked subjects will be of primary or subsidiary interest.

The organizational quality of linked subjects exhibitions has a considerable influence on their marketing merits. A clear separation or grouping of the component subjects helps the visitor to locate the stands of interest and to obtain a general impression of the offerings and is thus also of benefit to exhibitors. There are still organizers of smaller exhibitions who believe that mixing the stands of different subjects lures the visitor into areas which he would normally miss. All that such arrangements in fact do is to irritate the serious visitor and burden stand personnel in strategic positions with the task of acting as additional information bureaux.

When selecting exhibitions which are *combined with conferences or symposia* one is often faced with an additional selection problem, namely whether to participate actively or passively in these gatherings. Once more, decisions to participate should be based on an assessment of the events in relation to the defined marketing motives and to the quality of the contribution one could make. The decision then to be taken is whether to participate only in the exhibition, only in the conference, or in both.

The application of marketing criteria to science-based conferences may be anathema to some, but perhaps in time the realization will grow that spreading knowledge is, even semantically, not so far removed from marketing it; in other words, directing and encouraging its flow from those who generate it to those who want to use it. Of course in the case of scientific knowledge it should be done scientifically.

Participation in conferences and symposia is mostly subject to special charges and there are two schools of thought about the beneficial or deterrent influence of such charges. One view is that an exhibition of substantial marketing merit in its own right should be able to afford financially the mounting of a conference. Such an exhibition should be interested not only in the prestige value of an exclusive assembly of prominent names, but also in the widest possible dissemination of the subject matter.

The other view is that only an appropriate fee can provide the means for organizing the conference and securing the services of speakers. Fee-paying participants are usually reimbursed by their company, and for interesting events there may be too many candidates. Persons interested but not necessarily in the right department, or perhaps not of sufficient rank, have no access to those making the decision. A selection based on office nepotism is not necessarily the best way to spread the knowledge which the conference can impart to the most deserving recipients. The result is often that the same faces are seen and the same views are heard more than once and in time the social aspect becomes more important than the technical or scientific content.

The Risk Spectrum

When establishing a merit rating for an exhibition it is advisable to locate the critical risk elements involved. The relative importance of the risk spectrum of any particular exhibition and your own attitude to these risks will determine the influence of the risk factor on the final merit rating.

If you are a determined *security seeker* even marginal risks may deter you from exhibiting, but if you are a *risk taker* you will weigh the risks against other merits and so make your final decision. The risk spectrum usually comprises four types of risks or their various combinations:

> controllable
> assessable
> predictable
> unforeseeable

Some examples follow of risks which could affect the decision to participate or visit an exhibition, or sway the decision between choices of near equal merit.

Exceeding the exhibition budget is an *assessable* and *controllable* risk for experienced exhibitors and visitors, it should be *predictable* and *assessable* for newcomers who do their homework, but it becomes unforeseeable for those who plunge into exhibition activities without proper preparation.

Design stealing is a *predictable* risk, damage to exhibits *predictable*, *assessable* and *controllable*.

Vandalism and terrorism are mostly *unforeseeable*, very difficult to assess beforehand, and only in very unusual circumstances predictable.

Controllable risks should probably not qualify as risks, because they can be eliminated at extra cost. However, if you are a risk taker you may decide against the extra cost and for the risk. An example is an exhibition location where electricity supplies are subject to disruption due to overloading or natural forces, or where other services like compressed air or steam are likely to be inadequate or erratic. This factor may be critical for exhibits relying on these services for their display technique. Where such risks exist it is better to convert to static displays unless mobility is essential.

In some locations services may be erratic but fuel supplies plentiful. In such cases it may be possible to generate your own services for your stand only or in co-operation with other exhibitors. If your choice is between two or three exhibitions of almost equal merit but one of them has a propensity for disputes, delayed openings and cancellations it becomes the most favoured candidate for elimination. From past experience cr information you will deduce that in the best of cases your costs will be higher because of the likelihood of *extra-extra overtime*, your stand may not be finished to its best standard, your stand personnel may become disgruntled and your potential customers may stay away.

If you are involved in a cancelled exhibition and if it is technically feasible you may decide to counteract the loss of marketing opportunities by mounting a private exhibition. This is easier said than done and only a limited number of exhibitors could do it. The disruption, delayed opening, postponement or cancellation of exhibitions is a *predictable* risk at exhibitions known to be prone to labour disputes and strikes and it is also *assessable* in terms of expenditure, but not in terms of lost opportunities both at the cancelled event and at other events which could have served the same marketing purpose.

Health hazards and climatic hazards are mostly both *predictable* and *controllable* risks.

An exhibition which is a 'first of its kind' venture, particularly when the organizers are not very well-known, constitutes a *predictable* and *assessable* risk which can be reduced by limiting the scope of participation providing that such a limitation does not impair the achievement of a reasonable effectiveness of effort. Alternatively, a negative decision is preferable to a half-hearted participation.

Participation in exhibitions as a result of encouragement by governments, official or other bodies may involve an *assessable* expenditure risk when these ventures are based not on viable marketing motives but on national or regional prestige or propaganda aims.

A small firm attacking a quantity market runs the *predictable* risk that a very good response to its exhibition effort may overwhelm its production capacity. A premature display of new products can expose even a large firm to the same risk.

The risk of being exposed to staff recruiting manoeuvres is sometimes offered as an explanation for not staffing the stand by specialists. Apparently some exhibitors turn exhibitions into recruiting centres and some years ago it was reported that electronics manufacturers in the USA had hesitated to participate in one of the leading exhibitions, or even to send their observers to the show, for fear that some of their engineers would be hired away by competitors. For them it was obviously a *predictable* risk.

The incidence of competitive events is an ever-present risk, although in most cases it should be a *predictable* one. The fact that the exhibition organizers seldom mention, let alone emphasize, such competitive events, maintaining complete silence if they are exhibitions competing for the same customers, should not deter a prospective exhibitor from making his own investigation.

Non-exhibition events such as festivals, sports events, congresses and similar gatherings are often described as an added attraction to an exhibition taking place at the same time. Such claims need careful examination. It may be perfectly true that they will generate an increased flow of visitors, but there is the *predictable* risk that they may also create traffic and accommodation problems which could more than obliterate any potential benefits.

Legislation which may affect your decision to participate in an exhibition can be a *predictable* risk in countries with a propensity for sudden changes in legal or administrative measures and in some territories these changes may be to an extent *assessable*. Paradoxically or logically, depending which way one looks at it, in countries with a stable legal and administrative structure, changes when they do occur are mostly *unforeseeable*. There are of course omens of change which allegedly are very obvious to the initiated, although on closer inspection their foresight is mostly revealed as hindsight. If you come from an established and liberal environment to an exhibition located in a volatile and perhaps at the same time restrictive one, there is a predictable and controllable risk that, unless special preparations are made, your instinctive reactions when negotiating, your attitudes to demands for special safeguards or your irritation at what to you appear as petty and unnecessary complications may seriously affect the success of your exhibition effort.

Selection of Exhibitions

The selection process of finding exhibitions suitable for a particular set of marketing motives for exhibiting is a matter of individual assessments, of a search for optimum solutions and of judgement. When the marketing motives for exhibiting are defined and their order of importance is stated, the next step is a review of seemingly compatible exhibitions.

Broad term definitions of your marketing motives for exhibiting, of your target-markets and of your date and time restraints provide the background for the search and listing of exhibitions which, by virtue of their declared aims and scope, are seemingly compatible with your motives. A critical scrutiny of the general and specific marketing merits of these exhibitions will then qualify some of them for a short-list of prospective candidates for final merit rating and selection for participation.

The confrontation between, on the one hand, your stated motives for exhibiting and your material, human and time resources and, on the other hand, the short-listed most meritorious exhibitions will provide the basis for a final decision to participate in selected exhibitions. This confrontation may also reveal the need for a modification or revision of your motives, or of their order of importance, before they are translated into realistic objectives for the selected exhibition.

Ideally the steps would follow each other in orderly fashion, but in the real world neither motives nor existing knowledge of exhibitions, nor even the allocation of resources, are so well-defined and measurable as to allow such an orderly sequence. In reality the steps will interact, motives will be modified, objectives narrowed or extended and budgets cut back or enlarged before a final balance is struck.

The selection procedures used could be executed by one of a variety of techniques, such as using quantitative and/or qualitative merit factors for entering a niche market, or measuring the specific merits of short-list candidates against the objectives of a multi-market operation. You could use for the purpose comparatively simple graphical bar chart presentations, matrix analysis methods or complex three-dimensional modelling methods. You could have arrived at the merit rating of an exhibition by means of a sophisticated data processing technique or your personal experience told you that one exhibition was excellent for your purposes, another exhibition would be, if it were not held at an awkward time, and a third was held in a promising export market. A situation may arise where your merit rating for an exhibition can be set, without further investigation, at maximum value, but others which are new ventures need detailed analysis. Even so, it may be advisable to check a known exhibition for extraneous factors such as special competing events or changes in political or technological environments.

The selection of exhibitions for participation cannot be restricted to the examination and comparison of alternatives. If all obvious alternatives are inadequate to serve the principal motives for exhibiting—for example, if uncertainties or anticipated changes in the host country present a serious risk, or if the achievement of aims involves prohibitive costs—it will be necessary to consider different, possibly unorthodox, marketing media and techniques, perhaps even to create new ones as substitutes for a conventional exhibition effort.

A *marketing relevance selection procedure*, one of the many different techniques used, can be illustrated best by an exercise based on real events and locations, but with the omission of the name of the exhibitor and of the actual exhibition titles.

A complex, service prone engineering product sold in international markets to primary application customers and to end users caused serious problems. A decline in sales resulted from a spate of failures of a bought-in component. A radically improved design of that component not only eliminated the source of trouble but also opened opportunities for marketing the product in a new sector of applications. After the completion of extensive tests of the improved products a marketing strategy was evolved and the following main marketing motives for exhibiting were defined:

Recovery of market share in international market

Sales promotion of improved product in existing applications

Sales promotion of improved products in new applications

Contacts with existing users and operators

The company had many years of exhibition experience to its credit and it was comparatively easy to find exhibitions which were seemingly compatible with the four motives for exhibiting and the company's general international marketing strategy. Six exhibitions in four countries were identified and coded for matrix analysis:

Code	Exhibition
Exh. 1	Specialized Industrial Exhibition (UK)
Exh. 2	General Industrial Exhibition (FR Germany)
Exh. 3	Specialized Industrial Exhibition (FR Germany)
Exh. 4	Specialized Industrial Exhibition (France)
Exh. 5	General Industrial Exhibition (Italy)
Exh. 6	Specialized Industrial Exhibition (Italy)

The following general marketing merits of these exhibitions were listed and coded:

Merit code	General merit
M1	Validity of aims and scope when related to relevant markets
M2	Competence of organizers, effectiveness of their publicity and PR efforts
M3	Quality and numbers of visitors
M4	Quality of exhibitors
M5	Quality of the exhibition's internal environment
M6	Quality of the exhibition's sphere of influence

Quality rating values were applied to the general merits of the exhibitions according to the following scale:

Value	Quality
1	Fair
2	Good
3	Very good
4	Excellent

Exhibition code	General merits						General merit value
	M1	M2	M3	M4	M5	M6	
Exh. 1	3	3	2	2	2	2	14
Exh. 2	4	4	3	3	4	3	21
Exh. 3	4	4	4	4	3	4	23
Exh. 4	3	3	3	3	4	3	19
Exh. 5	2	3	2	3	3	3	16
Exh. 6	3	2	3	3	3	3	17

Table 1. General merits of exhibitions

The sums of the six merit values were taken as indicators of the general merits of the six exhibitions as shown in Table 1. Thus according to the values of their general merits their order of importance would be: Exh. 3, Exh. 2, Exh. 4, Exh. 6, Exh. 5, Exh. 1. The obtained general merit values were in turn subjected to an assessment of the international impact expected from participation in any of the six exhibitions. Based on the company's experience this evaluation was made by applying multiplicators:

Multiplicator	Expected impact
1	No special impact
2	Fair to good impact
3	Very good opportunity to make noticeable impact

The application of multiplicators transformed the general marketing merits into specific merits for the defined motives of exhibiting, as shown in Table 2.

Exhibition code	General merit values	Impact multiplicator	Specific merit values
Exh. 3	23	3	69
Exh. 2	21	2	42
Exh. 4	19	2	38
Exh. 6	17	3	51
Exh. 5	16	2	32
Exh. 1	14	2	28

Table 2. Specific merits of exhibitions

The order of importance according to the values of the specific merits of the exhibitions became: Exh. 3, Exh. 6, Exh. 2, Exh. 4, Exh. 5, Exh. 1.

Before a final selection was made, the six exhibitions were subjected to additional selection factors of expenditure, distance from base, availability of stand space and others.

In this particular case only six motives for exhibiting, four general merit quality factors, three specific merit multiplicators and only addition and multiplication are used for the sake of simplicity. More complex rating values and more sophisticated methods of merit rating can be employed, depending on the means available and on the actual need to use such methods. The method of weighting can be simpler or one can apply other than numerical criteria, or weighting can be left out altogether. The presented primitive method can be further developed on a three-dimensional basis or by programming a computer. The main objective is to arrive at a reasonable selection, using valid methods and sound judgement. In the context of exhibition activities the information gained by experience of past efforts is an excellent guide and analysis of such past efforts deserves the application of the best methods and best technical means available.

Selection of Exhibitions—Case Study 2

A company in the field of metals, in the widest sense of the term as basic materials and half products, with international buying and selling interests and operating through agents, wholesalers and distributors underwent a change of the chief executive. The change was initiated following a board decision to change the sales method from indirect to direct selling. It was implemented by premature retirement of the incumbent and the engagement of an executive with proven marketing success in another, somewhat related but narrower field.

Even before the change in office took place a review of exhibitions was initiated, the objectives of which were defined as follows:

Reason for review:
A change of sales method from indirect to direct selling

Objectives of review:
To locate relevant exhibitions suitable for participation
To compare the exhibition medium with other direct selling media

The review of exhibitions was entrusted to the sales department and delegated to the publicity department, normally engaged only in placing technical press advertisements of a general prestige character through agencies which also carried out all graphical work. The review produced a list of nine exhibitions which included in their title the general term metals or named metals. Up to that point neither the term nor the concept of marketing played any part in the procedure and at this stage the new chief executive of the company intervened. It became clear that what was intended as a change in overall marketing strategy was interpreted by the sales department (perhaps understandably as a result of long years of habit) only as a change in selling methods and not a very welcome one at that.

It was also established that company personnel had neither the technical resources nor the mental attitudes required to produce such a survey and that re-educating and burdening internal personnel with the task, while current activities were in a state of change, would adversely affect these activities and create unnecessary frictions. It was decided to enlist outside assistance and to commission a survey on the basis of revised and new objectives:

The assessment of exhibitions as marketing media suitable for the implementation of the new marketing policy was to be carried out in three phases as follows:

Phase one will be concerned with establishing a list of exhibitions which could be classified as coming within the scope of the defined objectives.

Phase two will be concerned with establishing the merits of the listed exhibitions, the material and human resources involved and the costing of selected exhibition activities.

Phase three will be concerned with a comparison of exhibitions and other marketing media.

The marketing elements to be used as guidelines in listing exhibitions were indicated as:

63

The needs of primary, intermediate and end categories of actual and potential customers, converters and users.

The implications of working, forming, fabricating, finishing and protecting techniques.

The implications of new developments in extracting, refining, ennobling and alloying and of combinations of metals with non-metallic materials.

The implications of substitutes for metals and of metals as substitutes for other materials.

The implications of predictable future working techniques and usages.

The task objectives of phase one were defined as:

To survey exhibitions relevant to the company's business and to the above marketing elements and to compile a list of exhibitions suitable for direct and indirect participation and for visiting and intelligence surveys.

At the briefing session it was pointed out by the outside consultant that the revised objectives were so widely drawn that almost the whole spectrum of exhibitions would have to be surveyed and that the brief sounded more like an elaborate marketing research assignment than a review of exhibitions. This was conceded, but it transpired that the review of exhibitions was intended as a preliminary step to later research and that the background to the formulation of the brief was the very successful use of exhibitions by the new chief executive, in his previous position. (If an aside by the author is permitted—this approach seems to be symptomatic of cases when a new chief executive is appointed on the strength of his marketing success in another less all-pervading field. His conceptual interpretation of the marketing task retains full theoretical validity, but its translation into a new reality requires the application of many critical restraints. But to return to the case study.) The consultant agreed to justify his criticism by preparing an outline of the areas which would be involved in the review. This outline was presented in graphical form (reproduced in Figure 5) and verbal comments were made at the explanatory meeting. It was pointed out that apart from cost and time considerations the outline had all the hallmarks of a long-range planning exercise rather than a preliminary to an intended marketing research investigation aimed at short- and medium-term targets. As a result of that presentation it was decided to limit the exhibition survey to five areas of marketing activities. Two were high volume and high turnover but low profit areas and three were areas in which competition had a much larger share of the market.

The selection of exhibitions for participation and visiting was made on the basis of the method of allocating merits and weights described in the relevant chapters here, but details unfortunately cannot be disclosed. The final selection was made by means of the matrix analysis described on page 61. The marketing motives for exhibiting were identified partly by selection from Checklists 7, 8, 9 and 10 (pages 78–81) and partly by defining special ones; the motives for visiting were defined by selection from Checklist 30 (page 170).

Exhibition Budgeting

Exhibitions are marketing tools and thus budgeting for exhibitions should be a part of the general process of budgeting for marketing expenditures. For companies recognizing marketing concepts and management accounting as essential ingredients of their

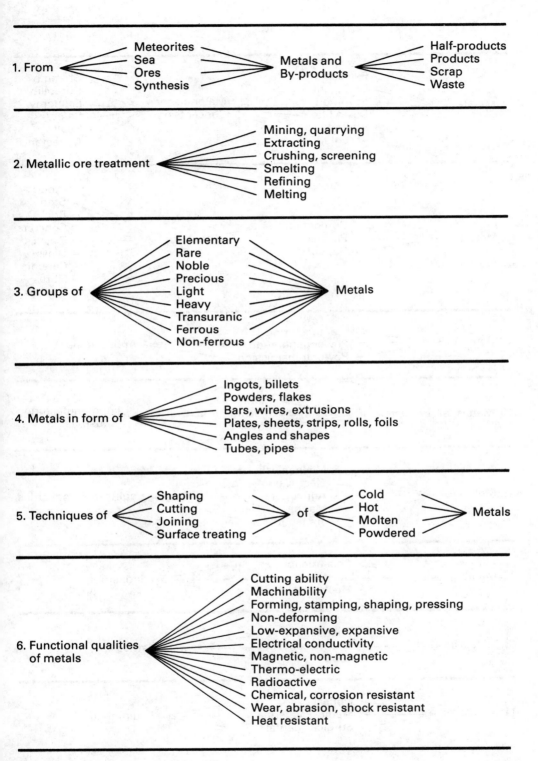

1. From ⟨ Meteorites, Sea, Ores, Synthesis ⟩ → Metals and By-products ← ⟨ Half-products, Products, Scrap, Waste ⟩

2. Metallic ore treatment ⟨ Mining, quarrying / Extracting / Crushing, screening / Smelting / Refining / Melting ⟩

3. Groups of ⟨ Elementary / Rare / Noble / Precious / Light / Heavy / Transuranic / Ferrous / Non-ferrous ⟩ Metals

4. Metals in form of ⟨ Ingots, billets / Powders, flakes / Bars, wires, extrusions / Plates, sheets, strips, rolls, foils / Angles and shapes / Tubes, pipes ⟩

5. Techniques of ⟨ Shaping / Cutting / Joining / Surface treating ⟩ of ⟨ Cold / Hot / Molten / Powdered ⟩ Metals

6. Functional qualities of metals ⟨ Cutting ability / Machinability / Forming, stamping, shaping, pressing / Non-deforming / Low-expansive, expansive / Electrical conductivity / Magnetic, non-magnetic / Thermo-electric / Radioactive / Chemical, corrosion resistant / Wear, abrasion, shock resistant / Heat resistant ⟩

FIGURE 5 (continued on pages 66–68)

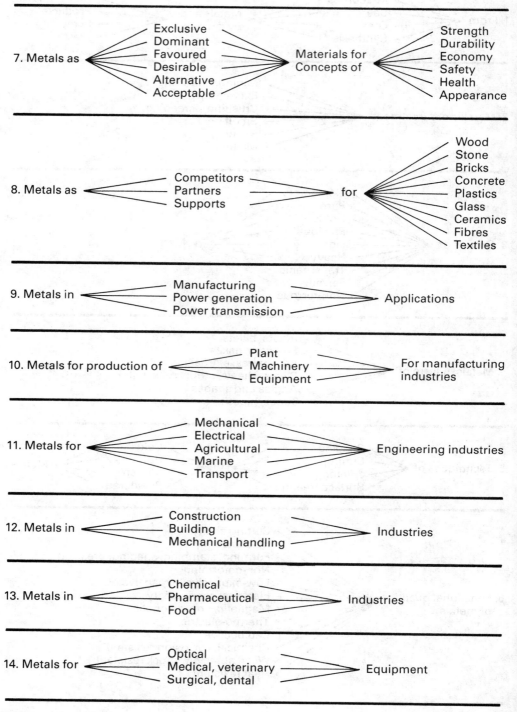

7. Metals as
- Exclusive
- Dominant
- Favoured
- Desirable
- Alternative
- Acceptable

Materials for Concepts of
- Strength
- Durability
- Economy
- Safety
- Health
- Appearance

8. Metals as
- Competitors
- Partners
- Supports

for
- Wood
- Stone
- Bricks
- Concrete
- Plastics
- Glass
- Ceramics
- Fibres
- Textiles

9. Metals in
- Manufacturing
- Power generation
- Power transmission

Applications

10. Metals for production of
- Plant
- Machinery
- Equipment

For manufacturing industries

11. Metals for
- Mechanical
- Electrical
- Agricultural
- Marine
- Transport

Engineering industries

12. Metals in
- Construction
- Building
- Mechanical handling

Industries

13. Metals in
- Chemical
- Pharmaceutical
- Food

Industries

14. Metals for
- Optical
- Medical, veterinary
- Surgical, dental

Equipment

FIGURE 5 (continued)

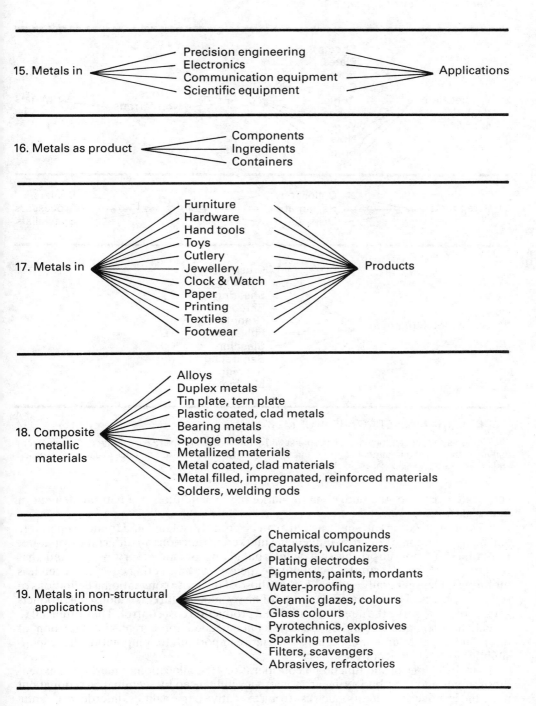

15. Metals in
- Precision engineering
- Electronics
- Communication equipment
- Scientific equipment
→ Applications

16. Metals as product
- Components
- Ingredients
- Containers

17. Metals in
- Furniture
- Hardware
- Hand tools
- Toys
- Cutlery
- Jewellery
- Clock & Watch
- Paper
- Printing
- Textiles
- Footwear
→ Products

18. Composite metallic materials
- Alloys
- Duplex metals
- Tin plate, tern plate
- Plastic coated, clad metals
- Bearing metals
- Sponge metals
- Metallized materials
- Metal coated, clad materials
- Metal filled, impregnated, reinforced materials
- Solders, welding rods

19. Metals in non-structural applications
- Chemical compounds
- Catalysts, vulcanizers
- Plating electrodes
- Pigments, paints, mordants
- Water-proofing
- Ceramic glazes, colours
- Glass colours
- Pyrotechnics, explosives
- Sparking metals
- Filters, scavengers
- Abrasives, refractories

FIGURE 5 (continued)

67

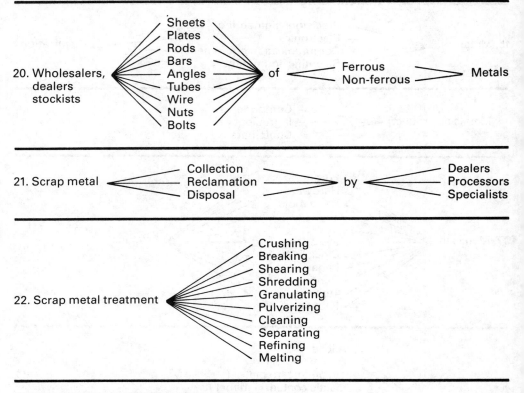

FIGURE 5. THE MARKETING AREAS OF METALS

The elements and concepts involved in the marketing of metals are shown in 22 activity groups ranging from primary extracting and treatment activities through working and fabricating of metals to usage, application and final metal scrap disposal and recovery.

corporate existence, the budgeting of marketing expenditures is a natural element of financial control.

In live organizations no single activity can be entirely isolated and treated separately and many overlapping or cross-influencing marketing functions are difficult to separate. It is therefore not surprising that actual budgeting practices vary widely and that definitions of what constitutes 'marketing expenses' or 'marketing costs' are even less uniform and less generally applicable than those of the more conventional definitions of selling expenses. The accounting systems of many manufacturers of industrial products were evolved to serve the needs of traditional production cost control. They often fail to reveal, and sometimes tend to obscure, data needed for a realistic allocation of marketing expenditures and, perhaps even more important, for pinpointing the responsibilities for such expenditures.

Apart from logical and functional considerations the allocation of marketing expenditure items and their budgeting are sometimes influenced by seemingly irrational but none the less decisive factors, such as strong executive personalities, interdepartmental politics, changes in executive appointments, entrenched departmental positions, new executive brooms, etc.

The methods of budgeting for exhibitions vary as much as those of budgeting for other marketing functions except that budgets for exhibitions are often based on what can only be described as motivations of imitation, faith, hope, hunch and feeling. The most frequently encountered methods of allocating exhibition expenditure practised by large, medium and small exhibitors alike are the following:

Percentage of the publicity budget
Percentage of advertising appropriation
Percentage of sales promotion budget
Fixed or variable percentage of selling costs
Fixed or variable budgets for specific products, territories, markets
Special budgets for selected projects.

Less well-defined exhibition allocations are made on the basis of 'me too' practices, following what competitors or 'the industry' spend, or on vaguely stated expectations of numbers of enquiries or orders that can be expected. Financial contributions by agents, distributors, official or trade bodies also influence the size of allocations. A senior marketing executive interviewed on the subject of exhibition expenditure allocations stated: 'we'll find money for any exhibition which shows promise of worthwhile returns'. When he was asked to specify these returns in measurable terms, the reply was: 'well—that's the problem'.

The degree of financial flexibility with which allocations are implemented depends as much on the internal structure and strictness of controls of individual companies as on the influence of external circumstances such as cost inflation, competitive pressures, powers of persuasion of interested parties, outside assistance and the financial situation.

The most popular of these methods, and at the same time the most facile but from an industrial marketing point of view least reliable practice, is to consider exhibition expenditures as percentages of general publicity or specific advertising appropriations. A prospective exhibitor searching for guidance in published sources would also find this method of exhibition budgeting to be the one most frequently quoted. Unfortunately, attempts to relate quoted percentages to real values founder on the very wide variations in both appropriations for advertising and percentages allocated for exhibitions. The fact that publicity or advertising budgets are also based on percentages, mostly of total sales or sales costs, adds another dimension to these variations.

A review of advertising and exhibition appropriations in thirty-nine groups of industrial products showed that advertising expenditure expressed as percentage of gross sales ranged from 0.16 to 3.0 per cent (with a median of 1.0 per cent) and exhibition expenditure in turn ranged from 5 to 25 per cent (with a median of 11 per cent) of the stated advertising expenditure. If a prospective exhibitor with gross sales of £100 million were to base exhibition budgets on these percentages, theoretically the appropriations for exhibitions could range from £8000 to £750 000. Thus at one end of the range participation in even one exhibition would be beyond reach, while at the other end participation in several exhibitions would be feasible.

Allocation of exhibition spending as a percentage of publicity or advertising spending, even if useful for purposes of media comparison, is an inappropriate device for exhibition budgeting. Publicity is a very important marketing function in its own right and it also plays a leading role in exhibition activities. It is nevertheless only one of a range of marketing functions performed at exhibitions. It does not seem to make very good marketing or financial control sense to budget for a complex activity embracing almost all vital marketing functions on the basis of a primitive percentage calculation related to only one of these functions. This is even less justified when that function itself

69

is the subject of many misunderstandings of its role and of controversies concerning its financial demands and their cost effectiveness.

The sound application of corporate resources demands that a given exhibition expenditure should yield a maximum return or alternatively that a given return from an exhibition effort should be achieved at minimum cost.

The most commendable, but also the most demanding method of exhibition budgeting is the method of *objectives and tasks budgeting*. This method requires the establishment of exhibition budgets on the basis of defined realistic marketing objectives, determining the tasks required to achieve these objectives and estimating the exhibition expenditures involved. Because objectives and tasks budgeting entails precision, judgement and discipline it is also the most likely to produce marketing-effective and cost-effective exhibition budgets.

One unorthodox view is that in economic reality exhibition expenditures are investments, sometimes long-term, and should not be treated as part of the current operating budget. *Exhibition budgeting* means translating the marketing motives for exhibiting into decisions to commit resources. Thus definition of the three basic elements of *expenditure, return* and *cost* becomes a crucial issue.

In theory, generally valid definitions of the concepts of expenditure, returns and costs could be constructed in a form valid for purposes of exhibition budgeting. In practice the prevalent variations in cost accountancy practices, sometimes reaching the point of fundamental incompatibility of principles, not only make the task a very difficult one but also provide a stern warning against construing general definitions which almost inevitably would mean different things to different interpreters. What may serve better are suggestions of possible attitudes and of lines of thought and a plea for the application of a marketing point of view.

The interpretation of these suggestions and the implementation of a method of budgeting will then depend on real situations, corporate aptitudes and personal talents, rather than on theoretical considerations. The following are some of the questions which have to be asked before budgeting can perform its task of saying what should be done, instead of simply repeating or revising what has been done in the past:

> What is the size of your organization, what are its resources and what are the methods of their allocation?

> What is the character of the chain of relations between departments, responsibilities and executives and what are the strong and weak links in that chain?

> To what extent does your market information, your marketing research and your market intelligence provide you with a rational basis for motivation and decision-taking?

> What are your methods of taking decisions in situations with a high degree of uncertainty?

> To what extent is your organization expense-conscious as distinct from cost-conscious and how does that consciousness manifest itself in normal conditions and how in crisis conditions?

Stand Expenditures

At first sight this term appears self-explanatory and for many items of exhibition expenditure it is. Charges for the stand space and structure, its erection and dismantling, packing and transport charges, stand services and consumable items both technical and culinary are all direct exhibition expenses which can be allocated to a particular event. Modular or standardized stand fixtures can be allocated to several exhibitions on a pro rata basis. Stand design and stands when appropriate can be treated in a similar way. When it comes to sales and technical literature, gifts, samples and souvenirs, the issue is not so clear-cut. Let us consider the most-important and most expensive of these items—sales and technical literature (see Checklists 33, 34 and 35, pages 173–175).

Special exhibition literature should be regarded as an exhibition expense but general, supporting and indirect publicity literature requires closer examination. It must be assumed that you have a complement of sales and technical literature catering for your markets. If participation in an exhibition reveals the need for additional quantities, for special issues or for translations, then obviously that need is based on the same marketing motives which decided your participation in the exhibition. The exhibition may have provided the stimulus for translations or modifications, but if your marketing motives have any validity, then these special issues or translations will be used in existing or potential markets in future routine operations and also in operations resulting from and following the exhibition. Furthermore, should a situation arise which would prevent you from participating in a particular exhibition, you would have to use alternative techniques to achieve the same marketing objectives and, providing your marketing motivation was sound to begin with, you would need all the material prepared for the exhibition. Depending on your method of budgeting you can allocate the expenditure connected with these special issues to general marketing expenses in that particular market sector or to any other sales and technical literature appropriation. Only in exceptional cases of one-of-a-kind exhibitions or perhaps participation motivated by singular indirect or remote marketing motives should an exhibition budget bear the whole burden of such items.

Similar considerations can be applied to other items of the material structure and material elements of the exhibition effort (Checklists 19 and 20, pages 121, 122) because an exhibition should not be regarded as an end in itself, a singular event, but as one of many tools used for performing marketing functions. The fact that exhibitions are usually more effective tools than any others should reinforce these considerations.

Stand Personnel Expenditure

The method of allocation of the monetary expenditure of staffing an exhibition stand will depend on your general cost accounting policy, salary structure, bonus and incentive plans, commission systems, expenses accounting, profit sharing, contingent compensation and all other factors entering into your overall scheme of expenditure calculations. Opinions, systems and practice vary a great deal. They vary according to the type of business, the size of the operation, management philosophy and attitudes. There is, however, one common denominator of personnel operations—the time expenditure factor, although that in turn is subject to variations of individual ability, working capacity and experience.

If time budgeting techniques are used in your field work, you will have no difficulty in applying them to exhibition activities where they are an indispensable ingredient of the operation.

Auxiliary stand personnel specially recruited for an exhibition in most cases represent a direct exhibition expenditure, although even here there are many special considerations. If auxiliary personnel are required to supplement the linguistic aptitudes of your own staff, you may have to discriminate between the needs of the specific

71

market which provided the principal motivation for your participation and the wider opportunities offered by an international exhibition, i.e. you discriminate between principal and subordinate marketing motives or perhaps between special and public relations motives (Checklists 7, 8, 9 and 10, pages 78–81). The application of these discriminatory considerations to time-expenditures will enable you to allocate appropriate monetary values, to separate them if considerable amounts are involved and to disregard them if the amounts are small or trivial in relation to the overall budget.

The assessment of the cost effectiveness of visits to and attendance at exhibitions is a fairly complex procedure, the complexity being characteristic for any evaluation of visits of personnel away from base. One of the difficulties is that any general formulation in terms of monetary values would depend for its interpretation on the cost accountancy method practised in individual firms and so defy independent comparisons.

There are, however, *person-time factors* which are generally valid, and their measurable values can be subjected to cost or expense allocations in accord with individual practice. These person-time factors are elements of the time management concept and the purpose of a detailed schedule of time elements is the application of time budgeting principles to exhibition activities to enable a time-cost analysis of personnel resources deployed at exhibitions.

The *time management concept* requires not only a systematic analysis of all time elements involved in reaching your objectives but also a realistic time budgeting for such elements as waiting time, wasted time, normal rest and extra fatigue time and a reserve time for unforeseen contingencies. In some situations a single task or a limited number of tasks can leave spare time on hand for which subsidiary or fringe interests tasks can be scheduled.

In the exhibition situation the events are of known duration and of predetermined date and geographical location. The feasibility of accomplishing one or more exhibition tasks depends on factors which are partly or wholly *controllable* or *uncontrollable*. The location, date and duration of an exhibition are outside the control of an intending exhibitor or visitor.

For exhibitors the preparation for participation in an exhibition is partly controllable as it depends on the time of application and on the availability of stands. For a visitor the preparation for a visit to an exhibition is entirely controllable. The time for travel is partly controllable as there is a minimum time governed by the fastest means of travel, while the choice of slower means will only result in an extension of that minimum time.

The number of hours which can be allocated as an 'exhibition working day' is partly controllable because it is governed by the exhibition opening hours (see Figure 12, page 150). For the exhibitor these opening hours are a required minimum as they represent stand attendance hours—which may have to be increased by providing relief personnel or by performing auxiliary tasks. For the visitor they represent a theoretical maximum which he can not extend but which he can arbitrarily reduce.

A topographical representation of the locations in which these activities take place is shown in Figure 1 (page 6). Stand design, construction, erection, dismantling, etc., are not included in the time schedule as they are often subcontracted activities costed as a whole or dealt with separately. All activities connected with stand construction combine time and material content so intimately that a generally valid elimination of the time element would be very difficult.

The *productive preparation time* for exhibition stand personnel is the time spent on briefing sessions, on the preparation of details of customers and potential customers and on listing any other contacts which have to be made. It may require liaison with other departments or divisions of the company and the co-ordination of different exhibitions interests. Technical preparations include such items as stand duty aids, technical data, price lists and discount schedules. The preparation for attending new ventures will normally take more time than that required for repeat participation, although even routine participation may require a new approach or an extension of the scope of the exhibition effort.

Unproductive preparation time is spent on travel technicalities, i.e. reservations, tickets and internal transport arrangements. It is usually absorbed as an administrative function, except perhaps in cases of intercontinental travel or large numbers of personnel, when the time factor can be allocated to specific attendances or visits.

Internal travel time is spent on travel from base to the exhibition within a moderate radius, mostly in one region or one country; it would be a minimum for exhibitions located in the vicinity of the base. Alternatively, internal travel is the time spent on travelling from a temporary base, such as a hotel, to the exhibition site.

External travel time is spent on international travel or on long distance travel between different locations in one country. Internal and external travel time definitions should not be regarded as rigid as they can overlap and change meaning, e.g. when international connections between two countries are simpler and faster than are nominally internal connections in others. In some cases internal travel time may be required to reach an airport or sea port, or between two modes of travel.

The *exhibition time* is the total time available within the confines of an exhibition. For the exhibition stand personnel it is the time required to prepare the stand, the time of stand attendance and the time required to close the stand. It includes rest and refreshment periods at the exhibition site.

The *exhibition task time* is the actual time spent on performing the allocated or programmed main and subsidiary tasks. For the stand personnel it consists of the stand attendance time and the time spent on such other exhibition contacts and activities as were specifically programmed.

The presentation of an independent visitor's day at an exhibition in Figure 12 (page 150) can apply with equal validity to an exhibitor's day at an exhibition except that, while a visitor can control, reduce or increase the visiting time, stand personnel must more often than not reduce or eliminate rest and meal times, stay late for adjustments to exhibits and arrive early to prepare the stand.

The reaction which this discussion of time elements sometimes provokes is: 'Well, if it's all that complicated and uncontrollable, why bother—let's just go and see what happens'. The reply given to opponents of time budgeting concepts is the same as that given to opponents of other management concepts: it may not always be possible to proceed as planned and it seldom is, but it will be possible to assess at each stage what has been achieved, what remains to be done, what should be left out and what must be done in the future.

Returns

The marketing motives (Checklists 7, 8, 9, 10 and 11, pages 78–82) on which you based your decision to participate in an exhibition also determine the nature of the returns demanded from an exhibition activity. Exhibition budgeting should also provide budgets of expected returns, firstly to establish bench marks to be aimed at and secondly to enable an assessment of performance. Motives with 'market share' objectives demand returns in terms of orders, serious inquiries, establishing of new contacts and maintaining or improving of existing ones.

If the making of otherwise 'elusive contacts' is a subsidiary motive then the return demanded is a quantitatively and qualitatively satisfactory number of such contacts and an effective exchange of relevant information. If 'redeeming a tarnished service image' is one of the motives, the demanded ultimate return may not become apparent for a long time, but the demanded interim return can be expressed in terms of numbers of visitors' queries which were satisfactorily dealt with and numbers and quality of visitors who were informed of the improved service.

Some of the returns can be measured quantitatively, some in monetary values. Returns in the form of orders and inquiries can be measured in actual or potential monetary values, other returns can be evaluated quantitatively and qualitatively, but some can be only assessed by subjective judgement. The achievement of some returns may be apparent at the conclusion of the exhibition but others mature after a period of time. The achievement of some demanded returns may be entirely dependent on the effectiveness of the exhibition effort, while the achievement of others may depend on the effectiveness of follow-up actions in the field, in the office or in the factory. The ultimate success of the exhibition effort—of which the returns are a measure—will depend on the totality and continuity of all involved marketing functions and activities.

Costs

The relation between the budgeted exhibition expenditure and the demanded or expected return determines the *budgeted cost* at which that return is expected to be achieved. The relation between exhibition expenditures incurred and returns actually achieved determines the *actual cost* of an exhibition effort. However, some exhibition functions and some expected returns defy direct assessment in monetary or other material values and once again judgement and discrimination have to be used.

• You may be able to record and assess the quantitative values of person-time factors as applied to the number of contacts, length of interviews, number of visitors to the stand, enquiries received, literature dispensed, demonstrations conducted and hospitality offered. Complications arise when qualitative factors are involved, particularly if they concern functions other than sales functions.

• You may have established reliable and effective criteria for the cost effectiveness of your sales force in the field and on a direct time basis you can compare their field effort with that at an exhibition. But what value do you allot to the assistance which your sales personnel receive on an exhibition stand where exhibits, specialists and service engineers can support and enhance the validity of their statements?

• What expenditure in money, time, personnel and material would you consider appropriate to secure 200 interviews with prospective customers? How would that overall expenditure compare with that required to mount an exhibition effort which would aim at the same numerical result?

• What value would you ascribe to the greater ease of securing appointments with important customers as a result of personal contacts made at the exhibition?

• How do you assess the value of the attendance of a marketing executive? Does his presence have a beneficial effect on the performance of the stand personnel? Does his authority improve the prospects of securing orders or long-term contracts?

There are no generally valid values which could be attributed to these factors in terms of monetary or material gain until perhaps their long-term effects become apparent. Identical exhibition techniques used by two different exhibitors can generate entirely different effects. Only practical experience, intelligent observation and systematic follow-up actions can in time provide answers to these questions.

There are numerous accountancy techniques dealing with costs and new approaches to old techniques as well as truly new ones, as distinct from merely novel ones, appear from time to time but may suffer from an inbuilt inability to distinguish between expense and cost and between cost control and budgeting.

In the context of exhibitions, effective cost control depends not only on the correct and logical choice of expenditure and return headings and subheadings but also on the allocation of well-defined responsibilities for expenditure and return to suitable executives. Provisions should be made for a reasonable amount of flexibility in exhibition activities and this will help to reduce the need for formalistic paperwork, which can so easily become an operational burden instead of being a tool used for cost control.

One of the budgetary control techniques suitable for exhibitions is the flexible or variable cost method. *Flexible or variable cost exhibition budgeting* is based on the proposition that general marketing expenditure should not be translated to an individual exhibition effort. By definition, fixed marketing costs would not vary within the limits of a marketing time period or within a given market area. Variable exhibition costs, on the other hand, are attributed to the exhibition effort that causes them. They are generated by the expenditure sustained to enable participation in a specific exhibition so as to achieve declared specific results.

The material elements of an exhibition stand and the comprehensive range of marketing functions which can be performed at an exhibition suggest that at least two methods of cost analysis used in engineering—*value analysis* and *function cost analysis*—could be applied with good effect to exhibition cost problems. Value analysis is concerned with the identification of basic functions and with evolving new means of performing these functions at lower cost. However, in exhibition activities there are often situations where the same function when performed in two different locations can cause vastly different expenditures, mostly of an unproductive or secondary nature, such as travel or transport to distant locations. While value analysis can reveal the relative merits of general functions if some form of cost control is already in operation, function cost analysis is better equipped to deal with individual or special target functions.

Time Budgeting—Case Study 3

At an exhibition abroad the stand of an engineering company was to be staffed by several sales engineers, a marketing executive, a secretary and a stand assistant. The duration of the exhibition was five days and the daily opening hours were 9.30 to 18.00, i.e. $8\frac{1}{2}$ hours.

An estimate of potential visitors was made on the basis of records of existing and prospective customers, market intelligence information, known merits of the exhibition and, most importantly, on the basis of the response to sent out invitations. An optimistic total of 260 visitors to the stand was forecast and a time budget for that number of interviews was prepared.

Past experience indicated two factors relevant to the time budget. One was that the first and last day of the exhibition were usually 'slack' days and the three days between them were 'busy' days. The second factor was that visitors could usually be recognized as belonging to one of five categories of importance and that different lengths of interview time should be allocated to these categories. The percentage incidence of these categories and the average interview time were known to vary depending on the location of the exhibition, its duration, stand facilities and other local factors. The values shown in Table 3 were accepted as valid for the particular exhibition discussed:

Importance of visitors	Incidence (per cent)	Average interview time (minutes)	Cumulative interview time (minutes)
Outstanding	10	60	600
Great	15	30	450
Medium	35	20	700
Moderate	20	10	200
Marginal	20	5	100

Table 3. Interview times for 100 visitors in five categories of importance

The personnel requirements for the exhibition effort were estimated on the basis of the time calculations shown in Tables 3 and 4. The theoretical total interview time for 100 notional visitors was 2050 minutes (Table 3) and thus for the estimated 260 visitors 89 hours of contact time would be required (as shown in Table 4 as the 'estimated cumulative time' of 5330 minutes).

Importance of visitors	Interviews numbers				Average times (minutes)		Cumulative times (minutes)	
	Estimated		Actual		Estimated	Actual	Estimated	Actual
Outstanding	10%	26	18	8%	60	47	1560	846
Great	15%	39	32	14%	30	35	1170	1120
Medium	35%	91	85	37%	20	18	1820	1530
Moderate	20%	52	62	27%	10	7	520	434
Marginal	20%	52	32	14%	5	6	260	192
	100%	260	229	100%			5330	4122

Table 4. Estimated and actual stand interview times

It was now necessary to relate the theoretical time requirement to exhibition stand realities. This was done as shown in Table 5 and resulted in a total 'practical contact time' of 27 hours per person for the five days of the exhibition.

Nominal daily operating time	8.5 hours
Preparations, meals, rest periods	−2.5 hours
Practical daily operating time per person	6.0 hours
'Busy day' operating time	6.0 hours
'Slack day' operating time	4.5 hours
Total practical operating time per person, for five days (three 'busy' days and two 'slack' days)	27.0 hours

Table 5. Practical contact time for one person for an exhibition of five days' duration

Normally four persons would be allocated to an 89 hours contact time but, in view of the attendance of the marketing executive, it was decided to assign only three sales engineers to the full-time task and to provide for half of the attendance time of the marketing executive to be available for contacts with visitors. For the five days of the exhibition the stand team was thus theoretically available for a total of 94.5 hours (27 × 3.5 = 94.5), i.e. for more than the required 89 hours.

The records of visitors to the stand, of their categories and of the actual interview times in the five categories were analysed at the conclusion of the exhibition. A comparison of actual and estimated figures is shown in Table 4. During the exhibition 229 interviews were conducted on the stand and the total time recorded amounted to 68.7 hours. There was a difference between the available stand contact time of 94.5 hours and the actual stand interviews time of 68.7 hours amounting to a spare time of 25.8 hours. About one-third of that spare time was taken up by unproductive early morning and end-of-day periods and by other gaps in stand contact time. During the remainder of the free time the team conducted a total of 16 interviews away from the stand with customers and prospects who were also exhibitors. In the time budget these visits were anticipated but only as an optional activity.

The total number of interviews conducted amounted to 245 interviews (229 + 16 = 245), an average of 70 contacts per person. In addition to the 16 'away from stand' interviews the team had about 3 hours of spare time per person for exhibition, other stands, competitors and other intelligence tasks (Table 6).

Total available exhibition contact time for five days	94.5 hours
Recorded stand interview time (229 interviews)	−68.7 hours
Spare time	25.8 hours
Unproductive time	−8.6 hours
Net spare time	17.2 hours
16 interviews 'away from stand'	−5.4 hours
Time available for other activities	11.8 hours

Table 6. Times of activities of a stand team during five days of exhibition

Within the framework of the exhibition effort analysis a comparison was made between the contact time and number of interviews actually achieved at the exhibition and a notional field operation of five days duration in the relevant markets.

The markets which provided the main motivation for participating in the exhibition had certain geographic characteristics which, combined with the location of customers and prospects, indicated that even with the strictest time discipline and effective programming a sales engineer could not make more than four visits per working day. Thus the maximum visiting capacity of sales engineers during a period of five days would be 4 × 5 = 20 visits.

Assuming that all visits in the field would have been arranged on a selective basis with a high proportion of 'outstanding' and 'very important' prospects, and assuming further that there would be no cancellations or postponements, an optimistic stratification of the visits would allow for not more than 8 contacts of 'outstanding' and 'great' importance and 12 contacts of 'medium' importance to be made during the five days of the field activity. Thus on a direct time budget basis we can compare the 70 contacts per person for the five days of the exhibition with 20 contacts made during the five days of the field operation.

Apart from the quantitative time comparison which could be evaluated in terms of expense and cost per contact or per interview hours, there was the qualitative aspect of the two types of contacts. At the exhibition the sales engineer was supported by exhibits, by hospitality facilities and by the presence of a marketing executive. Return visits were arranged, interviews were extended or curtailed—as each case demanded. Even gaps in visiting attendance were usefully exploited. Duties were shared and delegated, times rearranged and special customers afforded special treatment. In the 'away from stand' activities very valuable intelligence information was obtained.

Evaluation of the impact of these qualitative and other intangible benefits of the exhibition effort was undertaken at a later date.

77

Checklists 7–18

MARKETING MOTIVES FOR EXHIBITING	
Principal marketing motives:	
market share:	
increasing	
maintaining	
recovering	
market penetration:	
horizontal	
vertical	
lateral	
redirected	
market development	
market probing/exploration	
market infiltration	
Functional marketing motives	
sales promotion:	
exhibits (products, processes, services):	
established	
modified	
improved	
extended range	
rationalized range	
diversified	

Checklist 7   MARKETING MOTIVES FOR EXHIBITING (see also Checklists 8, 9, 10 and 11)

Checklists 7, 8, 9, 10 and 11 deal with a range of marketing motives arranged in five groups. One or two of the principal marketing motives (Checklist 7) may be sufficiently important for one exhibitor who will consider some public relations motives (Checklist 10) as optional activities of no particular significance for a particular exhibition. Another exhibitor will see the motive of challenging a monopoly situation (Checklist 9) not as a subordinate but as a main motive for exhibiting. The checklists could point to motives not considered in the normal course of an exhibition effort; they could also disclose gaps in marketing techniques employed at exhibitions. For the purposes of one exhibitor they could be reduced to a few items; for another they may have to be extended to cover exhibition activities of the various companies of a large group. The definition and ranking of motives for exhibiting will determine the merits of exhibitions in relation to these marketing motives and will also point to the techniques of exhibiting (Checklist 20) and appeal targets (Checklist 23) compatible with these motives.

	ALTERNATIVE MARKETING MOTIVES	
	Marketing of innovations and improvements:	
	exhibits in new application	
	exhibits with new features	
	offering new benefits	
	solving new problems	
	test exposure of exhibits with:	
	new qualities	
	new versatility	
	new method of operation	
	new design, shape, colour	
	new exhibits:	
	new to industry	
	new to market	
	new to market sector	
	introduction of:	
	new trade marks	
	new brand names	
	Marketing of pioneering concepts:	
	prototype exhibits	
	pioneering exhibits	
	exhibits in pioneering technologies:	
	intertechnology combinations	
	interdisciplinary combinations	
	'ahead of time' exhibits	

Checklist 8   ALTERNATIVE MARKETING MOTIVES FOR EXHIBITING

This checklist deals with important alternative motives of marketing innovations, improvements and pioneering concepts. These motives require a most discriminate selection of suitable exhibitions.

MARKETING STRATEGY AND TECHNIQUE MOTIVES	
Marketing strategy motives	
meeting:	
elusive contacts	
operators	
installers	
maintenance	
users	
challenging:	
supplier monopoly	
supplier oligopoly	
competitor's product arrogance	
Marketing technique motives	
inviting interest in:	
agency, distributorship	
wholesaler arrangements	
exploring opportunities for arrangements of:	
franchises, licences	
assembly	
manufacturing	
joint ventures	
support of parent company for:	
home or foreign branch	
agent, distributor	
co-operation of parent company with:	
foreign subsidiary	
associate company	
autonomous member of group	

Checklist 9   SUPPORTING MARKETING MOTIVES FOR EXHIBITING

The principal motives for exhibiting can be strengthened by marketing strategy and marketing technique motives, which in exceptional circumstances may become of decisive importance.

	PUBLIC RELATIONS ACTIVITY MOTIVES	
	Presenting corporate image of:	
	internationalization of activities	
	capability of new groupings	
	total scope of:	
	activities	
	outposts	
	facilities	
	capabilities	
	reputation:	
	establishing in new market	
	redeeming tarnished image	
	counteracting prejudices, antagonisms, hostility	
	Indirect promotion, exhibiting as:	
	'thank you' gesture for:	
	large contracts	
	official assistance	
	only means of extending hospitality to:	
	institutional customers	
	authorities	

Checklist 10   PUBLIC RELATIONS MOTIVES FOR EXHIBITING

The presentation of a corporate image and indirect promotion activities are usually only subordinate marketing motives for exhibiting and vary greatly in their importance. They are mostly of interest to large companies and multinational corporations.

SPECIAL MARKET OPPORTUNITIES	
Grouping of markets:	
political blocks	
economic communities	
Customs unions:	
trade agreements	
liberalization	
special privileges	
Trade booms:	
discoveries of natural wealth	
economic changes	
political changes	
Development and reconstruction:	
development plans:	
national	
regional	
local	
development aid:	
tied	
free	
reconstruction:	
planned	
special	
Financial incentives:	
credits	
loans	
investment privileges	
currency advantages	
Participation in exhibitions combined with:	
trade missions	
special promotions	
congresses conventions symposia	
Invitation, encouragement, participation in cost by:	
home government ⎫	
official body ⎬ to exhibit abroad	
trade association	
marketing grouping ⎭	
foreign government ⎫	
foreign regional authority ⎬ to exhibit in their country	
foreign importers grouping ⎭	

Checklist 11   MARKETING MOTIVES FOR EXPLOITING EXTERNAL MARKET OPPORTUNITIES

Market conditions of an external nature, independent of exhibitors' initiatives, may present favourable opportunities for participating in relevant exhibitions.

	GENERAL MARKETING MERITS OF EXHIBITIONS	
	Title and scope of exhibition:	
	relevance to:	
	motives for exhibiting	
	target markets	
	target visitors	
	Exhibition venue and structure	
	Exhibition organizers:	
	competence, reputation	
	exhibitors' previous experience	
	effectiveness of:	
	pre-exhibition publicity	
	publicity and PR facilities	
	services and facilities for:	
	exhibitors	
	visitors	
	stand erection, dismantling	
	SPECIFIC MARKETING MERITS OF EXHIBITIONS	
	Compatibility of general merits with:	
	marketing aims of exhibitor	
	exhibitor's resources:	
	personnel	
	material	
	financial	
	Convenience of date and duration of exhibition	
	Quality and reliability of information about:	
	numbers and status of visitors	
	participating exhibitors	
	Convenience of transport and travel:	
	external	
	internal	
	Existence of restraints and restrictions	

Checklist 12   GENERAL AND SPECIFIC MARKETING MERITS OF EXHIBITIONS

The critical review of the marketing merits of exhibitions provides the basis for a systematic procedure of merit rating and for the decision to participate in selected exhibitions compatible with your marketing aims.

EXHIBITION COMPLEX ENVIRONMENTS	
Location of exhibition:	
home country	
abroad	
Locale of venue:	
metropolitan	
urban	
provincial/rural	
industrial	
agricultural	
marine	
Spheres of influence:	
local	
regional	
national	
international	
Exhibition hall and display areas:	
quality (of items included in Checklists 4 and 5)	
Stands:	
quality of design:	
general	
competitors	
Exhibits:	
effectiveness of display:	
general	
competitors	
Technological and industrial, scientific	
Symposia and conferences	
National:	
economic	
political	
legal	
aesthetic	
cultural	

Checklist 13   MARKETING MERITS OF THE EXHIBITION COMPLEX

This checklist deals with the internal and external exhibition environment elements which affect the merit of an exhibition. Some of the items listed may be of no importance to your current aims, but may be well worth noting for future reference. There may be items not listed which need adding to the list. In any case the exhibition complex and its merits for your particular marketing effort are critical factors which not only influence your decision to participate but can also determine the effectiveness of your exhibition effort.

	VISITORS, EXHIBITORS, PARTICIPANTS	
	Visitors:	
	numbers:	
	estimated	
	audited	
	provenance:	
	national	
	professional	
	executive status:	
	top	
	medium	
	none	
	Exhibitors:	
	direct exhibitors:	
	total number of exhibitors	
	frequency of participation in last three events	
	numbers and quality of exhibitors:	
	main display groups	
	customers and potential customers	
	primary, intermediate, end users	
	market or market sector competitors	
	product or product range competitors	
	suppliers, direct, indirect	
	group exhibits (national or other)	
	foreign exhibitors (countries)	
	official participants—inland and foreign:	
	government, local government, municipalities	
	chambers of commerce, trade promotion offices	
	international development agencies	
	trade associations	
	professional institutions and associations	
	exhibitors or participants—indirect:	
	banking, credit, investment, leasing, insurance,	
	transport, shipping, packing	
	publicity, media, radio and television:	
	technical and trade journals, directories	
	technical and trade books, handbooks	
	research institutes:	
	market and marketing	
	economic	

Checklist 14   MARKETING MERITS OF EXHIBITION ATTENDANCE ELEMENTS

The qualitative and quantitative assessments of the attendance elements listed can be a matter of available records or may need checking. Their specific merits for your marketing aims should be subjected to scrupulous evaluation.

NOTIONAL MARKET FEATURES	
Territorial market concept:	
global	
continental	
international	
national	
regional	
local	
Industrial activity market concept:	
technologies	
industries	
disciplines	
services	
Market density:	
spacious	
open	
crowded	
overcrowded	
Market freedom:	
free	
sheltered	
restricted	
closed	
Market dynamics:	
developing	
static	
declining	
Market attitude:	
enthusiastic	
receptive	
indifferent	
unreceptive	
antagonistic	
Official attitudes:	
privileged	
friendly	
neutral	
restrained	
hostile	

Checklist 15 NOTIONAL MARKET FEATURES

This checklist deals with conceptual market features, market conditions and attitudes. The systematic steps leading to the selection of exhibitions and the assessment of quantitative and qualitative merits can be supplemented by the factors listed here. Some of these factors, e.g declining or static markets, can be assessed objectively; some are more difficult to define, e.g neutral or friendly official or unofficial attitudes. Where merits of several exhibitions are fairly well balanced, one or more of these supplementary factors can decide the selection.

	EXHIBITION STAND EXPENDITURE	
	Stand space charges	
	Stand structure:	
	furniture and fittings:	
	operational	
	protective	
	decorative	
	Exhibits:	
	main items	
	auxiliary display equipment	
	signs, showcards	
	Publicity display equipment	
	Stand transport charges:	
	to exhibition	
	from exhibition	
	mechanical handling	
	packing	
	Stand construction charges:	
	erection	
	dismantling	
	maintenance	
	auxiliary labour charges	
	General and operational expenditure:	
	services	
	communication	
	clerical and records aids	
	catering (staff)	
	hospitality	
	security	
	safety	
	cleaning	
	waste disposal	
	ad hoc repairs	
	consumable materials	
	insurance	

Checklist 16   EXHIBITION BUDGETING I

This checklist deals with expenditure related directly to the exhibition stand, which can vary within very wide limits determined by the scope of the individual effort. More detailed items which contribute to that expenditure can be found in relevant checklists. Thus, for example, stand structure is the subject of Checklist 19, exhibits are listed in Checklist 20 and publicity equipment is detailed in Checklist 37.

PERSONNEL EXPENDITURE	
Salaries, wages, bonuses:	
stand personnel:	
exhibitor's staff	
auxiliary staff	
other personnel:	
demonstrators	
intelligence	
service	
publicity and public relations	
visiting personnel	
Expenses:	
travel external	
travel internal	
hotel/accommodation	
out-of-pocket expenses	
personal equipment:	
special apparel	
cameras	
tape recorders	
other	

Checklist 17   EXHIBITION BUDGETING II

The checklist of personnel expenditure is intended as a means of apportioning emoluments and expense to an exhibition effort, so as to provide a basis for discriminatory analysis, e.g. of partial allocation to an individual exhibition, of allocation to direct or indirect marketing expenditure or to any other appropriate function. Checklists dealing with the activities which gave rise to items of expenditure can assist in such an analysis. The expenditure of 'visiting personnel' attending a scientific congress connected with an exhibition (Checklist 38) is ostensibly an exhibition expenditure, yet in fact would have been incurred just as well if that congress had taken place at another time or place. Intelligence tasks performed by an exhibitor's staff (Checklist 31) could be regarded as exhibition expenditure. On the other hand the opportunities offered by the exhibition may result in substantial savings in the expenditure that such a task would require if performed by other means.

PROMOTION EXPENDITURE	
Publicity and public relations:	
pre-exhibition expenditure	
exhibition expenditure	
post-exhibition expenditure	
Sales and technical literature:	
general	
special	
supporting	
Other publicity materials	
Catalogue entry and advertising	
Gifts, souvenirs	
Photography, cine, video and audio-visual	

Checklist 18   EXHIBITION BUDGETING III

Similarly to Checklists 16 and 17 this checklist indicates only some of the main headings of expenditure-incurring activities related to an exhibition effort without prejudging their actual cost allocation. Here again the whole series of checklists dealing with publicity and public relations will assist in the detailed analysis and apportioning of expenditures.

PART THREE

Exhibition Activities, Personnel and Preparations

Exhibition Activities

The total exhibition effort is an interacting blend of two groups of elements: a group of material structure elements—the exhibition stand—and a group of human elements—the stand team. Both are placed in the special, temporary, time- and space-constrained environment of the exhibition and its venue. An effective exhibition effort can be regarded as a real-time theatrical event which should be staged and performed in accordance with a well-conceived and well-prepared scenario.

The main material structure is the exhibition stand and its most important components are the exhibits. The location of the stand, the technique of featuring the exhibits and the facilities provided determine its visual impact, power of attraction and effectiveness. An accomplished performance by a well-trained and properly instructed stand team is decisive for the marketing success of the total exhibition effort. Shortcomings in the material structure not only defeat its main purpose but also impair the performance of the stand team. Incompetence by the stand team can degrade even the most spectacular exhibition stand to becoming nothing more than an impersonal three-dimensional advertisement.

Publicity, public relations and intelligence operate within the structure of the stand but also outside it and they enhance the impact of the stand and of the activities of the stand team. The crucial task of the stand team is the encounter with exhibition visitors. The discussion of transposition and confrontation and of buying influences of visitors deals with two important aspects of such encounters.

The Exhibition Stand

Stand Location

The location of the stand within the exhibition complex is important; the impact, consequences, merits and demerits of different exhibition hall environments were discussed previously (page 47). Not all exhibitors can secure the best locations, but if you have a stand of the right size, properly equipped, containing the right exhibits and staffed by knowledgeable and well-prepared personnel you will overcome the short-comings of a mediocre location, providing it is not more than that. A downright bad location should be avoided and other means, perhaps of 'indirect' or 'fringe' location exhibiting, should be considered.

Although the *exhibition stand* is the natural location of exhibits and in the majority of cases is the only one, other locations can also form a part of the material structure. Large and rich firms able to afford it have their own building or *pavilion* and, guided by long-term exhibition policies and the merits of particular exhibition events, may decide that this is the most economical method of participating.

Participation in *collective stand arrangements* is occasionally supplemented by a separate stand if organizational rules permit it. The size or layout of an exhibition stand is on occasions unsuitable for exhibits of large dimensions and the stand capacity is supplemented by attached or separate projection or cinema facilities. Thus the exhibits, or some of the exhibits, are displayed on these 'projection locations'. Products of component character can be exhibited on the *stands of other exhibitors*, who can be primary, intermediate or end users, either in their built-in state by emphasizing their presence, or as separate exhibits or both. In some cases just a show card can be used to indicate the application.

Open air areas can contain individual stands for exhibits, or can be reserved for demonstrations and tests of products exhibited elewhere. The open air aspect of many exhibitions is affected by the climatic conditions prevailing in the exhibition host country, where the optimistic expectations of the organizers seem to weigh heavier than the disappointing year-to-year experience of exhibitors. Considerations of cost obviously play their part. The question of how the attraction of a weatherproof arrangement can be made to bring in the added revenue required to compensate for that cost is a marketing problem which most other businesses have to solve almost daily but exhibition organizers seem to shun.

Some exhibition grounds provide facilities for free-standing displays of suitable products. Showcases, columns, pedestals and similar items can be used for displays outside halls or in their precincts. Often these facilities become available as a result of the imagination and initiative of exhibitors. Pumps operating fountains, shelters made from plastic, aluminium and stainless steel materials and open air sculptures made from tubes, rods, slabs and even from containers are examples of such 'special' locations for exhibits.

For products such as office and communication equipment a special location oppor-tunity arises in information centres, official offices and on other exhibitors' stands.

The exhibition site and exhibition halls can also provide opportunities of a permanent or transitory nature for exhibits incorporated in the physical structure of the exhibition. Examples of products suitable as such exhibits are passenger and goods lifts, escalators, catering equipment, public address systems, advanced or spectacular building methods for exhibition halls, tents, marquees, lamps, flooring, paving—the list is almost endless.

The policy of the organizers will determine the acceptability of such exhibits and the degree of publicity and recognition which they can receive. Once this is established the paramount concern of the exhibitor is to ascertain to his own satisfaction the functional suitability of the exhibits for their purpose and to ensure the highest possible degree of faultless operation, weather stability, appearance and, when necessary, refurbishing, renewal or replacement. Permanent exhibits are also seen by visitors to exhibitions mounted on the same site but not directly connected with the markets for these exhibits. For products with wide horizontal market characteristics, such as most material hand-ling or lighting equipment, this permanent exposure can be of great marketing value.

Some exhibitions provide display opportunities in town centres, at railway stations and at airports. Suitable products, such as special purpose vehicles, cranes or automatic vending machines, can be displayed on roped-off pedestals or similar locations. Smaller products, e.g. cameras, instruments or fastening devices, can be displayed in showcases provided in some hotels.

Stand Design

Exhibition stands should serve the same marketing motives that decide participation in exhibitions, that govern all exhibition activities and that determine the choice of exhibits and the techniques of exhibiting. In the overwhelming number of industrial exhibitions the exhibits, i.e. products, services, capabilities or concepts, will have a substantial engineering or technological content.

To be effective, stand designers need not only technical information, which will enable them to present to visitors the advantages and benefits of the exhibits, but also a thorough background knowledge of the exhibitor company and its activities and empathy with its corporate style and aesthetics.

Exhibition stand design is the subject of excellent textbooks in many languages and, like publicity, is the realm of specialists. But specialists have to be briefed and instructed in the wishes and aims of their task-givers, whether as members of the same organization or as outsiders. Stand design is not a matter of generally valid formulae, but an experimental process of reconciling the marketing aims of the exhibitor, the aspirations of the stand designer and the restraints of the exhibition site and of the most critical, although not the most important, factor—the budget. The great opportunity which an exhibition offers is that ingenuity very often can accomplish what expense cannot.

Aesthetic factors cannot be calculated or specified but the difference between functional excellence and gimmicky fussiness can be recognized, even if it cannot be measured by objective values.

Technicians and engineers have on the whole a less apathetic or hostile attitude to exhibitions than that frequently displayed towards all forms of publicity (discussed extensively on pages 162–165). Somehow exhibitions are more interesting, perhaps because they are more 'real' than publicity efforts or perhaps because there is a chance of a visit abroad. However, often when stand designers ask engineers to identify the unique features of their products which distinguish them from competitors, they are simply advised to refer to 'our expensive sales literature'. When confronted with the request for a new approach to the subject, engineers are inclined to reply that they have enough problems to produce new ideas for their products, let alone for stand designers' exhibits. When reminded that these are also 'their', i.e. the engineers', products they are somewhat surprised. There are of course laudable exceptions.

Engineers with a real understanding of stand designers' problems can make practical suggestions which not only overcome difficulties but are an inspiration to the designer. A stand designer grappled for years with the problem of displaying a colossal compressor which could be inspected only by climbing up a catwalk. He discussed the problem with an engineer and friend, who recalled his diploma project for which he had to design a similar compressor. He was at the time struck by the contrast between the beauty of the rotor and the ugliness of the housing. That was enough for the stand designer. At the next exhibition, a gleaming, slowly revolving rotor, suspended almost invisibly in mid-air with changing lights playing on its blades, drew great numbers of spectators to an exhibition hall normally only sparsely populated by the few visitors interested in very big machines. The display won an award and the following additional benefits were gained: transport and packing costs reduced by 62 per cent, accessible stand space increased by 31 per cent. The events related took place long before the advent of holography and its fabulous three-dimensional image projection capabilities.

In large halls of international exhibitions abroad some stands are raised conspicuously higher than floor level, some are lowered to give the impression of a sunken amphitheatre, but the great majority are at a sober floor level. There are elaborate giant stands in a curious style making somewhat clumsy allusions to what their designers think is modern art. There are stand designs which one sees year in and year out and which are obviously dedicated to a constant formula perhaps valid some years ago and retained ever since as safe and workable.

There are also many very good and some excellent stands in styles almost universally acceptable, proclaiming very clearly their marketing purpose by functional displays of products, by the regard paid to the flow of visitors and their temporary comforts and by an unobtrusive civility of the stand personnel coupled with determination to deliver their message.

Some stands are very good displays of the designer's ingenuity, well-applied when it serves the marketing purpose of the exhibits, misused when it serves nothing but the designer's urge to express himself.

Modular construction systems are playing an increasingly important role in stand design and construction. They have developed from a collection of a few extruded section elements and connectors to comprehensive sets of support elements, panels, ceilings, floors, walls, partitions and a full range of accessories. Parallel to the proliferation of exhibitions, more and more of these systems appear on the exhibition scene. Some claim that there are no limits to what you can do with them, some are more modest. Some offer a full stand design and consultancy service while some appeal to the do-it-yourself exhibitor. There is no doubt that modular systems have achieved considerable acceptance, particularly with exhibitors with a multi-exhibition programme.

While the early systems had too many pieces, obtrusive connectors, clips and inserts, many systems are now better designed and engineered and meet demanding criteria of rigid construction, versatility and good appearance. Some systems are still too fussy and elaborate and when used seem to proclaim their own virtues of modularity more loudly than behoves a background structure for the exhibits which they are supposed to serve. There are excellent systems which require only the ingenuity of stand designers to exploit fully their versatility and, very importantly, their cost-economy and multiple-use facility.

Conventional stand design techniques can be supplemented by modular scale model planning kits and by computer aided three-dimensional exhibition stand modelling techniques. The two key elements for a successful computer aided stand modelling system are a purpose-built data base and modelling software, similar to that used in modelling complex engineering processing plant.

Stand Aesthetics

A discussion of exhibition stands leads inevitably to the topic of aesthetics and its influence on the marketing role of the stand and exhibits and on the effectiveness of their contribution to the exhibition effort.

The response to aesthetic and style elements of industrial products is more complex than an appreciation of appearance. The principal visual stimuli of shape and colour can combine with stimuli of noise, smell and touch. Ergonomic factors play their part when human use, handling or operating are involved.

In the appraisal of machines and instruments we react not only to their general shape, but also to the arrangement and touch of handwheels, levers and control knobs and to the clarity of scales and dials. Depending on our personality and experience these arrangements may please or displease us, contributing to the general impression. Assessment of the operating efficiency of a piece of equipment can be affected consciously or subconsciously by shapes and colours. Our first favourable colour impression of an instrument can be modified by a clumsy arrangement of operating knobs; a well-shaped accessory is mentally rejected because of its, to the beholder, awful colour. A streak of oil, functionally fully justified, running down a clean light grey surface may suggest some malfunction; the same streak against the background of a narrow black band of paint would not even be noticed.

The aesthetic environment of exhibitions was briefly discussed on page 54. At an exhibition you are in a sense in a theatre except that not one, but many, stages compete for your attention. Theoretically, a product of inherent excellence of purpose and function and with good marketing merits to its credit should need no more than a bare stand as a stage to display its quality and the benefits it can bestow on the buyer. The theatre has used that device, if actors will forgive the simile of being marketable products. In practice we need a stand design.

Art Patronage

Art patronage is one of the areas which could enrich many a stale exhibition scene. The use of plastic panels, vacuum-formed plastics or the combination of light, movement and sound in art works should give some inspiration to exhibition stand designers.

If abstruse sculptures created by the application of metal welding and brazing techniques and by the use of glassfibre materials can move from sophisticated art galleries to the fronts of buildings and to courtyards of palatial headquarters, surely exhibitors of industrial products could do more than just adorn their stands with a row of flower pots. There are notable and sometimes spectacular exceptions, mostly on the stands of large corporations in the chemical and plastics industries. On the other hand, some pseudo-advanced banalities in encapsulation and what are intended to be funny personifications of components are examples of how not to use basically good ideas.

A neglected source of such artifacts is the apprentice schools of industrial firms. In one particular case a stand designer engaged by an exhibitor, a copper tube manufacturer, acquired some very good items of copper tube sculpture from an artist abroad. They did not know, and no one told them, that the firm's apprentice school, in co-operation with the local art college, produced prize-winning designs of no smaller merit than the imported items.

Stand Design Intelligence

Exhibition intelligence is the subject of a separate section (page 152) but it seems appropriate to discuss stand intelligence in the context of stand design.

The role of the stand design function ostensibly covers only the pre-exhibition period and perhaps the period just after opening. In fact, if not the function then its intelligence component should be active throughout the exhibition period. This need not necessarily mean the allocation of that particular duty to one person; it is enough if provisions are made to note the operational aspects of the stand and the effectiveness and impact of any new features or techniques and to observe difficulties experienced or benefits derived from such innovations. At exhibitions of high marketing merit or in an environment of sophisticated stand designs the intelligence task should extend to a survey of other stands, with particular attention to those of competitors and customers.

The influence of the stand design on exhibition effort performance is one of the analysis tasks (page 132). Structural and operational aspects of the stand that are the subject of visitors' complaints (or praise for that matter) should be noted, as should the observations of the stand personnel. There is no better way to improve future exhibition endeavours than to audit current ones.

Stand Reception Facilities

The reception facilities for visitors serve the basic purpose of the exhibition effort of establishing personal contacts and conducting them effectively. The range of interests, rank and personalities of visitors who can be expected at your exhibition stand, the design and size of your stand and the composition of your stand team will determine the nature of the facilities required to provide a cost- and time-effective set of reception facilities. If yours is only a small stand with the display element taking up most of the space then reception, conference and interview facilities will be physically non-existent, but a careful selection of stand personnel will enable you to entrust these functions to one person specially talented in that respect. Such a receptionist can do more for your visitors than the most luxuriously equipped reception area manned by brightly smiling but on the whole half-informed or buck-passing personnel.

Visitors' reception can be a loose-leaf book for recording details about visitors or it can be a reception desk with several receptionists in attendance and direct telephone connections to other stands of the same exhibitor and to his headquarters. Conference and interview facilities can range from a few chairs and tables to a complete suite of rooms on a floor above the stand. A modest conference room where a visitor can be served with sandwiches and coffee or a cold drink which he can consume in comparative comfort could do more for your image and goodwill than a lavish supply of alcohol. You may need that as well, because customers come in all shapes and partialities, but if you take the trouble to ask, instead of automatically assuming that everybody needs a drink, you will be surprised by the relief of many to be able to choose some light refreshment instead. At one exhibition stand a special effort was made to reduce to a minimum the use of stodgy food and to provide a choice of non-fattening savouries. The fame and memory of that stand among higher rank expense account executives persisted for three more exhibition events. It was the most cost-effective public relations exercise ever known by this exhibitor.

The stand office is an essential function of your exhibition activities. Here too it is the function which is important not the actual frame. An efficient stand manager, an experienced secretary, a tape recorder and a portable typewriter, inquiry forms and loose-leaf books of the same standard size issued to stand personnel with instructions to adhere to the one-page-one-subject rule can produce a record of exhibition activities and a dossier for follow-up action superior to a sophisticated enquiry card system operated by a multitude of bored helpers hired for the purpose from outside.

Plastic 'exhibition inquiry time-saver cards' and 'exhibition inquiry cards' issued by exhibition organizers allegedly '. . . ensure fast and accurate registration of your interest . . .' and this they may well do if the registration (on a properly functioning machine) is accompanied by a personal contact to ascertain the particular interest of the visitor. On the other hand the time-wasting delays often experienced in obtaining the 'time-saver' card to start with, and possibly at several busy stands, make the traditional visiting card ritual a more attractive proposition. In recent years customer questionnaires have made their appearance on exhibition stands together with attractively uniformed 'research assistants'. They persuade visitors and somewhat indiscriminately chosen passers-by to fill in so-called 'customer interest' cards which bear all the hallmarks of a surprisingly non-marketing exercise. They are so obviously designed for the convenience of the analyst rather than of the customer-victim, that one is inclined to add a remark: researcher research thyself.

Sophisticated electronic data processing devices are used on exhibition stands, in most cases with full operational justification but sometimes only as a matter of following current fashion and sometimes as an experiment on one occasion only to be discarded on the next one. Computer-oriented high technology companies are obviously inclined to use on their exhibition stands personal computers, fax or terminals connected to their headquarters. The extent of that use depends on such factors as cost, personnel aptitudes, stand size and general management attitudes. The advantages of providing 'instantaneous' responses to complicated enquiries, to requests for quotations or delivery dates and to similar questions have to be weighed against the disadvantages of too much reliance on the 'box', of embarrassment when the right response is not forthcoming from base and of queuing by stand personnel because there are not enough terminals on the stand to cope with an unexpected influx of visitors.

Publicity Material

The subject of sales and technical literature and other publicity material is discussed in the sections on publicity. The policy of literature distribution from the stand and the selection of recipients and targets will determine the method and arrangement required. It is very important to include in the instructions to stand designers not only quantities and types of literature but also details of the underlying policy, so that apart from space requirements such elements as accessibility to visitors, encouragement, restricted distribution and similar considerations can be taken into account.

An *open display* is readily accessible to visitors in the form of single items or a folder with a selection of items. In a fixed, covered display, leaflets or other items are firmly attached to a display board, preferably protected by a transparent cover. The individual items can be identified by reference numbers and, depending on strategy, can be requested verbally or by means of a request form on which the name and other details of the visitor are noted. The request can be met at the stand, by post after the exhibition or by a combination of both methods. Outdoor stands require special provisions, their scope again depending on your aims and distribution targets and also on local climatic conditions. An economic method of distribution is a weatherproof *fixed protected display* and distribution on request.

While some of the accessories for literature can be of modular design and serve several exhibitions, storage provisions for larger quantities are usually included in individual stand designs.

Auxiliary Equipment

The activities of the stand personnel should be supported by at least adequate, but preferably by the most efficient, material facilities. A well-qualified stand team deserves the best possible supporting auxiliaries to enable them to exploit their talents to the full. Numerical or quality gaps in the team should be compensated by suitable supporting elements.

Stand designers and the executives instructing them could be perhaps persuaded to rely less on at best purely intuitive attitudes and often simply accepted routines when dealing with so-called natural functions which are in fact ergonomic problems. The exhibition stand is a short-lived but crowded habitat of exhibits and people. The performance of people, which can be assessed and predicted by behavioural and biological measurements, is crucial to the effectiveness of the exhibition effort. Apart from all personal equations and the absorption of marketing principles, that performance will also depend on the nature of the stand facilities.

The mechanical and physical elements of stands, such as benches, tables, counters, the position of literature racks and the access to exhibits, are all designed to make life on the stand easier. When treated as an afterthought they not only hinder stand personnel in their main task but also display their inefficiency to observant visitors. The deep bottom drawer at the back of a display counter, proudly claimed as clever utilization of space, is in fact the source of back-breaking exercises because it is too low and so deep that the weight of leaflets jams it in its frame. The slotted rack for leaflets placed in front of the stand counter and below waist level is another example. It enables passers-by to take leaflets without the stand personnel being aware of it. There is nothing inherently wrong or underhand in that—but for the stand personnel the main task of making personal contacts and ascertaining visitors' needs is made more difficult.

Exhibits

The central and most important components of the material structure are the exhibits, the term being used in its wider sense and not restricted to physically identifiable products but also embracing services, capabilities, concepts.

Exhibits can be products, materials, half products and components in all the diverse forms in which they appear, as units in their own right, as parts of other units or incorporated in complex assemblies. Depending on their physical and dimensional attributes they can be displayed in their natural state or represented by substitutes. If their role in life is only fulfilled by incorporation in other products, the applications in which they are contained may act as exhibits. Processes, techniques and services can constitute independent offerings or can be media for demonstrating materials and products which can display their qualities only in association with, or against the background of, these processes, techniques and services.

Capabilities can be presented to potential customers as saleable contract capacities or alternatively they can be exhibited in combination with products, processes, techniques or services which can become negotiable only when supported by one or more of the capabilities, e.g. special purpose design, research or consultancy.

The demonstration of scientific, often esoteric concepts, sometimes combined with an exhibition of the relevant products, is a long-established tradition of learned societies now practised at exhibitions by governments, independent research organizations and professional institutes.

The choice of exhibits is governed by the marketing motives for exhibiting, by the marketing merits of the exhibition and by the stand and its environment. The different environments of the exhibition were discussed on pages 45–53 and exert their influence on stand location and design. The location and size of the stand can impose limitations or offer opportunities to stand designers and can also affect the choice of exhibits, particularly if they require special services. In your exhibition merit rating procedure you have already checked the availability of these services on the basis of the checklist of structural elements and by assessing the environment and organization merits of the exhibition. Another selection criterion for exhibits is the strategy planned for stand activities, the activity features to be emphasized and those to be toned down or eliminated. General marketing strategies may have to be modified to take account of special market opportunities in the exhibition host country, or perhaps of some local restrictions.

The range of exhibits which will be subject to that selection can vary for individual companies as much as for individual exhibitions. Some internal conflicts or pressures can also exert their influence. Engineers are inclined to insist on too many technical details as essential display items. Sales departments have a tendency to produce long lists of products which must be displayed as representative of the range. If these demands are not filtered through a mesh of marketing criteria the result is often that on the engineering side prominent technical features of an exhibit are obscured by an array of items of minor importance, and on the sales side exhibits representing products responsible for a very small share of sales occupy a very large part of the display area, relegating those with a much bigger share to a smaller stand space. This is, of course, a very crude generalization of observed phenomena, but it is quite revealing to find—by personifying the character of industrial products—how many elderly, big and clumsy characters who take up a great volume of manufacturing resources have a low market impact, while smaller, more compact, better built, one could almost say nicer members of the family not only sail through their production lines but also make a very good impression on the market.

Exhibits should be presented as solutions to specific needs and problems and occasion-ally it may be advisable to state clearly these problems. The emphasis should be on unique features, advantages and benefits of exhibits. For showcards, signs or graphs used to augment the exhibits, simplicity, easy legibility and a stand-compatible and corporate-compatible style are basic requirements.

Photographs of applications or end-use environments can emphasize the advantages of products, as can audio-visual presentations. Well-produced models can capture the essence of products which are perhaps too unwieldy or too susceptible to damage for transport and incorporation on an exhibition stand. Holograms can help engineers to show aspects of their products in three dimensions and to present configurations which it would be otherwise very difficult, very expensive or perhaps even impossible to display.

The basic importance of making strong efforts to gain the attention of the visitor is self-evident but the mere use of the unusual or of gimmicks can be counter-productive. In general terms, attention-getting devices should draw attention to specific exhibits, products, services and capabilities, help to tell the story of these exhibits and lead the visitor's mind logically from the attention-getting device to actual exhibits.

The techniques of exhibiting are many and varied and their effectiveness very often depends more on the ingenuity of a simple device than on the amount of elaborate equipment or lavish expenditure. Technical achievements of one branch of technology can help to display the advances of another.

Materials and half-products are often made prominently visible in other exhibitors' products and, in the attempt to emphasize their versatility, elaborate and ingenious devices are used to demonstrate their adaptability to shapes and contours, their suitability for a range of applications and the universality of their potential use. Many of the ideas used have the desired impact and clearly convey the intended message. Others exaggerate the technique to such an extent that what started as an ingenious device becomes an overcomplicated gimmick which not only loses its own credibility but by implication jeopardizes the reputation of the sponsored product. The illogicality of an all-aluminium, or all-steel, or all-plastic house or car body can hardly impress critical potential buyers who would rather see an equally ingenious but more purposeful demonstration of how these materials fulfil their role of benefiting real-life products and thus in turn are of direct benefit to them.

Visits to industrial exhibitions by the general public and particularly by group excursions and schools are regarded as a great nuisance and impediment by what is euphemistically called the trade, who frequently voice their annoyance in the technical press. From a marketing point of view, the educational aspect of exhibitions seems sadly neglected. A group of young potential future customers, who are obviously undergoing some form of education relevant to industrial markets, must surely present a medium-term marketing target for many industrial products. Apart from that, quite a number of industrial products would benefit in the market if they were presented in a fashion disdainfully described by engineers as *popular presentation*. Such a presentation would also benefit some specialized trade buyers who augment their half-knowledge of technicalities by pomposity and price bargaining.

The addition where practicable of popularized versions of industrial exhibits, combined with pre-exhibition invitations to selected technical colleges and trade schools, could yield a more tangible and lasting marketing impact than that apparently expected from a display of semiclad but otherwise uninteresting live embellishments of the stand.

Exhibition Stand—Case Study 4

The stand is sometimes the reflection of the source of information which was most active or most co-operative with the stand designer. In one case a stand was required for an exhibition in an export market in which the exhibitor had experienced serious service problems. A new service manager had been appointed there recently to overcome the troubles and it was decided, very sensibly, to call in the new service manager, so that his interests could be taken into account. As fate would have it this service manager had considerable practical experience of exhibitions, probably more so than the also newly appointed export sales manager who was functionally responsible for participation in that exhibition. The requirements of the service manager were stated in great detail and with so much appreciation of local exhibition conditions that everybody heaved a sigh of relief, and it was left entirely to him to instruct the stand designer.

The result was a very good stand displaying spares, service tools, locations of service depots in colour transparencies and a dummy dressed up in regulation overalls. Three service engineers were in attendance. The product, a horticultural cultivator, was on display, but in a somewhat shamefaced manner, as if apologizing for its existence. An analysis of visitors to the stand revealed that 4 per cent showed interest in the stand because they had had trouble in the past in locating spares for their cultivators and 17 per cent because they had experienced undue service delays, but 16 per cent were under the impression that the exhibitor was a service organization dealing with all makes of cultivators.

During the nine months following the exhibition the sales of spares in that territory increased by 63 per cent and the number of calls for service rose by 121 per cent, but this included 31 per cent of trivial calls, mostly for consumable small components.

Transposition and Confrontation

The most significant marketing characteristic of industrial products is the fact that the majority of them are used in connection with other industrial products, so that all producers and sellers of industrial products are at the same time buyers of other such products. In this *transposition process* some industrial products pass through several phases of incorporation and a considerable time span can elapse between the date the product is first manufactured and the date it reaches the ultimate user.

Many industrial products move through several industrial markets or across horizontal or vertical layers of the same industry. In their travel some lose their identity on the way from the first to the ultimate user. In some cases this is a requirement of the buyer, in others it is the unavoidable result of incorporation or assembly.

Very often, final users of a complete industrial product become aware of the conflicts and dilemmas arising from the incorporation factor only when they are forced to compare the publicity promises made for the complete product with disclaimers of responsibility for its components made in small print in the warranty.

A simple version of the transposition process is illustrated in Figure 6. Buyer *A* is the manufacturer of an auxiliary power unit. In the first transaction of the transposition process buyer *A* acquires a component from seller *B* and incorporates it in a subassembly. In the second transaction buyer *A* obtains a clutch, which completes one version of the auxiliary power unit. In transaction 3 the first transposition takes place and *A* becomes a seller, supplying the power unit to buyer *D* who is an engine manufacturer. Buyer *D* then obtains in transaction 4 a power take-off coupling from seller *E* and incorporates it in the complete engine assembly. In transaction 5, the second transposition takes place when *D* becomes a seller supplying the engine to buyer *F*, a manufacturer of industrial tractors. In transaction 6 the third and final transposition takes place when *F* becomes a seller, supplying the tractor to the user.

The final *confrontation* of a buyer and a seller and the placing of an order is the expression of the fact that at that particular instance a need of the customer has been satisfied and one of the cardinal aims of marketing has been achieved. At an exhibition of industrial products the frequency with which the placing of definite orders takes place and the nature of these orders varies considerably depending on the nature of the goods and on the preliminaries which preceded the exhibition.

Headlines which announce the placing or securing of spectacular orders also vary in the veracity of their reports. It all depends on whether you consider the signing of a document in the presence of press photographers to be the placing of an order, or whether to you the moment when specifications, deliveries and prices are finally agreed after months of negotiations is the actual order placing date. On the other hand, in some countries official purchasing agencies go to the length of extending negotiations to the time when they can be formally concluded at an exhibition. Whatever the motives for this procedure, it certainly has a great deal of publicity value for the exhibition and for the exhibitor.

There are of course many industrial products for which contracts are negotiated and signed at exhibitions. There are also situations in which an exhibition stand reverts to one of its ancestral forms and industrial goods are sold off the peg. Amazingly the objects of such transactions are more often than not large pieces of complex special purpose equipment probably never seen or heard of before in that market. In some restrictive markets the exhibition is the only medium through which certain types of industrial products can be sold so that exhibits are chosen for that particular purpose. In all these cases a final confrontation between buyer and seller has taken place, in fact or symbolically. At an exhibition the buyer–seller confrontation is the most frequent personal contact element, but by no means the only one. It is the strength and special merit of the exhibition as a marketing tool that contacts are made with so many other persons exerting their influence directly or indirectly on that final encounter.

The different functions, roles and personality attributes of these influence-wielding

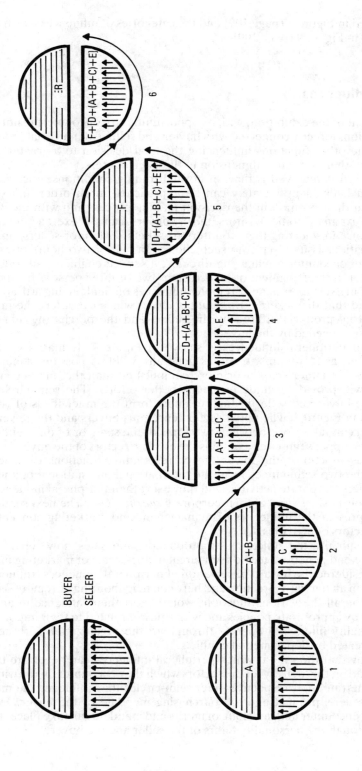

FIGURE 6. THE TRANSPOSITION OF BUYER AND SELLER ROLES

An example of six buyer–seller transactions, the transposition of the buyer role to the seller role occurring between transactions 2 and 3, between transactions 4 and 5 and finally between transactions 5 and 6.

people are listed in Figure 8 (page 108) and the categories of influences which they can exert are listed in Figure 9 (page 109).

Peripheral Influences

The environment of the exhibition, with its opportunities for encountering not only the orthodox functions directly connected with buying and selling of industrial products but also most of the other functions influencing the final decision to a greater or lesser degree, adds another marketing dimension to these encounters.

One of the factors involved is that, in normal trading conditions, once subsidiary influences have been identified they can be approached in an order and sequence compatible with their position in the decision-making process and with the weight of their influence. At an exhibition visitors, mostly buyers, can still exert a fair amount of control and choice in selecting their counterpart sellers. Exhibitor-sellers, apart from the direct invitations issued, have no such choice. In one or two hours of exhibition activity they can encounter a managing director, a service engineer, an irate user, a buyer, a designer, a chief engineer or on occasions two or three persons from the same firm. They all can exert their near or remote influences on final buying attitudes.

It is suggested that they exert *peripheral influences* which can affect the marketing merit of industrial products offered by the sellers and the purchasing mandate for industrial products needed by the buyers.

A diagram of peripheral influences is shown in Figure 7. It makes no claim to completeness and as it attempts to be as generally valid as possible it may not fit situations which are either simpler or more complicated than the one depicted. It is hoped that it will provide a guide for much better efforts. The semi-circles which represented the buyer and seller in Figure 6 now form the inner focus of two semi-circular sectors in Figure 7. The upper sector represents buyers and the lower sellers. The transaction can take place between two firms of the same or of different national provenance. The upper semi-circle contains the quarter-sectors of the buyers' manufacturing and sales functions, the lower the corresponding functions of sellers. The perimeters of the two semi-circles form the international and national boundaries of buyers' and sellers' corporate activities and they exert their peripheral influence on the definition of their business and of their corporate *raison d'être*. The next semi-circular ring-sectors represent the influences of management and marketing concepts which penetrate all sectors of activities.

Although nominally the functions of production and sales now separate, their influences in the end penetrate to the semi-circular ring-sector of marketing merits. So far we have considered the inward penetration of peripheral influences. Influences will be also exerted in an outward direction and between neighbouring or remote sectors. In an ideal situation all the various functions would exert their influence in an orderly manner guided by appropriate policies and with a power related to their importance. In real life personality filters will operate throughout the organization with additional disturbances created by departmental conflicts.

One could say that the rate at which peripheral influences can penetrate the inner focus will depend on the 'density' of the sectors which they encounter on the way. When they finally penetrate their respective inner semi-circles they influence the marketing merits of the seller's product and the purchasing mandate of the buyer. However, before the final encounter and matching of merits and mandate can take place, they also have to pass through the personality filters of the seller and the buyer.

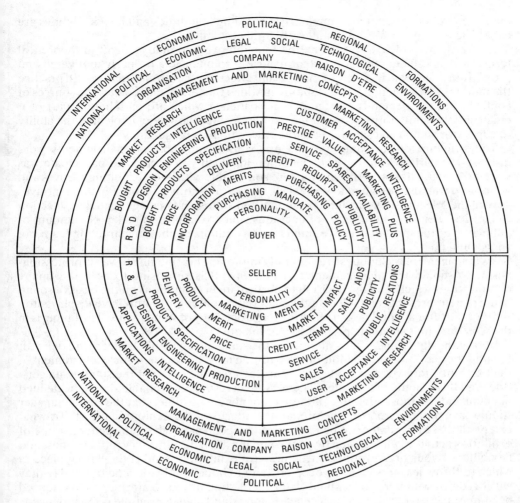

FIGURE 7. PERIPHERAL INFLUENCES OF THE BUYER–SELLER CONFRONTATION

The buyer–seller confrontation is subject to peripheral influences which collectively shape the final marketing merits of the product offered by the seller, the purchasing mandate of the buyer and, when filtered through the personalities of the seller and buyer, determine the compatibility of marketing merit and purchasing mandate, culminating in an order.

Exhibition Stand Personnel

Stand Management

If an exhibition effort is to succeed in its aims it must be competently managed. Exhibitions have their own specific structures and environments which can vary from venue to venue and from event to event. It is important to realize that irrespective of a company's divisional or functional structure an exhibition team will have to adapt to and master sometimes strange conditions, environments and time schedules. Whether the person entrusted with the exhibition stand management is described as a stand

103

manager or stand executive is immaterial providing that duties and responsibilities are clearly defined and powers and authority firmly established.

It is comparatively easy to define the function of stand management in theoretical terms. It would be enough to say that its task is to manage a properly motivated and properly briefed team in a well-organized and effectively controlled manner. In practice the motley environment of the exhibition in which the task is carried out, the sources of conflicts and the demands on stamina and patience which are an inherent part of it create anything but normal operational conditions. It follows inevitably that the ability to cope with an unusual situation requires more than usual qualities.

The structure of an exhibition and its external and internal environments were discussed in earlier sections. The exhibition in which you decided to participate was selected because its marketing merits were compatible with your exhibiting motives and your stand was also designed to serve these marketing motives. Similarly these motives govern the selection of your stand personnel and your stand manager and that selection is a critical element in the series of decisions which you have to make. No amount of publicity nor the most impressive stand can do what an exhibition marketing team can and should do.

As management techniques are generally improving and moving towards professionalism, so should the management of exhibiting. It is surprising to note that many organizations which take the decision to participate in exhibitions on the basis of sound management precepts and allocate the material resources for impressive displays stop short of the fundamental task of ensuring the proficiency of stand teams. The failing is in the selection, in inadequate preparation or in both.

Before the duties and responsibilities of the stand manager and his team are defined, the importance of the pre-exhibition preparation must be stressed. A clear statement of the exhibiting motives and strategies forms the essential basis for the stand manager's brief and programme of activities. The personnel resources available should be defined in detail and it is most advisable, although not always possible, that the stand manager should take an active part in the preparatory stages of the exhibition effort. To what extent all these postulates can be realized will depend as much on the general scope of exhibition activities undertaken by your company as on the efficiency, effectiveness and flexibility of your organizational structure. An exhibition stand is the wrong place in which to throw learners in at the deep end and to hope that by the end of the day they will become swimmers. In a stand team there should be a majority of experienced personnel and it is of course a basic tenet that the stand manager should be experienced.

The stand manager will also select a deputy, not necessarily formally but in fact, and use the opportunity to train the deputy for future duties. Good manners, tact and diplomacy are essential in dealing with visitors to the stand and are also important attributes of personal relations within the stand team. The team can include persons of different rank in the company, a mixture of personnel from base and field force, perhaps agents or distributors on temporary assignment to stand duties and, at exhibitions abroad, expatriates and foreign personnel.

The main burden of maintaining an effective and good mannered functioning of the stand team rests with the stand manager and, as he or she has to perform a great number of other stand tasks, the job is not an easy one. The following are some of the attributes which contribute to the making of an efficient and effective stand manager.

A basic requirement is organizing ability and flexibility in unusual environments and perhaps foreign locations. A thorough grounding in the marketing motives for exhibiting must be assumed as inherent in the appointment. A knowledge of general corporate policies and strategies is helpful in dealing with awkward problems, particularly when dealing with visitors of higher executive rank. In the case of exhibitions abroad a knowledge or preparatory study of the exhibition host country is very desirable, but there always has to be a first time for some occasions.

Tact and diplomacy are basic qualifications for stand managers, as without these attributes they cannot perform their duties. They have to give a good example to stand personnel and to visitors from outside and from their own organization. They have to exercise tact and diplomacy towards exhibition authorities, cleaners, technicians, hall supervisors, the press, officials and special visitors.

Ability to delegate must be assumed to have been already tested in an internal role in the company. At the exhibition it is perhaps more difficult to exercise as the choice of delegates is limited.

Stand Personnel

The marketing tasks of the stand personnel are defined by the motives for exhibiting, by the audience aimed at—the appeal targets—which can be customers, potential customers, users or visitors wielding varying degrees of influence. The selection of stand personnel is influenced by the aimed-at audience and by the expertise which is required to give the right emphasis to the features and benefits of the exhibits or services displayed.

The actual duties and their allocation to stand personnel is a matter usually decided in the pre-exhibition period, particularly when comparatively large teams are selected. Alternatively, if the team is familiar with the exhibition, the stand manager can make the final allocation of duties just before or at the exhibition. In the hectic conditions of an exhibition the allocation of duties must be flexible, and such flexibility will also benefit the all-round experience of the team. However, the need for flexibility does not remove the requirement to classify duties according to their importance. Classification methods will vary greatly, depending on the nature of tasks, the exhibits and the type of business, but chiefly on the motives for exhibiting. One method is to define:

> Essential stand duties
> Desirable activities
> External activities
> Special activities

Essential stand duties are those for which stand personnel were trained and of which they have knowledge and experience. Most stand duties revolve around the establishing of personal contacts with visitors, and in greatly simplified form they can be summarized under four headings:

> Invite visitors to your stand
> Inquire about their needs and interests
> Inform them of what you can offer
> Impress them that what you offer will bring them benefit

Like most slogans, these can mean as much or as little as is read into them.

The invitation to the stand could be no more than a polite gesture, but it can also be a lengthy conversation with a potential customer. The inquiry about the visitors' needs can be a brief note on an inquiry form or alternatively it can mean several pages of specifications and a set of drawings.

Another way of indicating the relative importance of duties is to describe them as:

Main duties
Secondary duties
Supporting duties
Auxiliary duties

They can be further distinguished by their location as:

Own stand
Other stands
Exhibition site
Extramural

The list of stand personnel qualifications shown in Checklist 21 (page 123) is only an example of items which could be checked. You may already have full details of the educational background, training, etc. of your personnel and all you need to assess are attitudes to exhibitions, or perhaps contacts of an employee who recently joined your team. On the other hand you could draw up an entirely different list specifically adapted to one particular exhibition effort.

Stand Personnel and Visitors

The variety of visitors and the possible permutations of their corporate and individual personality traits pose a special problem in the unique exhibition situation.

Here a relatively small contingent of stand personnel is exposed to a much greater number of visitors with different interests, occupations and ranks and with different degrees of competence and influence. The encounters take place in a small confine of space, often in crowded conditions. Opportunities for generating conflicts are extensive.

Visitors can act as observers only, as partners in a person-to-person confrontation or in both roles. The manner in which they act out their roles depends on their individual personalities and on the motivation which brought them to the exhibition. Person-to-person contact is the primary aim of the exhibition effort and it is important to appraise the actors in the play that will be enacted on the stage of the stand.

Experienced stand managers can to a large degree assess the personality traits of their team—after all they participated in their selection. But what kind of visitors will they encounter, how will they establish rapport with them, what kind of dialogue will develop and what strategies of behaviour should be used?

The social behaviour and social techniques of visitors will vary as much as the social and ethnic groups from which they come and, at important international exhibitions, the variety will be very great indeed. However, from a marketing point of view the organizational background of visitors and the motivation for their visit provide the most significant guidelines for a *dialogue strategy*.

The information intake capacity of visitors depends on a combination of environmental and behavioural factors and the restraining effect of the time and space concentration of the exhibition. On the other hand the exhibition situation can in some cases offer an opportunity for a return visit prompted by the visitor's need to 'know more' or made in response to an invitation extended by the exhibitor. The information output capacity of stand personnel is similarly affected, with the important difference that by judicious staff selection and training and by the provision of proper stand facilities and aids the capacity of the stand personnel can be maintained near the optimum attainable level.

In a high *customer density* exhibition, stand personnel will be subject to considerable physical and mental strain during the whole working day. Often time spans which would normally be rest or break periods are disrupted by visitors or taken up by urgent work. It is advisable, even if at times difficult, to insert some rest periods into the schedule. A stand staffing arrangement which provides sufficient personnel to allow for work rotas and rest periods on the face of it requires a higher budget allocation but in the end is more cost-effective.

Figure 8 indicates the categories and individual functions and some personality traits which stand personnel can encounter. The influence of personality traits and attitudes is sometimes questioned, but long experience has taught that a delayed flight, rain soaked shoes and an oncoming cold can make all the difference between an order now and perhaps in three months' time, as much as the 'legitimate' factors of discrepancy in the specification or a difference in price.

Figure 9 gives examples of possible variations in buying influences. Peripheral influences were discussed on page 102.

Languages

The value of talking to a visitor in his own language needs no special advocacy, except that in the environment of an exhibition it receives the added emphasis of the overall importance of person-to-person contacts. The correct understanding of the needs and requirements of customers and potential customers is just as important as the added power of persuasion which it gives to the conduct of negotiations. At international exhibitions the minimum requirement is a knowledge of the language of the host country and, if possible, of one more additional language which is important in a particular situation.

Surveys of the importance of different languages in commercial, technical and scientific activities are valuable guides for international corporations with worldwide interests. From the point of view of exhibitors the emphasis is not on the objective ranking of any one or more languages as much as on the relevance of that ranking to their marketing objectives and to the exhibition task currently in hand. The nationality and linguistic aptitudes of expected visitors, particularly of potential customers, will provide a guide to the language requirements of each particular event. If your own language is one which is widely understood, do not assume that a heavily accented version of it, or a local dialect, will be comprehensible to your visitors. The use of regionally coloured idiomatic expressions or local figures of speech will not have the same meaning, if understood at all, as at home.

Sectors of commerce and industry often develop their own jargon and some large organizations use their own phraseology liberally dotted with only internally meaningful initials, symbols and artificial word formations. They are all very bewildering to newcomers, outsiders or foreigners.

Using your foreign customers' language is a matter of courtesy and of good business practice, but when you have only a poor command of it, the courtesy is of doubtful value and as a business practice it can do more harm than good. A foreign language as such is not an asset unless it is backed by knowledge of the subject and an understanding of the customers' needs. To include persons in your team only because they know a foreign language has serious limitations. The effectiveness of such linguists is in direct proportion to the size of your team. The smaller the team, the less effective the linguist will be. If your team is fully staffed in accordance with your exhibiting strategy, then the linguist can be very useful as assistant, as interpreter and for helping in social duties.

INDUSTRIAL	OTHER	CONCEPTS
Buyers	Economists	Management
Sellers	Statisticians	Marketing
Users	Sociologists	Technology
Operators	Academics	**STATUS**
Engineering	Consultants	
Production	Technologists	Chief executive
Maintenance	Students	Senior executive
Services	Apprentices	Executive
Research & Development	Visitors' companions	Staff
Design	Parties	**VISIT TO COUNTRY**
Projects	Excursions	**VISIT TO EXHIBITION**
Process	Sightseers	
Laboratory		First
Testing	**LEGAL**	Frequent
Despatch	**INSPECTORATES**	Regular
Packaging	**STANDARDS**	Last
Storage	**APPROVALS**	Planned
Transport	**OFFICIAL**	Ad hoc
Administration		
Clerical	Government	**PERSONALITY**
Publicity	Local government	Enthusiastic
Public relations	Municipal	Balanced
Market research	Trade missions	Apathetic
COMMERCIAL	Associations:	Hedonistic
	trade	Puritan
Banks	professional	Hypochondriacs
Investment	Trade unions	**ATTITUDE**
Finance	Consumer protection	Positive
Insurance	Military	Neutral
Surveying	Civil defence	Negative
	Police	Objective
	Security	Prejudiced

FIGURE 8. CATEGORIES AND PERSONALITY TRAITS OF EXHIBITION VISITORS

Knowledge of your customers' language is also most helpful in informal personal contacts and at delicate discussions in which the presence of an interpreter could be embarrassing or unpolitic. If you rely on foreign nationals from branches, agencies or subsidiaries to provide the linguistic capability on your stand, make sure that the people

108

BUYING INFLUENCES		
CHARACTER	CATEGORY	FUNCTION
Buying	Customers	Decisive direct: placing orders Decisive indirect: initiating orders
Recommending	Customers	Non-buying personnel (peripheral)
Advising	Consultants Others	Outside advice, comparative tests Independent assessments
Selecting	Customers	Technical, commercial, reciprocity
Screening	Customers	Comparison (products of equal merit)
Advancing Obstructing	Users	Direct, intermediate, end use
		Contractors, operators, installers, inspectors
	Publications Publicity Media	Editorial, comparisons Test reports, surveys

FIGURE 9. BUYING INFLUENCES OF EXHIBITION VISITORS

selected know your own language as well, so that communication is possible between them, other stand personnel and visiting executives. This will apply particularly to foreign personnel on a medium level of responsibility. It must be assumed that senior foreign executives know the language of their principals.

Exchange of Information

The mission of the stand team is to communicate the marketing message to visitors to the stand and to note both the items of information disseminated and those received, i.e. questions, enquiries, requests for quotations or even orders, but also complaints and criticisms. The quality of these messages is affected by the fact that at an exhibition they are received against a background of noise, interference and distortion, in both the acoustic and communication meanings of the phenomena. Fortunately the effects of these disturbances can be reduced by preparation and the better the preparation the better the reception.

To be able to cope with the quantitative and qualitative variety of visitors the stand personnel must be very versatile indeed; such versatility can be achieved only by purposeful special training tailored to the general and exhibition marketing objectives of your company. The ramifications of the required versatility and therefore of the training programme can range from a short briefing session of experienced personnel to a full-time training course conducted internally or attended externally. If you have an extensive exhibition programme you can compile records of instructions and experiences in an exhibition manual, but only if you are determined enough and have the resources to keep it up-to-date and to ensure implementation.

In the instruction and training of stand personnel it is important to stress that in person-to-person contacts at exhibitions anyone at any time may have to assume the role of the solitary representative of the company and what it stands for. On sparsely staffed stands this is quite often the case and to be courteous in manner and cautious in pronouncements is not always easy under stress or at the end of a tiring day. But the easy way out, the excuse often heard of: 'I am only an assistant, the chief will be here tomorrow', is a sign of bad training at base or of a defect in stand management or both.

The efficiency of handling, occasionally perhaps even manipulating, both disseminated and received information is a critical factor in the assessment of the proficiency of the stand team. The use of forms, inquiry pads, contact record forms and more sophisticated accessories and electronic communication devices depends on the one hand on the information management system practised by your company and on the other on the size and design of the exhibition stand. The environment of an exhibition may require adaptation of existing devices or provision of special ones geared to your type of exhibits, products or services or other items on which you hope to obtain information.

In the world of industrial products generally and of engineering products in particular, the use of data collecting devices in person-to-person situations is a sensitive issue. Irrespective of the size of your stand and the strength of your stand team, data collecting devices should comply with certain basic requirements.

All personal portable accessories, such as notebooks, enquiry pads or mini-cassette recorders, should be strictly functional, unobtrusive and 'user friendly'. Any devices used should be tried and proved reliable and where necessary spare parts or replacements should be available. Thorough familiarity with these devices by persons using them is an obvious requirement. Forms and questionnaires, and indeed questions, should be time-economical and designed to ensure priority to the acquisition of essential data. No questions should appear to be trivial or ponderous or indiscreet, so that your respondent is neither bored nor alienated.

Other areas of information gathering activities, such as competitor and product intelligence, exhibition merit intelligence or visits to customers-exhibitors, will be defined by the objectives and scope of the exhibition effort. Even the best laid plans for these 'away from stand' activities can be affected by an unforeseen high influx of visitors or an unexpected absence of personnel. When there is a strong probability of such occurrences outside assistance can be engaged for special tasks.

The exhibitor's visiting personnel attending for more than a fleeting visit can contribute to the performance of special tasks, both technical and social. On the other hand top echelon executives gracing the stand for a few hours can seriously disrupt the efforts of a well-organized team by demanding a guided tour of the exhibition, a summary of 'all that happened so far on this expensive stand' and of course a critical assessment of all competitors.

It is the duty of the stand manager to supervise the efficient collection and recording of data and when necessary to supplement the preparations and instructions which should have preceded the exhibition by providing *ad hoc* guidance. In the bustle of a busy exhibition it is difficult to note all relevant observations and details, even with the help of the best aids and accessories. The nature of inquiries, the categories of visitors and incidence and density of visits can all change from one event to another in a manner which cannot be foreseen.

When exhibiting in new markets or at exhibitions not attended before, even the best pre-exhibition intelligence cannot fully compensate for the lack of experience. In such cases it is good practice for the stand manager or the executive in charge of exhibition activities to hold a short and informal analysis session at the end of each working day. The relaxed atmosphere of such a session generates an exchange of observations which are still fresh in memory, emphasizes problems of a symptomatic nature, reduces single complaints to their exceptional status and provides warnings for required corrective measures. Modified strategies can be discussed, tensions released and successful approaches more generally adopted. Such a session also gives the executive in charge an opportunity to observe the strengths and weaknesses of his staff and indicates where support is required and where initiative can be given a free reign.

It may be going too far to start with the educational background and methods of teaching which contribute to the state of the art of receiving, noting and sending of received technical information in an industrial marketing environment. It is, however, sufficient to trace the path of any one of hundreds of incomplete or garbled inquiries, even orders, and then to retrace the return path of queries, delays, misunderstandings and recriminations to find lack of schooling or sheer subject illiteracy as the basic cause of trouble.

The omission of one critical dimension, of a detail of material compatibility, of accuracy required or dimensional freedom allowed, any of which it would take only a minute or less to establish and to note, can be very costly. The fact that the costs of such omissions are difficult to assess or perhaps that they are taken as natural ingredients of industrial activities covers up, but does not do away with, their iniquity. If you are a small but specialized firm and the customer who made the inquiry is a large corporation you may have a difficult task to penetrate their bureaucratic jungle and get hold of a specification clerk or junior draughtsman who is responsible for that small but important detail.

Large projects in an advanced stage of completion have been known to wait for days to establish the correct position of an ominous decimal point; complicated machinery had to be dismantled because no one suspected that an essential detail could have been omitted. The plea is therefore made to stand personnel to take their notes with care and, to management, to provide stand personnel with aids which will make their task easier. There seems to be a false notion around that to make scrupulous notes on proper forms or in notebooks is the occupation of pedestrian minds while the nonchalant scribbling on the backs of envelopes is the sure sign of superior mental powers.

It really does not make sense to travel to a far-away exhibition at great expense, to work hard, to make excellent contacts, to come back with an order rating a press notice in an exalted newspaper and then to spend hours on telex messages and telephone calls to clear up details. It is cheaper, and impresses the customer as well, to try hard, to persevere and to return home fully briefed.

Despite the increasing acceptance of marketing concepts, the penetration of marketing attitudes into all spheres of an organization must of necessity vary in degree. In all organizations, whatever the degree of penetration, there will be functions which due to their special duties or skills are more remote from direct marketing functions than, for instance, sales or publicity.

The motives for exhibiting and the resultant strategies or choice of exhibits may require the inclusion in the stand team of personnel from these somewhat remote areas. In such cases it is not enough to issue them with instructions to pack their bags and go and see what they can do. It is essential to imbue them with the marketing aims of their function and prepare them for exposure to the different kinds of interrogators they will encounter at the exhibition. Designers, draughtsmen, research and laboratory technicians, chemists and clerical staff can be called upon to perform stand duties, either because their presence is important or because there is no one else available. In many cases their superiors may resent the temporary loss of their services, even when convinced of the marketing justification or more so if they are non-believers in exhibitions.

An exhibition provides a good occasion to preach the marketing concept gospel in these more remote areas, to the benefit of all.

Events with Long Duration Times

Exhibitions with long duration times, particularly if they are geographically remote from exhibitors' bases, can present problems with the staffing of stands. This applies particularly to general trade fairs. Local sales organizations, branches or agencies can be called on to assist in the staffing of the stand but unless there is definite knowledge available of the persons who would be assigned for the task this can be a risky procedure.

At international exhibitions with a strong influx of visitors from many countries there might be a conflict of interests between the local agent and a buyer from a third market, particularly if delivery times and perhaps prices and discounts are a problem. On the other hand, if the emphasis of the exhibition effort is on the local, regional or national market of the exhibition host country, well-screened and well-instructed local personnel can be a great asset to a stand team.

The inclusion of local personnel in the exhibition team can provide a good opportunity for their sales training and on many occasions headquarters personnel can learn a lot by judicial observation of local practices, reactions, customs and prejudices.

Contacts between executives on different levels of responsibility carried out in the informal, and of necessity co-operative, atmosphere of an exhibition can be of great value to current and future relations. The establishing of such relations requires a conscious effort by executives of higher rank. The rewards are not only a more effective exhibition performance, but also the opportunity to assess the capabilities, strengths and weaknesses of those involved.

Exhibition Stand Manners

'In these degenerate days' we oft hear said
'Manners are lost and chivalry is dead.'
No wonder, since in high exalted spheres
The same degeneracy, in fact appears.

Lewis Carroll, Solution to 'Puzzles from Wonderland'

By participating in an exhibition you are extending a public and general invitation to all interested parties to come and visit you. In many cases you supplement that public impersonal invitation by asking organizations or firms to visit your stand and you also extend personal invitations to specially selected persons. Apart from all business and public relations considerations and the benefits which you expect to derive from them you have, as an exhibitor, the plain obligations of a host. The way you treat your visitors becomes thus a matter of good manners which should consciously range from the full business treatment given to a customer or potential customer to the polite but nevertheless firm dismissal of the long-winded nuisance visitor.

Circumspection in the treatment of visitors, whatever their importance, is not only inherent in good manners but also helps you to husband your resources. In some situations good manners must be raised to the level of diplomacy and extra-cautious tact employed so as not to offend historical, political or hierarchical susceptibilities. If the substance of good manners is consideration for others, and if these others are visitors to your stand, then good manners become good marketing practice and that, after all, is the main purpose of the exhibition exercise.

Indifferent or absent stand personnel, inquiring visitors leaving stands with a massive supply of literature but without being asked for their name, lengthy social chats between neighbouring stand personnel or among personnel on their own stand, so obvious to outsiders because all involved are sporting their name badges, stand personnel retiring to the hospitality area or to the hidden parts of the stand—all these and some other manifestations of this failing are there for all to see, to provide food for comments and probably to influence the reputation and image of the exhibitor.

To hand a visitor a sheaf of leaflets and to dismiss him with a paternal smile, saying 'You'll find all the data in these', is tantamount to saying: 'You have wasted your time and money coming to our stand, you could have obtained the same information for the price of a postcard, telephone call or reply paid numbers card'.

On the other hand, to force a somewhat unwilling visitor to listen to a description of exhibits which is no more than a verbose repetition of the catalogue entry is to waste his time and yours. The obvious question is when to do what. The answer is briefing, experience and most of all intelligent observation. One or two questions will soon disclose the seriousness of the interest and the difference between a rubberneck, a remote prospect, a seriously interested potential customer and a snooping competitor.

In the absence of good briefing the technical shortcomings of stand personnel are not wholly their own fault, but even the most tolerant visitor will blame them entirely for their personal failing in good exhibition stand manners. In many cases the composition of the team on an exhibition stand is the result not of planning and purposeful selection but of haphazard last minute arrangements or of internal manoeuvring for overseas service by volunteers, who imagine that nightclubs are natural extensions of exhibition stands.

Executives of exhibiting firms when questioned *before* an exhibition about this particular organizational task will readily concede its importance, and will regard it as self-evident that due attention should be paid to it. When confronted *after* an exhibition with evidence of failing, the response depends to some extent on whether the inter-viewed executive actually visited the exhibition or not. The response can range from offended incredulity to assurances of strong corrective action and improvement in the future.

It is interesting to note that failures of this aspect of the exhibition effort can be observed as much on stands of large firms as on those of medium and small ones, although on large and elaborate stands these shortcomings are perhaps not so obvious or not so glaringly displayed as on smaller stands.

Occasionally lack of attention to visitors and passive rudeness by high-powered executives from headquarters can be observed during visits to a stand. There are of course those *real* chief executives who on a busy stand take on any duty required but unfortunately they are not very numerous. It was a heartwarming experience to see a well-behaved junior clerk save the reputation of a bumptious executive by offering to an obviously interested but tired visitor a chair on the stand. It was late in the day and the keen executive seeing just one more visitor keeping him from his prepared drink asked the junior to dismiss the visitor and tell him 'to come back tomorrow'. It was later learned that the man in question was a deputy minister responsible for approving tenders which this exhibitor had recently submitted. It also transpired very much later that the visitor noticed the whole manoeuvre but, being the man he is, took it in good humour. It is also sad to relate that the executive did not mend his ways until his company was taken over and he had to mind his manners in a new management environment.

Stand personnel cannot be expected to be accomplished psychologists or socio-psychologists, nor should they be expected to be cunning manipulators. But for the effective performance of their tasks and for the achievement of set goals they need to be very good persuaders. To round off their skills they should be acquainted with the customs, conventions and codes of conduct of the environment in which they operate.

In the Middle East the practising and expecting of strict punctuality will gain no particular merit points and insistence on it, or reproaches about it, can cause conflicts and otherwise unexplainable setbacks. By the same token delays and postponements accompanied by transparently lame explanations will incur no penalty points. In Scandinavia punctuality is regarded as a natural ingredient of good manners which, when transgressed, can release reactions of disapproval ranging from a grave frown for minor offences to a temporary break in negotiations when fixed time appointments are not strictly kept.

Stand Personnel—Case Study 5

Industrial exhibitions were the subject of a seminar in which the lecturer identified three basic attitude types of stand personnel.

Negative types don't believe in exhibitions; they consider exhibiting or visiting exhibitions as a tiresome, time-wasting and generally unproductive activity. They only attend exhibitions when forced to do so by the sales department rota or by some other form of official compulsion. They perform their duties with a minimum of exertion. They sometimes seek confirmation of their disbelief in exhibitions by commiserating with tired visitors and asking at neighbouring stands whether they too consider it all an infernal nuisance. They usually report that nothing much happened at the exhibition.

Passive types are usually sales managers or export managers of small or medium firms, who think that they are overworked and their office is understaffed, and sales engineers who think that their territory or area will be neglected or open to competition (disregarding the fact that most of the competitors are also exhibiting).

When management considers that design or engineering specialists should attend exhibitions, some of the more desk-bound or bench-bound think that all important work will stop during their absence—forgetting that nothing like that happened during their last illness. On the exhibition stand they perform their duties fairly effectively although without any special enthusiasm; this they leave to their exhibition-mad colleagues. Their reports are somewhat formalistic, sometimes patronizing and contain statistics of the number of visitors to the exhibition, etc. copied from exhibition bulletins.

A few of them, after attending several exhibitions, realize that there is more to it than they thought and in time they become converted to active participation.

Active types know that participation in exhibitions is a normal marketing activity. They make provisions for attending by arranging their other activities accordingly, they take considerable trouble in preparing their supporting materials, they inform customers and other interested parties about the dates of their attendance and they co-ordinate their attendance with other colleagues. Their reports are usually concise, they emphasize the importance of the contacts made and they recommend follow-up action.

114

Customers—Case Study 6

A marketing executive defined the following three types of customers who are likely to visit the stands of the company participating in a number of specialized industrial exhibitions and indicated the attitudes which the stand personnel should adopt:

Potential future customers. The numbers that will visit our stand will depend on our preparatory work, on the number of personal invitations we have sent out to prospects, on the number of special calls which our sales engineers made and generally on our publicity and direct mail efforts. Apart from the special attention which they will receive on the stand, you will suggest to them a visit to our works whenever they are in the area. You may even invite a decision-making executive of a really important potential customer to visit our works at our expense.

Lapsed customers will constitute a small group unless special efforts were made to attract them to the stand. Among them will be some who perhaps are not as pleased with the change as they expected. Handled tactfully they are candidates for a return to the fold. Persuasion has to be exercised and be seen to be exercised to give them a justification for reversing their course once more.

Present customers should be numerous because they will all know about our stand from our invitations, from press announcements, from the special note in our current advertisements, from stick-on labels in our correspondence or because we are usually participating in exhibitions which they usually visit. They deserve full attention—perhaps they should meet some of our executives with whom they usually have no contact. Are there any new names in their buying or technical departments? They should be given special but tactful attention.

Customers' Attitudes—Case Study 7

A stand manager concluded one of the briefing sessions for the stand team, held on the eve of a mechanical handling exhibition, with the following words:

We have discussed our new equipment and the strength of two new features, we have also talked about what we can expect from our competitors. I think that we are quite well prepared for the ordeal but I would like to stress once more the importance of probing into our customers' needs. You have your inquiry forms. Please pay special attention to the items marked as critical. Just for those who are new to this exhibition I should like to make a remark or two about our present and potential customers. Among the lapsed, present and potential future customers who will visit our stand there will be at least three typical categories and one rare one requiring special attention.

● **The negative attitude type**. They are almost inarticulate when required to define their needs in a positive statement. They hint at them indirectly in complaints about the shortcomings of our equipment. By judicious questioning you may be able to extract some vague remarks as to what, in their opinion, the equipment should do. In reply to your deliberate provocative question how *they* would improve our equipment a few may have some suggestions, many will plead 'I don't know' and some will reply with varying degrees of smugness: 'that's your business—I am only interested in buying the right piece of equipment at the right price'.

You must display considerable patience with negative types and guide them gently towards a decision. You could suggest or perhaps write out a pro forma order and ask them whether the types, quantities and delivery dates are what they had in mind. In the end they usually respond to a concrete proposition. With some it may be advisable not to press for a decision and to suggest a return visit to the stand, but only if you have found out that they are not leaving the exhibition at once.

● **The neutral attitude type**. They are, on the whole, fairly satisfied with our machines, but then they consider our main competitor's machines to be probably just as good. Their needs are mostly in the areas of prices, discounts and deliveries. As to the future—they will probably require about the same type and quantity as last year—perhaps 5 per cent more or perhaps 10 per cent less—who knows—it depends on their sales.

With neutral types you must be factual, you must also have ready answers to any questions on comparisons with competitive equipment and if tactically necessary, but only then, you can prove your points by referring to our equipment comparison dossier. If they are potential prospects make sure that they have received all data, ask whether anyone else in their organization should be sent details and inquire about the best times for a personal follow-up visit.

● **The positive attitude type**. They have definite ideas about our equipment and its virtues and vices and their relative importance. They will give you definite, sometimes detailed indications of their present and future needs. Of course some may completely redesign our equipment in a way which would make it virtually impossible to manufacture economically, but even their out-of-the-way ideas may contain something more than the grain of salt with which you will take them.

Discussions on performance in the field, endurance and service and spares facilities will find their ready ear. If they say that they are going to place an order they usually mean it and you can respond by saying that you in turn will make out a provisional works order to ensure delivery. What is more you should make out that order and at the same time make the necessary arrangements for an early follow-up visit to secure confirmation.

● **The prominent company type**. Visitors from large companies come to our stand in all shapes and sizes. Some are buyers with limited powers, some are executives with a decisive voice in the business. They mostly know exactly what they need and, if they have had any dealings with us before, we also know what they require.

There is only one type you have to watch and that is the small man in a large company. He grows taller with every hour he spends at the exhibition. He hints at colossal orders at low prices and even bigger repeat orders next year. He expects lavish entertaining, but he will be evasive about his status in his firm and never carries a visiting card. He can take up to an hour of your time and although he does most of the talking, you soon feel that it is not you but himself he is trying to convince. If you can manage it without being too obvious, pass him on to our competitors.

Negative, neutral or positive—they all are, or could be, our customers. Please note what they have to say—be good listeners and poor interrupters.

Preparations

The preceding sections have dealt with the structure of exhibitions and their merits, with motives for exhibiting, with budgeting, selection and exhibition activities. In a strict time sequence preparations should follow the decision to exhibit and the selection of exhibitions for participation. However, the discussion of preparations was placed deliberately in its present position to enable interpretation of the preparation requirements in the light of the discussion of the full range of exhibition activities outlined earlier.

Exhibiting requires preparation not only because it is a complex marketing activity but also because of its intensity and concentration and of its propensity to expose shortcomings. On the other hand the intrinsic value of effective preparation and the resulting economic use of resources employed is enhanced by the extrinsic value of the resulting smoothness of the exhibition operation and the general good impression created.

Depending on the organizational structure of an exhibitor and on the ramification of the exhibition programme, exhibition preparation can mean as little as a do-it-yourself exercise by a small exhibition team or as much as the operation of a fully fledged special department.

One advantage which an exhibition effort has over other marketing activities is the ease with which specialist outside help and subcontracting can be called in for parts of the total effort. Stand design, stand production, erection and dismantling and some publicity and public relations functions are obvious candidates for outside help; so is training of your own personnel and recruiting of auxiliary stand personnel. All this can be successfully accomplished providing that overall management guidance and instructions remain firmly and unequivocally in your own hands.

The range of preparation activities for an exhibition effort is defined by the marketing motives which decided participation, by the material structure of the exhibition effort and of the stand and by the tasks set for the personnel. Irrespective of the size and scope of the operation, exhibition preparation activities are concerned with the deployment of personnel and material resources during specified activity periods and for specified purposes.

But just as exhibiting should be a part of integrated marketing activities so preparations for exhibiting should be integrated into the general scheme of marketing services. As exhibiting embraces many marketing functions, routine preparations for such functions contribute their share to the special aspect of exhibiting. Preparations for the issue and maintaining of stocks of sales and technical literature and publicity materials, preparations concerned with packaging and transport and preparations for demonstrations, tests and trials can all be adapted and extended for the special requirements of exhibition efforts. From a timing point of view exhibition preparations can be related to routine times, to the active preparation period, to the immediate pre-exhibition period, the exhibition duration, the immediate post-exhibition period, the analysis time target and the duration of the follow-up period.

Preparations related to time elements are best illustrated by reference to appropriate checklists.

> Checklist 2. The frequency of the exhibition will influence the preparation period between applications for stand space. If the date of the exhibition is movable, a close check must be kept on changes of dates. In some locations cancellations and other changes are more likely than in others. Some competing events may be known a year in advance but some may become known only weeks, or even days, before the opening of an exhibition.

> Checklists 7, 8 and 9. Changes in assigned tasks and duties may require additional preparation. Close scrutiny may indicate the need for additional personnel or throw doubt on the feasibility of accomplishing the task.

> Checklists 11 and 13. Changes, additions, cancellations, congresses, symposia, cultural events and special functions can influence drawn-up time schedules and may require their modification.

> Checklist 15. Changes in official attitudes, e.g. a move from a neutral to a friendly or privileged attitude, may require more frequent or longer attendances at official functions.

Material structure preparations. The preparation of the material structure of an exhibition effort is so closely defined by its scope and content that general remarks are of limited value. For one exhibitor attending a number of exhibitions, preparations of the material aspects are matters of experiences brought up-to-date at each event; for another exhibitor participating in as yet unknown events in difficult locations the preparation can assume the dimensions of a major operation.

When an exhibition takes place in the environment of an established market, the extent of the necessary preparations can be easily assessed as the features exhibited, their locations and the techniques of exhibiting (*Checklist* 20) will be reflected images of the marketing techniques already employed in that market. When a new market is explored (*Checklist* 7) or exhibits new to the market are introduced, effective preparation may be a critical factor which could determine the success or failure of the effort.

A thorough scrutiny of checklists dealing with the material structure elements of the exhibition effort and the supporting publicity and other materials and an examination of the facilities and services available at the exhibition will provide a guide to the preparations which are required and to their timing.

Personnel preparations. The establishing of personal contacts is one of the main tasks of any exhibition effort and deserves the best preparation. The motives for exhibiting indicate the areas in which contacts should be sought and the most appropriate means of encouraging new contacts, i.e. visits to your stand, can be selected from the relevant checklists.

For alert exhibitors an exhibition of high marketing merit provides many facilities for encouraging visits to the stand, for publicity, for press releases, for invitations to demonstrations, etc. Meticulous preparatory work is required if these facilities are to be fully exploited during the pre-exhibition period when persons staffing the media services are more receptive and less overworked than during the actual exhibition period. The use of checklists to assess the preparations required is shown by the following examples:

Checklist 3. Suitable material should be submitted in time for inclusion in pre-exhibition publicity, press releases and press conferences.

Checklist 6. Catalogue entries should be checked for correctness in time for the final catalogue issue, with particular attention paid to new products, translations of texts, addresses and telephone numbers.

Checklists 9 and 10. If support for an agent is one of the motives for exhibiting, the preparatory activities of the agent may need checking, advice or guidance. Public relations activities may require careful preparation of timing and of suitability of material and checking of compatibility of personnel, even when the exhibition environment is similar to that of your home ground. In locations with marked differences, the preparation could amount to an investigation in depth well ahead in time of the actual activity. Many a distorted image or questionable reputation was established as a result of insufficient preparation or inept adaptation to local conditions. Marketing executives following in the wake of such campaigns have to repair the damage done instead of reaping the expected benefits.

Checklists 21 and 22. The need to prepare personnel attending an exhibition for the first time needs no special emphasis. The task of personnel with established contacts can be eased by the preparation of material aids, advance invitations, gifts, etc. The personality traits and attitudes of stand personnel may need checking, correcting or encouraging, particularly if experience of a particular country or exhibition is lacking.

Checklists 2 and 27. The geographic location of the exhibition may indicate the need for advice and perhaps for the provision of special clothing appropriate to the climatic conditions, the season of the year or the environment. Exhibition activities located in agricultural, mining or marine environments may require special clothing. In addition to its primary protective function, the provision of such clothing also indicates to customers the exhibitor's capacity for foresight and planning.

Checklists 13 and 14. The national environment of the exhibition may impose certain sartorial demands perhaps not known to newcomers to an exhibition. In some countries at official functions and receptions formal dress is expected, even if not stipulated, and informal dress is regarded with disapproval.

Checklist 3. Restrictions on the nationality of stand personnel or of visiting executives imposed as a result of political events or changes in regime can occur after all preliminary preparations were made. In locations prone to such changes vigilance right up to the date of the exhibition opening may be necessary.

Checklist 10. When 'thank you' gestures or hospitality to highly placed customers is an exhibiting motive, the status, compatibility and social technique aptitudes of stand personnel or persons delegated for the duty is of the greatest importance.

Preparation of information aids. An important and often neglected aspect of preparations is the provision of aids for stand activities, interviewing, inquiries, intelligence and generally for enabling information to be gathered in a reliable form without being an operational burden. It is the task of the preparation function to examine aids which are available on the market as to their suitability for a specific exhibition event. The temptation to take the path of least resistance is often great and sometimes based on entirely irrational reasoning. In one case it was administratively easier to order 'exhibition record cards' of a commercial pattern in expensive loose-leaf binders than to justify a request for specially designed and cheaply duplicated cards. The fact that the 'bought in' cards could be charged as 'general stationery' but specially designed cards would be charged as 'exhibition expenses' decided the issue.

The company in question participated in about eleven exhibitions annually, but no one seemed interested in the fact that specially designed and internally produced cards would have reduced the overall annual expenditure on this item by about 67 per cent. In the context of the total budget of eleven exhibitions the actual amount which would be saved was not very significant but the operational end results were nevertheless fairly damaging. The commercial pattern cards were for obvious reasons designed for a wide range of applications with an emphasis on consumer goods. Neither the headings nor the spaces for entries were suitable for inquiries concerning the sophisticated industrial products exhibited and when used the cards had to be supplemented frequently by additional pinned on or stapled bits of paper, many of which were eventually lost before they reached the analysis desk.

There are situations where the character of the exhibition location or the type of product exhibited, or perhaps the audience aimed at, is not suitable for noting too many details of inquiries or interviews. A tape recorder placed in the stand office can provide a way to record summaries of interviews, comments and impressions, preferably not later than at the end of each span of duty.

The aids provided in one form or another should be examined for their suitability for record purposes, for analysis and where appropriate for follow-up activities. The ultimate utility test of such aids is in the first place their purposeful design and ease of handling, which together should encourage their use, and only in the second place the convenience of reproducing, storing and analysing them. The ideal aid meets both requirements with an equal degree of effectiveness.

Preparation for travel. Travel arrangements, visas and other formalities require varying degrees of attention, depending on the location of the exhibition. In one location the length of time required to obtain a visa determines the starting date for that aspect of preparation work while hotel reservations present no problem; in another no visa is required, but hotel reservations must be made 10–12 months ahead.

In one case all arrangements can be made with ease from the exhibitor's office by telephone or telex while in another it is imperative to employ none but the best of specialized agents dealing with that territory. The task of the preparation function is to find the optimum means of achieving the desired results, and when expedient to abandon the ambition of doing it all without any outside help. For many exhibition locations advance preparation of visits to customers and of other marketing activities scheduled before and after an exhibition can yield substantial savings in time and expenses, providing that a valid marketing goal is the guiding motive for such arrangements.

Checklists 19–27

	MATERIAL ELEMENTS OF EXHIBITION STANDS	
	Display elements:	
	exhibits	
	literature	
	other display elements	
	Visitors' reception elements:	
	reception	
	conference rooms, interview rooms	
	refreshments/bar	
	cloakroom	
	Literature display:	
	open display:	
	assortments/folders	
	individual items	
	fixed protected display:	
	request forms, reference numbers	
	dispensers, hall stands	
	dispensers, open air stands (weatherproof)	
	Literature distribution:	
	open choice	
	restricted choice	
	invitation to take	
	invitation to request:	
	from stand	
	to be sent on	
	storage facilities	
	Stand facilities:	
	office	
	rest room	
	kitchen	

Checklist 19   THE EXHIBITION STAND COMPLEX

This checklist deals with the focus of exhibition activities—the stand. The requirements of individual exhibitors and the opportunities offered by individual exhibitions range over such a wide spectrum of size, cost, design and sophistication that a checklist can provide no more than an indication of what needs to be checked, initiated or dispensed with.

The activities of the stand personnel must be supported by at least adequate but preferably very efficient material facilities. The best qualified stand personnel deserve the best auxiliary facilities to enable them to exploit their talents to the full. Numerical or quality gaps in the stand team may have to be compensated by suitable supporting material elements.

The reception of visitors serves the basic purpose of the exhibition effort of establishing personal contacts and conducting them effectively. The range of interests, ranks and personalities of visitors which can be expected at an exhibition stand will determine the nature of the facilities required to provide a cost- and time-effective reception background.

FEATURES EXHIBITED	
Exhibits:	
products	
product ranges	
applications	
processes	
techniques	
services	
Capabilities:	
research	
development	
projects	
design	
consultancy	
Concepts:	
technological	
intertechnological	
interdisciplinary	
LOCATIONS	
Individual stands	
Pavilions, kiosks	
Stand or booth in collective arrangement	
Projectors	
Cinemas	
Stands of other exhibitors	
Open air area stands	
Special locations	
Locations outside exhibition site	
TECHNIQUE OF EXHIBITING	
Static displays	
Moving displays	
Demonstrations	
Tests	
Static models	
Animated models	
Visual and audio-visual presentations	

Checklist 20   EXHIBITS

Exhibits are the manifestation of the essence of exhibiting. They are the fundamental core element of the exhibition effort and their presentation is an expression of your marketing aims. The motives for exhibiting may call for special techniques of exhibiting and the feasibility of using them may have to be checked against the facilities and services provided at a particular exhibition.

STAND PERSONNEL QUALIFICATIONS	
Educational background:	
general	
professional—technical	
special (lecturing, demonstrating)	
languages	
Training:	
marketing	
sales	
service	
exhibitions	
languages	
Exhibition experience:	
this exhibition	
other exhibitions:	
home country	
abroad	
stand duties:	
executive	
routine	
special	
First time experience:	
exhibition host country	
abroad	
in this role	
Established contacts:	
in exhibition host country:	
in exhibition location (town, region)	
with customers:	
exhibition sphere of influence	
local	
international	
with other exhibitors	
with exhibition authorities	

Checklist 21   STAND PERSONNEL ACTIVITIES I

The basic qualification requirements of stand personnel are determined by the motives for exhibiting and by the exhibition strategy. This checklist provides a means of checking to what extent these requirements can be met and what measures need to be taken to compensate for any shortcomings. Technically qualified personnel may need linguistic support. Special or local exhibition experience may indicate that an allocation of executive duties should be made, perhaps even disregarding formal seniority considerations.

STAND PERSONNEL—PERSONALITY TRAITS	
Personality:	
manners	
appearance	
presence	
self-confidence	
general attitudes:	
adaptable	
irritable	
co-operative	
stand attitudes:	
orderly	
indifferent	
negligent	
attitude to exhibition environment:	
enjoying	
accepting	
hostile	

Checklist 22   STAND PERSONNEL ACTIVITIES II

In the exposed arena of the stand, personality traits of the stand personnel are an important aspect of their encounters with visitors to the stand and with other contacts at the exhibition. Personality traits of newcomers to the company and/or to the exhibition scene should be noted, the need for special training observed and exceptional talents encouraged.

	STAND PERSONNEL APPEAL STRATEGY	
	Appeal targets:	
	customers	
	users:	
	primary	
	intermediate	
	end	
	indirect influences:	
	operators, installers	
	service, maintenance	
	installation, contractors	
	Exhibits appeal features:	
	design	
	appearance	
	weight	
	performance	
	economy	
	operation	
	Capabilities appeal features:	
	design	
	research and development	
	consultancy	
	Services appeal features:	
	product availability, deliveries	
	service:	
	range and scope	
	service contracts	
	training of customer's personnel:	
	operating, maintenance, servicing	
	spares:	
	availability	
	distribution	

Checklist 23   STAND PERSONNEL ACTIVITIES III

This checklist is concerned with the appeal strategy of exhibition stand activities. The motives for exhibiting will govern the selection and ranking of features of exhibits and services which will be presented to visitors and also of the categories of visitors which should be the subjects of special attention. Thus in some market situations the presentation of service availability and training can be ranked as 'most important' when visitors are end users, while the features of operating techniques and training of operators may command a higher priority in others.

	EXHIBITION STAND	
	Design	
	Material structure	
	Exhibits	
	Display elements	
	Reception elements	
	Stand facilities, amenities	
	Information aids:	
	visitors record cards	
	literature request cards	
	product intelligence forms	
	stand intelligence forms	
	Exhibition site elements	
	Extra-mural elements	
	Administration elements:	
	stand space	
	catalogue entry	
	services	
	hired items	
	packing	
	transport	
	insurance	
	security	

Checklist 24   PREPARATION OF NON-PERSONAL ELEMENTS

The extent of the preparation for all non-personal elements of exhibiting is so closely governed by the scope of the individual effort that the headings of this checklist should be regarded as no more than reminders pointing to the areas for which preparation and anticipation is required. More details can be found in the series of checklists dealing with the relevant exhibition elements.

PREPARATION FOR PERSONNEL	
Exhibitor's personnel:	
stand and exhibition site personnel:	
commercial staff	
technical staff	
demonstrators	
service personnel	
special task visitors	
visiting executives	
publicity and public relations staff	
Auxiliary personnel:	
interpreters	
technical	
clerical	
catering	
PREPARATIONS FOR CONTACTS	
Customers—current, potential, lapsed	
Users—current, potential, lapsed	
Indirect influence contacts	
Non-buying contacts	
Suppliers	
Invited visitors	
Other exhibitors	
Authorities—officials	
Visitors from exhibitor's:	
associated, subsidiary company	
agencies	
representations	

Checklist 25   PREPARATION FOR PERSONNEL AND CONTACTS

This checklist indicates some of the categories of the exhibitor's staff for whom preparation is essential for the performance of their tasks or who could greatly benefit from it.

For preparations to be effective they must be related to the persons concerned, anticipated situations and perhaps to encounters deliberately contrived to achieve desired results. Not all situations can be anticipated and some encounters may not take place, but the waste of a superfluous preparation is much to be preferred to the disadvantages of no preparation. Preparations for exhibitor's personnel can be frugal or generous, but they should never be perfunctory. In some cases the scope and quality of the preparation can be a critical factor, e.g. in difficult market conditions (*Checklist 15*), in locations with language problems, when stand personnel have no exhibition experience or when auxiliary staff are engaged. By reviewing the list of persons expected to visit the stand and of contacts which should be made, the preparation of the exhibitor's personnel can be made to better purpose. Specially invited visitors may require attention not only in business matters, but also some consideration for personal needs or problems connected with the visit. In such cases preparation should be attentive without being obtrusive. At the same time stand personnel should be prepared, i.e. warned that some visitors not only expect exceptional treatment but on occasions show no reticence in demanding it. Unfortunately nothing short of a crash course in firm but tactful diplomacy is a sufficient preparation for such visitors.

	PUBLICITY AND PUBLIC RELATIONS	
	Programme, importance, participation:	
	events:	
	stand	
	exhibition	
	extra-mural	
	special	
	contacts:	
	general	
	special	
	official	
	high rank	
	Stocks, translations, suitability:	
	sales and technical literature:	
	general	
	special	
	other publicity and PR material:	
	routine items	
	special exhibition items	
	outside-exhibition items	

Checklist 26   PREPARATIONS FOR PUBLICITY AND PUBLIC RELATIONS

A timely review of contacts, targets, events and the availability and suitability of all publicity and PR material is particularly important when some or all tasks are assigned to outside help. Ineffective publicity and PR actions and perhaps even embarrassment and negative publicity can result from lack of attention, failure to communicate or failure to give explicit and clear instructions.

	PREPARATIONS FOR PERSONNEL	
	Travel and personal transport arrangements:	
	pre-exhibition	
	during exhibition	
	post-exhibition	
	Hotel reservations:	
	special requirements:	
	secretarial service	
	conference facilities	
	banqueting facilities	
	Other staff accommodation:	
	private rooms	
	caravans-trailers	
	aboard ship	
	hotel-trains	
	PERSONAL PREPARATIONS	
	Personal welfare:	
	protection (health hazards)	
	remedies (personal susceptibilities)	
	apparel:	
	climatic conditions	
	protective clothing	
	Personal formalities:	
	passport	
	visas	
	special permits	
	currency, credit cards	
	insurance:	
	general	
	special risks	
	letters of introduction	
	Personal aids:	
	visiting cards (foreign language)	
	phrase book, pocket dictionary	
	personal/portable computer	
	camera	
	tape recorder	
	portable typewriter	

Checklist 27   PERSONAL PREPARATIONS

The supreme importance of personal efforts has been stressed throughout the study. In the environment of an exhibition the effectiveness of performing tasks depends not only on qualifications and aptitudes, but also on the absence of intrusive irritants unrelated to the tasks but hampering them and on the availability of personal aids easing these tasks.

This checklist provides examples of such items. Some are essential, some optional but all require attention either by the person concerned or by the exhibitor's administrative function charged with preparations. At first sight the items listed may appear obvious or trivial, but their neglect can cause considerable delays or loss of time.

PART FOUR

Performance Analysis, Audit and Follow-Up

Evaluation of the Exhibition Effort

An exhibition effort, like any other marketing activity, is a resource-conversion process expected to generate benefits which are related in a cost-effective way to the marketing objectives of exhibiting. The nature of exhibitions and their wide marketing scope provide excellent opportunities for the application of almost all elements of the marketing mix and thus for the expectations of a variety of tangible and intangible benefits. Exhibition efforts, in the quest to reap these benefits, can range from regular participation in one event to a comprehensive programme of participation in numerous exhibitions around the world.

From the point of view of a general marketing strategy the analysis of the exhibition performance and the audit of the exhibition effort are critical links in the chain of exhibition activities shown in Figure 2. The conclusions drawn from the analysis or the judgements and recommendations of the audit will influence the scope and volume of future exhibition initiatives and the choice of venues and events.

The question arises of whether an analysis report of exhibition activities, i.e. only of external activities, can provide a good enough basis for decision making or whether a full audit of all exhibition activities, i.e. internal as well as external ones, is the only rational approach for evaluating the whole of the exhibition effort.

Large organizations with an extensive exhibitions programme, a commensurate exhibitions budget and a modern management information system will find the practice of exhibition auditing a natural and valuable management tool. It is suggested that exhibition auditing is equally important for medium and small companies, particularly for companies relying on exhibitions as their main marketing tool. Smaller companies may be reluctant to add one more chore to the duties of their overworked staff for—as they see it—no other reason than to give a fashionable name to an exercise which they have been doing for years, guided by experience, intuition and hope.

Whether exhibition effort auditing is a full-time function or only a part-time or *ad hoc* assignment is a matter of company structure and organizational convenience; what is important is that exhibition effort auditing, whatever its description and form, should be practised in an effective professional manner.

Analysis of Exhibition Activities

All exhibition activities and all of the material framework in which they are performed represent the theoretical totality of elements which should be the subjects of analysis. In practice a selection of such subjects must be made, as otherwise the extent of the task would defeat its own two-fold objective of providing a speedy purposeful guide for future action and an assessment of the performance of the current exhibition effort. The exercise of selecting and listing the exhibition elements which should be observed and noted for an analysis in turn creates a salutary opportunity for a critical assessment of the intended exhibition effort.

The need for exhibition performance analysis is widely recognized in theory but in practice it is implemented with varying degrees of insistence and with varying degrees of success.

Received information. The main task of the analysis is the systematic scrutiny of all received messages (orders, inquiries, requests for information, opinions and impressions) and their arrangement in distinguishable interest groups related to the objectives of exhibiting. In addition to the substantial data acquired in encounters on the stand and away from the stand there is a host of other observations or remarks perhaps not directly related to the objectives of exhibiting and more difficult to define. They are mostly well founded, unfounded or anecdotal value judgements, perceptions, rumours and stories rarely encountered in the normal course of business but voiced deliberately or unwittingly in the freer atmosphere of an exhibition. Notices in the press and comments on radio and television are also potential contributors of such observations.

The range of marketing motives for a particular event will determine the nature of the interest groups, their fragmentation, their claim for priority of response and also the selection of messages which have to be allocated to individual groups. The interest groups most commonly encountered are the following three in order of importance: sales interests, service interests and information interests. Within the individual groups internal priorities could be established. Thus the order of priorities for the sales interests group could be: production orders, trial orders, specific requests for quotations, general requests for prices. The priority order for service interests could be: warranty problems, general service problems, spares and replacements orders, service and spares inquiries. Information interests could be arranged in the order of: specific requests for product data, requests for general technical information. In the course of an exhibition of five or more days' duration, orders and requests for quotations and for information can be fully or partially actioned during the course of the exhibition, but it is essential that these actions should be included in the analysis schedule under their appropriate headings.

Visitors and contacts. Closely connected with the analysis of received information, and relying to a large extent on the contents of its messages, is the analysis of visitors to the stand and of all other personal contacts. The categories and traits of exhibition visitors were shown in Figure 8 and their buying influences in Figure 9. These provide a suitable background for analysis purposes. While the list of buying influences indicates the most frequently encountered areas of competence, different areas, both wider and narrower, can result from delegation of duties, changes in roles or peculiar internal

131

organization structures. The position in the company and the rank of a visitor usually enables a correct interpretation of the exerted influence. There are also cases when the influences of two or more visitors are exerted simultaneously and it is difficult to assess the dominant influence. Only energetic follow-up action can provide the answer.

Stand personnel. A critical review related to the objectives of exhibiting is required of the composition and competence of the stand team, of the effectiveness of teamwork, of the response to assigned duties, of the correctness or otherwise of the definitions of these duties and of the resulting capacity of personnel to cope with them. Observation of the activities of stand personnel and of their effectiveness is a delicate matter to be carried out with tact and diplomacy but is none the less an important aspect of performance analysis. The marketing and social behaviour of stand personnel is crucial to the realization of the exhibiting objectives. But beyond that on the open stage of an exhibition stand and in the more secluded precincts of stand offices or special rooms, the image and reputation of the exhibitor can be influenced by impressions from personal behaviour to a degree quite out of proportion to the status, position and importance of the individuals whose manners and attitudes generate these impressions. Strange roles, unusual situations, tiredness, subconscious or even overt xenophobia, self-deprecating criticism of one's own products, company or country, disinterest, commercial or technical arrogance, odd personal habits—all these and many more are the factors involved. It is not the task of stand managers to be accomplished psychologists but a popular paperback on the subject read on the dull journey to the exhibition could give quite a few hints as to what to look for in personnel behaviour and the reasons for it.

Exhibits. The main items for scrutiny are the following: the relevance of the exhibits to the stated objectives of exhibiting; their functional and aesthetic effectiveness related to the special marketing tasks of exhibiting and to general corporate marketing aims; the response of visitors, their praise and criticisms; the support which exhibits gave to the efforts of the stand team or their shortcomings or failings in that respect.

A subsidiary task is a critical comparison of exhibits of direct and indirect competitors and the implications of the observations made. Award-winning exhibits or exhibits which attracted exceptional publicity, both your own and those of your competition, deserve critical appraisal.

Exhibition stand. An assessment is required of the functional effectiveness of the exhibition stand when related to the exhibiting tasks, the reception of visitors, the ease of operating, the comfort of the stand personnel and the prestige and standing of the exhibitor. An assessment is also required of the size and visual impact of the stand when compared with stands of competitors and with stands in the immediate neighbourhood. Restraint must be exercised lest the magnitude of the analysis task should defeat its objective, but Checklists 19, 20 and 23 (pages 121, 122, 125) and the discussion of stand design (page 92) will provide a basis for selecting subjects for analysis which are most appropriate for the particular event attended.

Exhibition merit. A critical scrutiny is required of the merits of the exhibition attended, in relation to the merit values credited to it at the time that the decision to participate was taken. The checklists dealing with the structure of exhibitions (Checklists 1–6, pages 31–36) and with the marketing and environment merits of exhibitions (Checklists 11–14, pages 82–85) will indicate the scope and extent of the scrutiny that may be appropriate for an individual exhibition effort.

Publicity and public relations. Scrutiny of the performance of the publicity and public relations activities is a specialized task which is in most cases outside the competence of the stand team. It is, however, appropriate to examine the degree to which opportunities for publicity and public relations efforts offered by the exhibition were in fact exploited to the best advantage.

132

Analysis Report

The composition and contents of this report are governed by two factors: the corporate character and organizational structure of the exhibitor and the scope and magnitude of the exhibition effort. A very large corporation can, where appropriate, participate in a specialized exhibition with a modest stand, albeit of high quality. A medium-size firm relying on exhibitions as a main marketing tool can participate in a number of exhibitions with quite sizeable and elaborate stands.

In one case the exhibition report can be addressed to an executive of a division or perhaps of a subsidiary of a large corporation, in another to the chief marketing executive of the firm or to its managing director. One report will consist of a page or two of terse comments and a summary of good or bad results, another will be a complex essay compiled on the basis of an analysis carried out by means of the most sophisticated methods available. At both ends of the scale the validity of the conclusions will be determined by the quality of the data collected and their intelligent interpretation and only to a limited extent by the means by which they were processed.

The methods and techniques which exhibitors could use for processing exhibition data would cover a spectrum which is as wide as the variety of their corporate sizes, wealths and organizational skills. There is, however, one fundamental requirement of performance measurement and analysis—that the parameters used should be meaningful in their own right and that they should be relevant to the special needs and aims of an individual exhibitor.

Each report should present salient conclusions and recommendations for action under three main headings:

> A summary of the intake of marketing messages received as a result of exhibition activities and of their general follow-up implications.

> A review of the performance of the stand personnel and of the effectiveness of exhibits and stand in relation to the stated objectives of exhibiting.

> A review of the effectiveness of the exhibition as a medium for achieving the stated marketing objectives.

The summary and main body of the report should be concise and should be written— in keeping with marketing principles of regarding the customer—with the recipient in mind. If necessary it should be subdivided into suitable sections, which can be separated physically so that recipients with specialized interests can be served without burdening them with redundant matter. If the report is compiled from contributions by several persons, different methods of presenting the report can be employed. At best the several reports or parts should be submitted to an editor who creates out of the parts one comprehensive whole and also assumes overall responsibility. It is sometimes a matter of mistaken policy, or a case of shunning responsibility, that a collection of separate reports is presented in a form in which the common outer binding is the only unifying factor. Such a collection usually carries open or hidden marks of individual authorship and the contributions are mostly coloured by personal opinions, to the detriment of objectivity and factual reporting. Objectivity in reporting is a discipline which should be taught and practised as talents in that area are very rare. Many an internal conflict and the settling of interdepartmental scores have their origin in deliberately provocative or subtly distorted presentations of basically indisputable facts. One comparatively tame example will illustrate the point. The following are extracts from three reports written by three persons who followed each other in the rota of stand duties on the same stand:

. . . as it was known that the exhibition takes place in June and that the hall would be extremely hot, it is surprising that a closed design was adopted and that no provisions were made for air conditioning.

. . . our stand was so hot and the air so stifling that it was impossible to conduct normal business.

. . . it is suggested that next year it would be advisable to adopt an open-stand design, to provide several low speed fans, a refrigerator or ice cube making machine and to arrange for a facility to serve cold drinks to customers and staff.

The first extract contains a direct accusation of incompetence, the second an exaggerated ('impossible') complaint and only the third makes a positive suggestion allowing the reader to draw his own conclusions or to ask the appropriate questions. The writers of reports realize too late that their essays are read by senior executives not only for their factual content but also as voluntary confessions of personal talents, failings and attitudes. On the other hand the reason for technically and otherwise deficient reports can be often traced to inadequate preparation and training and the lack of management guidance. Finally, the presentation of success analysis in a report is just as important as that of failure analysis. It is imperative to establish the sources and origins of success and failure. The analysis of symptoms, however detailed and penetrating, very seldom provides a prescription for the required cure or for the energetic pursuit of healthy exercises.

Exhibition Effort Audit

An exhibition effort audit is a synthesis of the analyses of all internal and external activities involved in an exhibition effort. Internal data will be obtained from the information system used by the individual company and external data will be obtained from the analysis report which deals with exhibition activities, i.e. with information obtained on the exhibition stand and as a result of away from stand activities.

The purpose of an exhibition effort audit is to provide an objective and, when necessary, critical review of the whole complement of internal and external activities, an evaluation of the resource-mix cost inputs into the exhibition effort and an evaluation of the yield of benefits generated by exhibiting. The task of the audit is to provide not only a measure of the effectiveness of the exhibition effort, i.e. of the degree of attainment of objectives, but also to make considered judgements of the reasons for success or failure. The question is whether these judgements can be made on the basis of adequate, reliable and relevant information.

It is true that it is often difficult for the auditor to determine measures of degree of attainment of objectives and of values of benefits, partly because of the uncertainty factor inherent in any evaluation of the interaction of people and partly because of the time delay between a short-lived exhibition and the carry-over and cumulative efforts of follow-up and other marketing actions resulting from the exhibition effort.

Many attempts have been made to build an exhibition-response model but unfortunately most of them go no further than defining the costs of exhibiting in great detail. They retreat before the problem of evaluating less tangible benefits and use as benchmarks of achievement such facile but unreliable measures as a headcount of visitors, amount of sales literature dispensed, number of inquiries, unit cost of contacts or cost of exhibition versus cost of advertising per estimated audience.

An exhibition event can be affected by an array of independent, interdependent, separate, overlapping, favourable and unfavourable influences and in the past a meaningful evaluation of exhibition efforts was very difficult. Today the computer can remember and interrelate a large number of factors and given a set of reasonable instructions it can trace the consequences of various interactions and of alternative decisions; it can be persuaded to identify alternative or new relationships between people, actions or resources; it can enable an intelligent and experienced user to find solutions to problems hitherto regarded as intractable.

One of the most difficult tasks of the audit is the evaluation of intangible benefits from the exhibition effort. For some of the marketing motives related to image presentation and other public relations aims, the analysis of exhibition activities can at best provide only indications of the actions taken by publicity and public relations. The effectiveness and impact of these actions in most cases only become apparent after a lapse of time, although occasionally almost immediate acknowledgement is forthcoming. The nature and measure of the impact will in time emerge from follow-up activities or can be made the subject of special marketing research surveys. The internal reports of the publicity and public relations functions also provide an indication of the attainment of objectives, assuming that at the exhibition they operated from a specified and agreed upon platform.

Similar considerations apply to such benefits as improved team spirit, learning of marketing skills, incentive to learn languages, improved communication skills and training in communications technology. The frontiers between tangible and intangible benefits are not always clearly defined. Speed of response to service problems, improvements in product quality or introduction of new products can produce both tangible benefits in the form of orders, or at least serious inquiries, and intangible benefits of an enhanced reputation, of an improved position in the industry.

The audit of a particular event will establish whether, and how well, the exhibition served your general marketing aims and your specific motives for exhibiting and whether a lesser effort could have done as well or whether a more substantial effort could have achieved much better results.

The actual audit document can range from a one-page executive summary of conclusions and recommendations to a multi-page, suitably subdivided and indexed report. It all depends on the nature of your company and on the magnitude of the exhibition effort. The main requirements are that the audit should be produced with your individual needs in mind and that its recommendations should be able to be implemented within the framework of your resources, capabilities and talents. If at all practicable, it is advisable for the auditor to visit the audited exhibition; this is particularly important in the case of new ventures, of a strong presence of competitors or of large, elaborate and expensive stands.

The extensive complement of checklists presents ample opportunities for selecting subjects for auditing which are particularly relevant to one event or a series of them. An audit can be simplified, elaborated or perhaps even dispensed with and the analysis of exhibition activities can be relied on as a source of information for decision-making. The following description of headings of an imaginary audit is no more than an attempt to illustrate what could be achieved.

Notional Audit of an Exhibition Effort

The audit of a fictional, exemplary exhibition effort endowed with comprehensive and purposeful human and material resources would produce opinions, assessments, value judgements and recommendations on the following subjects:

The validity of the selection of the exhibition when related to the stated marketing motives

The validity of the marketing objectives when related to the scope and merits of the selected exhibition and its various environments

The effectiveness of purpose and quality of preparation

The cost effectiveness of the stand design and construction

The operational effectiveness of the stand and its facilities

The validity of the selection of exhibits and the effectiveness of attention-getting devices

The quality and proficiency of stand management

The quality and proficiency of the stand team

The degree of attainment of marketing objectives in terms of quality of contacts (visitors, prospects, customers, users)

The quality of intelligence information

The degree of attainment of publicity and public relations objectives

The quality of resources allocated to follow-up activities

The quality of the resources mix allocated to the exhibition effort

The internal dissemination of information and intelligence gathered at the exhibition

The quality of contribution of the existing information system to exhibiting decision-making

The marketing merit of the exhibition for current, near-future and future marketing aims

Considerations of decision-making concerning future single, selective or sustained multiple participation in exhibitions

Follow-Up

The follow-up of an exhibition effort is the activity most intimately connected with the continuous marketing function of contacts with customers and prospects. If these contacts are normally maintained in a regular and organized manner, the co-ordination and inclusion of exhibition follow-up activities will present no problems. On the contrary it can strengthen that function by providing additional interest, by opening new doors and easy access, by creating new opportunities. Publicity initiated in connection with the exhibition, gained as a result of the exhibition effort or timed for post-exhibition impact can also contribute its share to an intensified sales drive.

The follow-up activity directives emerging from the analysis of interest groups, of gathered information and of visitors and contacts should be supplemented by information from records of previous marketing activities so that a final evaluation can be made of priorities and degrees of importance. This supplementary information is particularly important when it concerns service-prone products, built-in products or customers who were supplied with prototypes; in short, all cases where previous contacts of technical or commercial importance are on record. Reference to marketing records will also disclose habitual inquirers who year in and year out visit the exhibitor's stand, collect some literature, leave their visiting card and indicate their interest in one or two exhibits. A follow-up visit, paid in the course of routine duties, will then disclose whether there is perhaps a genuine interest hampered by internal obstacles or whether it is enough to maintain goodwill by a formal response.

In overseas markets the exhibitor's service or delivery reputation can influence the timing and character of follow-up actions and in some locations background infor-mation may indicate that the normal procedure of leaving follow-up actions to the local agent or distributor will not meet the case and that a special visit to the territory is required. The effectiveness and economy with which human and material resources can be deployed in follow-up activities is thus strongly affected by the capability and efficiency of the information retrieval system operated by the exhibitor.

The techniques used for follow-up activities vary, depending on exhibitors' corporate ego, on the extent of their exhibition efforts, on the range of exhibits and of course on the motives for exhibiting. When large numbers of visitors express interest in a range of medium-priced products which are also extensively advertised, a general direct mail action supplemented by individual approaches to potential large customers will be sufficient. In the case of high value capital goods, follow-up action may involve an executive's visit to the prospective customer, an invitation to visit the location of existing applications and an invitation to the exhibitor's works, possibly all at the exhibitor's expense. Between these two extremes there is the personal letter, the telex or telephonic request for an appointment, the so-called personal cold call or any combination of these techniques.

The timing of follow-up actions is as important as the timing of other marketing activities. The requirement for promptness of action is self-evident, but speed alone has no intrinsic value. When speed is applied to a well-prepared action aimed at serving the individual needs of prospects and customers it produces its own marketing justification. When lip service is paid to promptness by an indiscriminate despatch of stereotype acknowledgements of visits to the stand and a vague promise of later attention, speed is of limited value and is very often counter-productive. An effective exhibition effort can be sufficiently provocative to induce competitors to react promptly by mounting their own sales drive, even before a successful exhibitor can analyse results let alone follow them up.

Just as speed and co-ordination of follow-up can earn rich rewards, so tardiness can cause considerable damage. Some exhibitors demonstrate their interest and attention by an attentive immediate follow-up—others, mostly large corporations, reveal by long delays the gap between the modern image implied by their magnificent stand staffed by a multitude of well-dressed attendants and the sad reality of a heavy-handed bureaucra-tic response. If the considerable expenditure of resources which is involved in any exhibition effort is to make economic and marketing sense, then follow-up must be regarded as an essential and productive part of that effort.

Follow-up deserves careful preparation and requires efficient execution and inte-gration into the framework of the exhibitor's general marketing activities. It is the last link in the closed chain of exhibition elements (see Figure 2, page 10) and the results of follow-up activities can strengthen, weaken or modify marketing motives for exhibiting and can influence the decision to exhibit in the future and the selection of exhibitions.

Checklists 28–29

	EXHIBITION PERFORMANCE ANALYSIS	
	Analysis, interpretation and report tasks:	
	messages and information:	
	sales interests	
	service interests	
	information interests	
	visitors and contacts:	
	customers	
	users	
	indirect influences	
	exhibitor's personnel:	
	stand team	
	visitors to exhibition	
	other functions	
	exhibits:	
	effectiveness	
	comparison with competition	
	stand:	
	effectiveness	
	utility	
	comparison with competition	
	exhibition:	
	merits for exhibitor	
	general merits	
	expenditure	
	publicity and public relations	

Checklist 28 EXHIBITION PERFORMANCE ANALYSIS

The analysis of the basic exhibition activity and material elements indicated in this checklist should yield purposeful directions for follow-up actions and an assessment of the exhibition effort in relation to aims and objectives. Such an analysis need not be restricted to the eight main elements listed: the relevant checklists can provide many more details which could be included if justified by the scope of the effort and by the capability both to analyse and to follow-up.

AUDIT OF EXHIBITION EFFORT	
Validity of:	
marketing motives for exhibiting	
marketing objectives for selected exhibition	
marketing merits of selected exhibition	
Quality of:	
stand design	
stand facilities	
intelligence operation	
information system	
Proficiency of:	
stand management	
stand team	
supporting personnel	
Cost effectiveness of:	
stand design and construction	
resources mix	
total exhibition effort	
Operational effectiveness of:	
training	
preparations	
publicity and PR efforts	
follow-up activities	

Checklist 29   EXHIBITION EFFORT AUDIT

The audit of the exhibition effort embraces both internal and external activities involved in the exhibition effort. Like many other checklists, this one provides no more than guidelines for procedures to be adapted to individual (wider or narrower) requirements. In view of the diversity of exhibitions, exhibitors' marketing aims and the nature of companies participating in exhibitions, this seems to be the only practicable approach.

PART FIVE

Visiting Exhibitions, Exhibition Intelligence, Publicity and Public Relations, Projects and Training

Visiting Exhibitions

This section is concerned with visiting exhibitions, an activity pursued by a great variety of persons for a wide range of purposes. In social hierarchy visitors range from heads of state, royalty, ministers and chief executives of international corporations and financial institutions, to humble buyers, users, consumers, apprentices, students and schoolchildren. The decision to visit an exhibition can be prompted by a casual sightseeing interest, by an optimistic hope that something useful will be located or by a well-founded assessment of what the exhibition can offer. One government official will do no more than ceremoniously open an exhibition; another will show a genuine interest and knowledge of its objectives and aims. Some visitors paying the price for the laxity of their preparation will conclude at the end of their visit that they had wasted their time; others will find that they benefited in time, expense, acquired information and contacts even more than their systematic preparation led them to expect.

Visitors of different provenance, occupation and rank also differ in social behaviour, attitudes, temperament and other personality traits. Some of the categories of visitors encountered at exhibitions and some of their traits are listed in Figure 8 (page 108).

Motives for visiting and visiting tasks will be discussed in detail and the implications of visiting time management will be illustrated by a case study.

Visitors with defined exhibition interest can be independent visitors or exhibitors who act as visitors to other stands or to other sections of the exhibition. There is no basic difference in the requirements for preparation, definition of objectives and tasks as far as the three categories of visitors are concerned, except that performance of the tasks will be technically easier for exhibitors acting as visitors. They have a base from which to work and make arrangements, they can reciprocate hospitality and they have access to internal exhibition information and services. On the other hand, unless they are specifically assigned to visiting tasks, their stand duties take preference and their time is not as easily managed as that of independent visitors.

Visiting Motives, Tasks and Interests

The identification and definition of *visiting motives and interests* and the preparation of the visit are the two main activities preceding a visit to an exhibition. Both these activities are time-consuming elements but within reasonable limits they are not subject to date or time span constraints. On the other hand the actual exhibition visit is strictly circumscribed by the event, the date and the time span available. Details of the definition of interests and preparation for the visit can be modified and corrected in the light of changing circumstances. The task activities of the actual visit can be modified and corrected only to a very limited extent because they are usually performed on the basis of a tight schedule. If special provisions can be made for such corrective actions, they should be included in the actual brief and as such become part of the main task, eliminating the need for later adjustments. The statement of objectives and tasks, the auxiliary documentation and other task aids, the time allocation and schedule of contacts, in short all that is contained in the preparation of the visit, exert their influence on the person assigned for the visit and are subject to personal interpretation and response; first before the visitor reaches the exhibition and then during the visit, when the exhibition environment exerts its own cross-influence. The exhibition environment can affect the exhibition task time that can be comfortably sustained. This applies particularly to conditions such as open-air stands at exhibitions which take place early in spring, when unexpected frost and snow or persistent rain can occur, or exhibition halls with overheated and/or dust-laden atmospheres or with unheated and/or draughty halls. Unsatisfactory catering arrangements and lack of cloakrooms and rest facilities also affect the bearable time span.

Good exhibition facilities, such as efficient post office services, banks, interpreters, snack bars, refreshment trolleys and rest facilities, enable a better use of the time available. The opening hours of the exhibition, distances between different locations of exhibition halls or areas, exhibition ground transport and ease of orientation are other important time factors.

Exhibition opening times vary within comparatively narrow limits of six to nine hours, the majority being in the eight to eight and a half hours range. To what extent these opening hours can be exploited by a visitor depends on such a diverse collection of influences that it is not only hard to generalize on the best way to achieve maximum exploitation but also not advisable to do so, lest the application of such generalizations generates more sources of conflicts than precepts for effective action.

The need for the systematic planning of participation in exhibitions is generally recognized, even if not fully implemented, but visiting of exhibitions is unfortunately often left to last minute arrangements. The securing of an air ticket and of hotel reservation is regarded as a sufficiently important organizational achievement needing no further elaboration. The topography of an exhibition (Figure 1, page 6) and the review of exhibition time elements discussed on pages 148–152 and in Checklist 2 demonstrate the need for advanced planning of exhibition visits in the interest both of an economic use of human and material resources and of an effective accomplishment of tasks.

The advent of computer-generated stand location services makes the task of visiting much easier but does not absolve the visitor from making systematic and purposeful preparations. The planning of a visit to an exhibition should be based on a statement of aims and objectives, the character of which will depend on individual needs. The effectiveness with which these objectives are reached can be measured only if they are clearly defined in qualitative and quantitative terms.

Exhibitions catering for your product, your market, your customers or for industries connected with or influencing your market are natural targets for your visit. Your visiting strategy will be governed by the merits of the exhibition *per se*, by its merits for your particular needs or objectives and by the reconciliation of your aims with your resources.

Motives for visiting exhibitions usually fall into three main interest categories: *buying*, *customers* and *intelligence*. Depending on the scope of the exhibition the main interest categories can be supplemented by optional fringe interests. A special motive is the visiting of exhibitions in combination with marketing or other activities in the area.

The time restraints affecting exhibition visiting activities suggest that, in addition to a statement of objectives, the different tasks which must be performed to achieve these objectives need some qualification of relative importance. Intending visitors who by their status or function are intimately involved in the motivation process of visiting will be naturally conscious of these qualifications, but when the visiting task is delegated to other persons a more formal procedure should be adopted. At the same time even in the best organized schedule some scope should be left for serendipity discoveries of unexpected items, which subsequently may prove to be of considerable importance.

Visiting Tasks

The tasks required to deal with defined visiting interests can be active, passive or combined active-passive.

Active tasks are usually concerned with establishing personal contacts, which can be pre-selected if the persons are known or defined by company, product or industry, with an indication of the rank or function to be aimed at. Active tasks can be also concerned with negotiations and with receiving information as well as giving it.

Passive tasks are mainly concerned with gathering non-personal information and data, with making observations, witnessing tests and demonstrations, etc.

In the course of performing passive tasks, non-scheduled personal contacts are occasionally made and then pursued as active tasks to a degree depending on their importance. The *combination of active and passive tasks* is the most flexible technique for achieving visiting results, but this flexibility calls for a considerable amount of preparation, self-discipline and time control.

Each of the three types of tasks is in turn subject to a further qualification. They can be of intrinsic or extrinsic character. The terms intrinsic and extrinsic are used to emphasize the flexibility which is essential in performing exhibition tasks—the terms essential and non-essential would be much too strong and absolute.

Intrinsic tasks are tasks of primary importance to the achievement of the stated objectives. These tasks are the subjects of specific instructions, require a systematic execution and should be specifically reported on.

Extrinsic tasks are of secondary importance. They can be observations of general attitudes, noting of opinions and rumours, making of incidental and social contacts and gathering information on subsidiary or fringe interests.

The classification of tasks, like so much else in the exhibition scene, should not be regarded as requiring rigid divisions which must be adhered to. The underlying purpose of the definitions is to analyse as far as possible the elements which constitute a complex whole and thus to assist in the assessment of their relative values in relation to the main objectives.

Authority of the Visitor

Persons assigned to visit an exhibition should be given a detailed definition of their tasks and of the ramifications of their authority to act on behalf of their organization. This applies particularly to the following activities:

Supplier contacts:
   placing formal inquiries
   requesting tenders and/or quotations
   discussing orders
   promising orders
   placing orders

Customer contacts:
   soliciting orders
   discussing, dealing with and/or settling warranty and service claims
   discussing and/or accepting requests for modifications of products, conditions, prices, etc.
   accepting and/or approving product modifications, price alterations,
   changes in delivery schedules, credit arrangements or cancellations.

Other contacts:
   social activities, entertaining, invitations to visit home base, participating
   in official functions, political events, publicity or public relations.

At first sight it might appear that awareness of company policy and of marketing directives should provide sufficient safeguards for the proper execution of visiting tasks. However, even in the best of marketing-oriented companies the rate of penetration of policy into different strata of the organization can vary considerably. These variations, which affect the appreciation and response of policy precepts, can have several sources. The most obvious one is that of natural variations experienced in human communications channels stemming from the differences in the qualities of senders and receivers. Then there are differences in interpretation due to disparities and conflicts of divisional, departmental and personal interests, both real and imagined.

From the point of view of the activity of visiting exhibitions, a very significant factor is the change of roles. A visitor to an exhibition is often cast in an external role which is different—and mostly extended in scope—from an internal role as defined by the position in the organization. Some enjoy the new role; on others it imposes a severe strain; some use it to pay off old scores; some disclose capabilities far beyond their current internal position. The majority of tasks which a visitor-presumptive performs in the internal role are of a well-defined and mostly intrinsic character and are carried out under supervision and in an environment with built-in controls and opportunities for correction. Extrinsic tasks are usually in the minority and subject to various restraints. In the external role as visitor to an exhibition some of the extrinsic, mostly social, tasks are new or assume greater importance than they had internally. The restraints are different and in the case of foreign exhibitions the added complication of a strange environment is perhaps further confused by an unfamiliar language. If several persons from the same organization are visiting an exhibition, the need for a definition of tasks and authority becomes the more important, the larger the organization.

If there are taboos in some areas or *carte blanche* permissiveness in others these should be clearly stated. There is hardly a more disconcerting experience than for two persons from the same organization to meet unexpectedly on the same stand but pursuing different inquiries, or for one visitor to follow unknowingly in the footsteps of another and to be unaware of what information was sought or imparted by a predecessor.

Visiting Contacts

The establishing of personal contacts is so obviously a natural aim of all exhibition activities that it may become a self-sufficient objective leading to neglect of other assigned tasks. It is therefore of interest to examine the character of such contacts and to attempt to grade them in order of importance. Contacts made by a visitor have the following type, time, technique and frequency characteristics:

Contacts made by special appointment can be assessed in respect of their duration, although this assessment will be subject to considerable correction factors depending on the location of the exhibition. A special appointment made at an exhibition in Scandinavian countries can be timed from start and finish to within 5 minutes; in South American countries the limits would be more in the region of one to two hours. Special interest contacts which yield no immediate results but need no more than one repeat visit in one country once your requirements are stated but in another country three to four return visits are required to achieve results.

A qualitative and quantitative assessment of the planned contacts, corrected by local attitude factors and related to a particular exhibition, will provide an indication of:

time and personnel requirements
feasibility of fulfilling the task
expense and cost values

On the basis of these indicators decisions can be made as to whether visiting an exhibition is the best way of achieving the expected results or whether alternative means are available and, if so, at what expense and cost.

TYPE OF CONTACT	CONTACT TECHNIQUE	CONTACT TIME	CONTACT FREQUENCY
Special interest	By appointment	Short (5–10 min)	First
General interest	Planned	Medium (15–30 min)	Single
Auxiliary interest	Ad hoc	Long (1–2 hours)	Repeat
Fringe interest			Multiple
Routine			
Courtesy			

FIGURE 10. VISITING CONTACTS

Visiting Interests

Buying interests

Buying interests can be considered within fairly flexible limits as mainly resale-oriented, product-oriented or plant-oriented. Materials, components, complete products can be purchased for resale. Basic materials, half products, components and finishing materials bought for incorporation into your own products are product-oriented purchases and so are auxiliaries, accessories and some complete products. The same items when sold as spares or replacements can be purchases for resale. Machine tools, processing equipment, materials handling and storage equipment are typical plant-oriented purchases.

The different buying interests may require special expertise, they may be channelled through central buying functions and they can be subject to an established routine or a matter of *ad hoc* decisions. The co-ordination of the different buying interests, the importance and urgency of individual tasks and the merits of exhibitions relevant to these tasks will determine the choice of events most suitable for visiting. The analysis of timing, cost and resources will narrow that choice to an optimum selection.

If buying interests are the main motive for visiting an exhibition, the stands to be visited and the contacts to be made can be pre-selected before the visit, provided catalogues or lists of exhibitors are available well in advance of the exhibition, which is unfortunately still far from a common practice.

The majority of tasks performed should be active and preparation for the event should include specifications, drawings, delivery schedules, price margins, credit requirements and other elements of the purchasing activity relevant to the particular products, processes or services which are of interest to the visitor-buyer. At the exhibition the visitor can encounter any one of the three basic groups of suppliers: present suppliers, potential suppliers and lapsed suppliers. The suppliers in each group require a different approach.

The exploration of opportunities for agency or distributor arrangements, manufacturing licences, franchises and joint venture arrangements can be considered as resale or product-oriented interests, depending on your organizational structure and the character of the arrangement aimed at.

Present suppliers

All contacts with current suppliers should be active. It would be a strange relationship indeed if there was no reason at all to praise or to blame, to promise more orders, to warn of cut-backs, to talk as well as to listen. At the very least, there is the reason to pay a courtesy visit to the stand of a supplier so as not to give offence by ignoring him.

Benefits can be derived from contacts with otherwise elusive executives and technical personnel. Information can be gathered about future developments, about competitors' activities and about large orders placed by competitors which may affect deliveries of your own not so impressive orders. If your supplier is a smaller company than yours, you will show an appreciation of their good service, give reassurance about the future, impart reasoned and well substantiated reprimands about shortcomings and generate a modicum of general goodwill.

If your suppliers are much larger companies than yours they should, by virtue of their marketing expertise, appreciate your reliance on their supplies and your importance as a customer. If that is not the case, you may have to probe a bit deeper to find more weighty influences than the ones encountered. On the other hand, your own advanced methods or far-sighted planning will encourage them to give you some preference in the supply of new or improved products. An important supplier may be able to impart interesting information about the intended use of the products by your competitors, information not necessarily secret but normally not broadcast.

Suppliers' stands and largesse in hospitality will encourage many visitors, providing them with opportunities for contacts with interesting people and probably with competitors, with whom an exchange of views would otherwise be unlikely. Many a market conflict and impending price war can thus be avoided.

Potential or new suppliers

Contacts with potential suppliers can range from a passive collection of information through placing of well defined inquiries to placing of definite trial or quantity orders. As buyer or potential buyer the visitor is in the most favoured position for receiving full attention. Caution is sometimes required so as not to allow a tentative inquiry to be taken or deliberately interpreted as a serious intent to change sources and then being flaunted as such to the discomfort of the present supplier. An exhibition is an easy field for such manoeuvres, which have been known to upset relations with well-established suppliers, to harden their attitude when granting discounts and to cause other upsetting reactions. The fact that from a marketing point of view this is the wrong way to react makes little difference to the actual outcome. Large suppliers with a near monopoly position or with a very strong hold on the market are particularly susceptible to take unreasonable umbrage at the daring of a smaller customer to seek new sources of supply.

Lapsed suppliers

You may have severed relations with an otherwise good supplier because of some failure, e.g. deliveries, price or a technical detail. There may have been personal reasons for the severance: a clash of personalities, delicate questions of fringe benefits or a change in buying policy. You have reason to believe that the sources of the conflict have been corrected. In all such and similar cases, it may be difficult to re-establish normal contacts without some real or imagined loss of prestige or pride. The hospitable background of an exhibition offers an excellent opportunity for both parties to come together again, neither losing face in the process.

Customer interests

Customer interests are mainly concerned with contacts with direct and indirect customers and users. If such contacts are the main motive for visiting an exhibition, then its merits in that respect must be fairly substantial to justify such a visit. If that is so then, regulations permitting, serious thought should be given to participation in the exhibition, because all marketing interest tasks can be performed more effectively by an exhibitor than by a visitor.

If your customers know that you are usually in the habit of visiting a particular exhibition in which they participate, or if they have invited you, they will expect your routine or special visit to their stand. A number of situations can develop.

Depending on your relations with them, their importance to you and their standing in their industry, your customers may have some ideas of the rank of the visitor whom they expect. They may think that the person delegated is lower in your hierarchy than their expectation. If the exhibition is an important one for the industry concerned, your customers are perhaps surprised that you are not exhibiting while your competitors are. Several of your customers are exhibiting and they may be sensitive about the order in which they are visited, the length of the visit and the importance of the visitor. All these attitudes may seem trivial, but they remain trivial only as long as you, as a visitor representing your company, are aware of them and are prepared to deal with them in a serious or lighthearted way, whichever fits the situation better. You must be ready with a plausible explanation of why your company is not exhibiting. If you are not as 'important' as they expect and if it shows in their reception you will take it in good grace and prove, by your preparation for the visit, how seriously their problems are taken. Preparation and tact will establish your position and pave the ground for your follow-up visit.

If you are a senior executive, make a special effort to visit customer-companies smaller than yours, particularly if you discern in them signs of future growth. Visits to your customers' stands can provide opportunities to hear comments by users and in critical situations, e.g. of service or spares complaints, it may be advisable to offer your customers assistance in dealing with users. Such an offer implies that you were aware, when planning your visit, that such contingencies might arise, and that you made an appropriate time allowance in your visiting schedule.

An indirect customer interest task is the support given by visitors from an organization to the stand personnel of its subsidiary, branch, agent or distributor participating in an exhibition. In this case, however, the visitor assumes the role of an exhibitor.

Intelligence interests

Intelligence is usually an integral part of buying, customer and marketing interests, even if not declared as such. The visiting of information centres, trade associations, official or semi-official representations or bureaux can be part of a specific interest task or an intelligence task.

Attendance at conferences, symposia and lectures is mostly a passive information-gathering task subsidiary to a main interest task. Active participation by a visitor who is not an exhibitor is usually an information-imparting exercise with a content of marketing elements, while a resulting discussion can be of intelligence value. In some situations, one or more of the visiting interests are declared as requiring only observation and gathering of information and they then become intelligence tasks. On rare occasions personal contacts are expressly excluded from these tasks. This is not a very effective way of performing intelligence tasks and the results are usually as poor in quality as the concept. There is also the danger, in some countries, of contravening laws of industrial espionage. Genuine intelligence interests are usually generated by market and marketing research activities and the tasks are sometimes entrusted to visitors to exhibitions engaged in other tasks. In such cases there is a great risk that unless the intelligence task briefing is very explicit and an adequate time allocation is made for it, a systematic intelligence task can degenerate into a superficial *reconnaissance exercise*. A special intelligence task is the evaluation of the merits of an exhibition. This can be a general assessment made for record purposes, or an investigation for a specific objective of marketing or future exhibiting.

Visitors undertaking intelligence tasks are on their own and must rely on their own systematic preparation. They can obtain such assistance as the exhibition organizers provide and can perhaps find a friendly exhibitor-customer or supplier willing to extend hospitality. However, as debts of gratitude are the most difficult ones to repay caution is indicated.

Fringe interests

In addition to the specialized tasks defined by the main visiting objectives, an exhibition is a good occasion, if time permits, to review product design, display techniques and selling methods in your own field, as well as in others related to, or even remote from, your main interest.

Your main tasks may be of a product-oriented interest but depending on your knowledge and experience you may notice resale opportunities. The review of products for resale may be your main task, but new developments in storage and handling techniques relevant to your business, if exhibited, may prove of additional interest.

For one category of visitor, works canteen equipment can be a plant-oriented interest; for another this would be only a fringe interest. The review of fringe interests provides not only useful information for your own sphere of activities, but can also serve as a refreshing interlude to your main task and can help in gaining a new perspective on your own activities. You may find that others do things in a way that could be applied with benefit to your own activities; you may also note with satisfaction that your own way is the best, or at least as good as that of others.

Combined visits interests

When the marketing functions of a company contain a substantial element of visits to international markets, the visiting programme will in most cases include some or all of the following elements:

> Visits to subsidiaries, branches, agents and distributors
> Visits to customers
> Visits to users
> Visits to exhibitions, congresses and symposia
> Special sales campaigns

The frequency of the visits will vary depending on the market structure, the product, the replacement cycle, service requirements and the resources available. In the interest of economy the visiting of exhibitions should be integrated, whenever possible, with other external visits. The economics which can be achieved by including exhibitions in the visiting programme will depend on the number of exhibitions relevant to the marketing strategy and whether active participation, visiting only or a combination of participation and visiting is required. The further away from base such visits take place the greater is the influence of integration on the cost effectiveness of the human and material resources employed for the purpose.

Time Elements of an Exhibition Visit—Case Study 8

This case study relates the story of one visit to an exhibition of mechanical handling equipment abroad. The story started in an uneventful way and was related by a consultant who was visiting a company in connection with a diversification problem and incidentally became involved in planning a visit to an exhibition. The company manufactures special-purpose attachments and Mr Smith, an engineering executive of the company, was interested in finding an alternative source of supply for a built-in component unit. In the past the company had participated in an important biennial exhibition abroad but in the wake of an economy drive the participation in exhibitions abroad was severely curtailed 'because exhibiting abroad is more expensive'. The company exported 36 per cent of its output and as several overseas customers were overdue for a visit, the opportunity of seeing them at the forthcoming exhibition and locating a supplier of the required unit was an obvious solution. Mr Smith decided to send his assistant for a one-and-a-half-day visit to the exhibition and travel and hotel arrangements were put in hand. This decision was taken in January; the exhibition was scheduled for March of the same year.

The subject was casually mentioned to a consultant at lunch for no other reason than that he was known 'to be interested in exhibitions'. His reaction was that the visiting time seemed rather short and he suggested that the occasion should be used for an exercise in the systematic planning of an exhibition visit. The suggestion was accepted with slightly indulgent smiles. The first step in the exercise was to define the motives for visiting. These were stated as:

To contact several customers
To locate one or two potential suppliers of the built-in unit

It was pointed out that as a matter of principle this definition was too vague. The definition of motives and objectives of the visit was revised and emerged as:

Courtesy visits to customers
 at least four customers are known to exhibit and another three are likely to exhibit

Visits to potential suppliers
 eight to ten potential suppliers of the required unit are likely to exhibit

 offers to be sought for units complying with company's specifications, delivery dates and price range

 suppliers to provide evidence of service and spares facilities in seven countries (three very important)

Visits to users
 sixteen to eighteen users of equipment incorporating the unit are likely to exhibit; their opinions should be obtained on the units made by potential new suppliers.

The numbers of likely customers, suppliers and users were deduced from an examination of the available catalogue of the exhibition of two years ago.

In the time budget of the visit the following considerations were taken into account: the time allocation was based on informative short contacts of 20 minutes' duration, on probing contacts of 30 minutes' duration and on negotiating contacts of 60 minutes' duration. The allocation of the three types of contacts to customers, suppliers and users was tabulated as shown in Figure 11.

Interviews with:	Customers							Suppliers										Users															
First contacts	1	2	3	4	5	6	7	1	2	3	4	5	6	7	8	9	10	1	2	3	4	5	6	7	8	9	10	11	12	13	14	15	16
Short (20 min)	●	●		●		●	●			●	●	●	●	●	●	●	●	●	●	●	●	●	●	●		●		●	●		●	●	●
Medium (30 min)			●		●			●	●																●		●			●			
Long (60 min)																																	
Repeat contacts																																	
Short (20 min)			●	●	●								●												●		●				●		●
Medium (30 min)									●	●																							
Long (60 min)																																	

	Interviews
Customers	8x20 min = 160 min
	2x30 min = 60 min
Suppliers	9x20 min = 180 min
	4x30 min = 120 min
Users	17x20 min = 340 min
	3x30 min = 90 min
	43 interviews = 950 min = 15 hours 50 minutes

FIGURE 11. TIME BUDGET FOR A FOUR-DAY VISIT TO AN EXHIBITION

A time budget for three types of contacts for interviews with seven customers, 10 suppliers and 16 users. A total of 43 interviews consisting of 33 first contacts and 10 repeat contacts.

It was anticipated that three customers, three suppliers and four users would require repeat contacts. According to this schedule 15 hours and 50 minutes of net exhibition time would be required to accomplish the task.

The time elements of the exhibition were:

Daily opening hours: 9.30 to 18.00 hours
Travel time from hotel to exhibition: 40 minutes
Travel time from exhibition to town: 50 minutes

The catering facilities at the exhibition were good, but a sit-down meal would take at least one hour.

On the basis of these data it was found that the available daily exhibition task time would amount to six hours (Figure 12). Taking all these factors into account, the theoretical minimum time for the visit would be three exhibition visiting days. This would not allow for any excess waiting time or for wasted interviews, nor for any contingencies such as delays in the open air area due to bad weather and the like. No time would be available for visits to more than five customers, for visiting non-scheduled stands or for any fringe interest visits. It was clear that in reality four days at the exhibition would be required to achieve the set objectives.

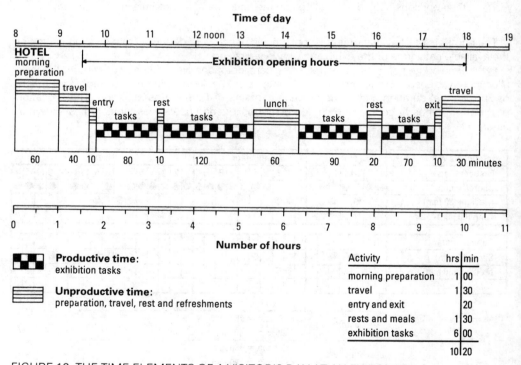

FIGURE 12. THE TIME ELEMENTS OF A VISITOR'S DAY AT AN EXHIBITION

The one-and-a-half day visit originally proposed would allow contacts with not more than two customers, four potential suppliers and six users. The operational advantages of a four-day visit became apparent. Such a visit would provide flexibility in making contacts, a minimum of irritation resulting from unavoidable time wasting, and the probability of completing the task early on the fourth day of the visit, enabling return by an earlier flight. This last possibility opened

150

the question of any contacts on the route of the return flight. In fact, a visit to a prospective customer located on the path of the return flight was overdue and tentative arrangements for that visit were made.

Preparations for the visit included:

Specifications and installation details of the built-in units and a questionnaire concerning service and spares facilities

Brief dossiers on ten customers

A simple, duplicated form in A5 format listing critical points of built-in units and providing space for noting users' opinions in code

Travel and hotel arrangements were made by the company's travel agent. Three of the company's overseas agents were notified of the visit by telex. Two confirmed their own visit and in turn gave details of how they could be contacted.

The end result of the visit was summarized as follows:

Visits to customers' stands
in fact seven customers exhibited, all were visited and five repeat visits were paid.

Contacts with visiting customers
four customers from three countries were contacted through the foreign visitors' reception bureau and discussions with them were held at the exhibition and at their hotels.

Suppliers of built-in unit
the stands of twelve potential suppliers were briefly surveyed and their literature collected during the first day of visit; short discussions were held with four and subsequent negotiations with two of the last four suppliers.

Users of built-in units
twenty users exhibited, fifteen of whom were users of units made by the four most promising suppliers; these fifteen were each visited once and three twice.

Company's overseas agents
two agents were contacted and the standing and service facilities in their territories of the two short-listed potential suppliers were discussed.

Trial orders for three units each were placed with two suppliers for compatibility tests and technical evaluation.

The exhibition task was completed at noon of the fourth day and several fringe interest stands were visited. Contacts made by telephone and telex with potential customers located in the path of the return flight resulted in meetings with two potential customers and a trial order from one of them, who incidentally specified the make of one of the built-in units which were the subject of final negotiations. A total of eleven customer contacts and two potential customer contacts were made, fifteen users were interviewed and two overseas agents were contacted.

In a final review and discussion of the exhibition visit a question was asked about the significance, if any, of a cost per contact figure, as used in assessing a salesperson's efforts. The answer was that in a mixed task situation like the one encountered even the total cost effectiveness can be assessed only after a considerable time has elapsed and when the results can be evaluated. A cost per contact assessment would have to provide some weighting of contacts as obviously two 30-minute contacts with customers cannot be directly compared with three 20-minute contacts with users. The contacts with customers could result in orders, the contacts with users could be abortive. On the other hand, the contacts with customers could produce no more than some goodwill but the contacts with users could prevent a serious mistake in the selection of suppliers.

This rudimentary example of time budgeting for exhibition visiting not only shows the benefits of such an approach but also highlights a phenomenon seen again and again in large organizations and small. Engineers breathing mathematics, eating calculus for breakfast and modifying several PERT diagrams out of recognition between lunch and tea, treat a visit to an exhibition with less mathematical forethought than they would a family picnic.

Exhibition Intelligence

Exhibitions are the most fertile grounds for industrial intelligence, i.e. for the acquisition of information about products, markets and competitors, about marketing and exhibiting techniques, about customers' and users' praises and about complaints and unfilled needs.

An exhibition intelligence task is the application of *organized curiosity*. As exhibiting or visiting are marketing functions, exhibition intelligence becomes a marketing intelligence function, usually initiated and organized by marketing research who also sort, evaluate and analyse the obtained material. Marketing intelligence tasks are best performed by specialists from marketing research or perhaps even by a special marketing intelligence function, but there are complex engineering products, sophisticated conceptual systems and complicated chemical formulations which require an intimate knowledge of their properties to be able to discern the differences, changes and faults which could be the subjects of an intelligence task.

Exhibition intelligence can be carried out by internal resources, assigned to an outside organization or carried out by a combination of internal resources and outside assistance. Internal personnel and time resources have their limitations even in organizations with large marketing research departments, let alone in medium and small firms. The accomplishment of intelligence tasks becomes thus a matter of delegation to personnel engaged on stand duties. In the context of a busy exhibition this can impose severe strains and affect both stand duties and intelligence tasks adversely.

The requirements for intelligence tasks must therefore be included in the personnel and time budget of exhibition activities. Depending on the scope of the exhibiting effort and the exhibition environment this may mean additional stand personnel or at least additional junior personnel to provide the necessary assistance and relief, or alternatively personnel primarily engaged in intelligence and only assisting in stand duties. The danger is often stressed of using sales personnel for intelligence tasks because of lack of objectivity and potential conflict of interests. That sales personnel are most frequently singled out for these doubts is understandable on several counts. Firstly, sales operations in the field are a natural source of intelligence and sales personnel are engaged in these operations. Secondly, intelligence tasks are often misinterpreted as marketing research tasks in which case the doubts would be justified. Thirdly, in the industrial products sector service engineers, maintenance engineers, operators and others could be just as well charged with intelligence tasks and the same objections of bias and conflict of interests would be raised. However, the problem of objectivity cannot be confined to personnel outside the marketing research function as even highly skilled and experienced researchers will show different degrees of objectivity.

Let us take the case of two research assistants assigned to the same intelligence task. Research assistant A is a member of an independent market research organization;

research assistant B is a member of the company's market research department. Apart from personality traits, educational background and training, in the real world the objectivity of A (the outsider) may be affected by loyalty to his organization or by personal ambition. The objectivity of B, in her internal role, may be affected by interdepartmental intrigue or by the wish to outdo the outsider A, to prove herself and to demonstrate that it wasn't really necessary to engage outside help. Of course it need not happen and both may be willing and anxious to co-operate to the greater glory of the task in hand.

When there is a mixture of research and other personnel of the same organization similar conflicts can arise. Market research departments are sometimes resentful of a possible infringement of their preserve if some of their duties are delegated to others. Sales departments are apprehensive about the encroachment by market research on their territories and on their contacts with customers. The segmentation, empire building, bureaucracy and departmental rivalry which can be found in any organization large or small must be taken as normal and only then can counter-measures be taken.

The performing of intelligence tasks by specially assigned personnel not involved in stand duties has very great advantages. The stand provides a good base of operations. An exhibitor has access to information and data not available to visitors and assistance in technical matters by specialists, interpreters or clerical staff; even the opportunity for rest and refreshment may greatly ease the intelligence task.

The concentration of *intelligence targets* at an exhibition and the opportunity to accomplish the task in a set time usually fully justify special assignments on time-person-expense grounds alone. Cost effectiveness, a great saving in time and valuable experience are mostly additional benefits.

When delegating intelligence tasks to personnel visiting exhibitions or to stand personnel, it is important to assess their capacity and capability to perform the task. The personality, experience and knowledge of the person may not be compatible with one type of task, but ideally suited to another. The task may appear too trivial to one, or too strenuous to another.

What must be avoided at all costs is to treat intelligence either as something which is 'to be done when the time is available' or as a duty which 'is at least as important if not more than anything else you do'. If the task is only of marginal importance, then why waste the time of a person otherwise engaged? If it is all that important, it deserves the efforts of a person specially assigned to it.

Another pitfall to be avoided is to invest an intelligence task with a false glamour by describing it as 'really a bit of market research' and adding a benevolent pat on the back for good measure. Many an environment and location of an interesting exhibition intelligence task is much more glamorous than that of a dull, slogging piece of desk research legitimately described as market research. If conditions require a modicum of public relations before you can achieve your objectives, why not stress the 'intelligence' which is required to perform the task, the opportunity of extra knowledge, nay expertise, to be acquired, the satisfaction of tangible immediate and reportable results?

Each situation will require individual treatment but the basic precepts are the same:

Definition of intelligence task aims
Preparation, instruction and provision of task aids
Designation of minimum and optimum task goals
Selection of personnel compatible with defined tasks

The quest for absolute objectivity, although desirable in itself, should be somewhat tempered in the definition of aims. Although the basic requirement for acquiring factual data and noting factual information must be clearly stated, room should be left for the reporting of some non-objective information providing it is marked as such and for the expression of opinions if declared as such. An exaggerated demand for objectivity may generate an inclination to present all collected data as objective or to select only those that will pass the test.

If people can be persuaded not to be afraid to say 'in my opinion' in a report and then express that opinion concisely, a great deal can be gained. Apart from other considerations, subjective pronouncements of impressions and observations will reveal personal prejudices, preferences, aptitudes, frustrations and powers of judgement which eventually can be checked against facts. The resulting assessment of personality traits may be very important for future assignments. The programmed tasks of an executive visiting an exhibition will have an inherent or self-assigned intelligence content. If his role is that of a visitor only, the intelligence element will be related mainly to specific interests and, depending on personality and other factors, perhaps private interests will be extended into other areas. If the executive visits an exhibition in which the company participates, intelligence should also include the stand, performance of the stand personnel, merits of participating and merits of the exhibition.

At an executive level of responsibility a systematic preparation for a visit to an exhibition is usually formally accepted, although not always implemented in practice. Intelligence tasks are usually left to *ad hoc* decisions. This is due partly to the fact that at executive level intelligence tasks are rarely defined as such and partly due to a widely accepted view that 'one will not know what to look for until one gets there'. It is also sometimes thought, consciously or subconsciously, that to prepare specially for an intelligence task may reflect unfavourably on one's own executive status. Only participation in a live performance of an exhibition intelligence mission will convince an executive of the benefits of discharging intelligence tasks intelligently; in other words, with proper preparation. This preparation may be no more than a few brief notes about the subjects to be observed and the people to be met, or it may run to a full dossier of products, designs, competitors, customers and the points about which intelligence is required.

If no special intelligence tasks are planned, a deliberate, even if modest, intelligence effort added to normal duties will amply repay the effort. It will provide background and colour to exhibition activities on which reports may later be received. It will enable the executive to add personal impressions not only to the subject of the reports, but also to the image of the people who wrote them.

From a general management point of view it is important not to isolate the intelligence function as one performed only when required. *Intelligence vigilance* should be preached and instructed as an integral element of any marketing activity, to be practised by everybody with varying degrees of emphasis regulated by the importance of current main tasks.

Intelligence interviews

Interviews with customers, suppliers, users or any other respondents are easier to arrange at an exhibition than in the normal course of business. There is at an exhibition an atmosphere of an easy exchange of views. The danger of alienating respondents by probing questions about competitors or customers is much less likely at an exhibition where the comparing of competitors is a natural function. Operationally the exhibition offers unique advantages. You know that your respondents will be at the exhibition for a set time, you can revisit them to check on information received and you can repay the courtesy shown before by imparting interesting information. If you are fortunate enough to perform your intelligence task with the backing of an exhibition stand, you can perhaps request the support of a specialist in an interview, where his qualifications are more compatible with those of the respondent you intend to interview than yours. Stand personnel could also give you assistance with linguistic or social skills. The importance of intelligence tasks deserves a remark about technicalities. Intelligence is a systematic discipline and requires the recording of information. If we start with the basic element of notes made on paper the plea is made not to use large cumbersome clipboards more suitable for stock-taking in a general merchandise stock room than for a task which, while probing, must be tactful, and while intruding, should remain unobtrusive. At the other extreme the making of notes on odd bits of paper when interviewing a senior executive can give the impression that you are not really very concerned about what he or she has to say. A whole range of sophisticated aids is available, from loose-leaf books, through pocket tape recorders to miniature cameras. The aids should be not only suitable for the task but should also comply with the legal restrictions and regulations of individual exhibitions. The issues of ethics, espionage and design stealing are in the realm of individual or corporate conscience.

Language problems

Intelligence tasks at exhibitions held in foreign countries with difficult or unfamiliar languages can present a problem. The essence of intelligence tasks is not only a matter of noting facts but also of registering shades of meaning and interpreting understatements and exaggerations. When such difficulties are foreseen in time it may be possible to employ local, preferably bilingual, personnel to perform the task at the exhibition.

The bilingual requirement is to ensure good understanding between the instructing researcher and the person charged with the task. When properly instructed, university or technical college students engaged in studies with some affinity to your problem or free-lance journalists dealing with your area of interest can perform intelligence tasks very successfully.

General survey intelligence

At exhibitions of a high marketing merit, observation of the numerical incidence of an exhibited product or product group can give an indication of market saturation trends, product ranges and shortages. Once again it must be stressed that the task of intelligence is to observe facts and note them carefully. Marketing research has the task of co-ordinating, analysing and drawing conclusions.

A report saying 'we have observed a greater number of air-cooled engines installed in earthmoving equipment than last year' means very little in terms of intelligence, except to confirm that such engines are used as before, which everybody knows anyhow. A report giving the names of 30 models of equipment and the makes of the 27 engines installed in these 30 models, together with technical data of both earthmoving equipment and engines or including the relevant technical literature, is all that is required.

It is possible to receive the first type of report without asking for it or because the questions asked were not specific. It is also possible to receive the second type of fully informative report without requesting it. It all depends how intelligent the intelligencer was. It is comparatively easy to ensure that only the second type of report will be received. A purpose-made questionnaire, a sufficient supply of pre-printed forms in a handy format or an indication of minimum and optimum information limits results in great satisfaction all round.

Product intelligence

The additions, refinements and changes in appearance, colour, shape and functions of products are more easily detected at an exhibition, where immediate comparison with other products is possible and where observations already made can be repeated, omissions corrected and impressions noted and, if necessary, confirmed.

User intelligence

When your exhibits are industrial products which are auxiliaries, accessories or other built-in components, user intelligence is an important task.

Quality or performance is often judged by the user subjectively and as a result of factors other than the actual properties of the product. An excellent accessory can be judged unsatisfactory because it is difficult to fit or remove. The dissatisfaction generated by the awkward handling properties and difficulty of opening of a container is affecting the judgement of the contents. A combination of one very good and one indifferent component is not so serious although it lowers the opinion about the good one. A combination of a good and a bad component invariably gives both a bad name. Systematic intelligence gathering of user attitudes can make a very valuable contribution to product improvement.

Technological intelligence

The technological environment of an exhibition was discussed on page 51. Technological intelligence tasks can be directed towards selected targets within your sphere of interests, for example:

Improvements and innovations
Manufacturing techniques
Needs for new products or processes

Technological intelligence tasks are best performed by specialists. In the case of the above three targets they would come from research and development or design, production and market research functions. Although the requirement for systematic preparation is valid for technological intelligence tasks as much as for any other, there is a different attitude in the execution of the task. The observation and probing is more free-ranging and at the same time more discerning. Imagination plays an important role in relating the intelligence gathered to your own skills and resources. When technological intelligence is subjected to the test of market research and long-range forecast analysis it can also trigger off promising speculative developments.

A typical and rewarding technological intelligence task is the identification of gaps between the technology available and the technology actually used in your sphere of activity. However, before initiating a 'gap identification task' you should carefully assess the merit of the exhibition in that particular respect. A general industrial exhibition in which several branches of your technology participate is a suitable medium; a highly specialized product-oriented exhibition will yield better direct product intelligence material but only by inference technology intelligence material.

An unconventional, not quite systematic, approach to intelligence can also yield results if used by persons of suitable talents. To see something done better outside your field can on occasions show an imaginative designer how to short-circuit a more elaborate procedure. The shortcomings of competitive products can provide an early warning of potential pitfalls.

State of art intelligence

The state of art intelligence is closely related to technological intelligence except that it mostly concentrates its attention on the achievements of a defined object rather than on its environment. Where technological intelligence is inclined to be synthetic, state of art intelligence tends to be analytic. It can be applied to single products, to a system of equipment, to a process or to a function. A state of art intelligence task must be carefully organized and there is no room for deviation from the brief. All collected observations and data should be objective facts; any information thought valuable but not objective should be declared as such. It cannot be stressed too often that a requirement for objectivity does not exclude all other information but only insists in prefacing it with the appropriate adjective.

Sales and technical literature

The acquisition of sales and technical literature on competitive products and products related to your direct marketing interests is a basic intelligence task which should be performed as a matter of routine not requiring special instructions. When stating that requirement it is assumed that your personnel are sufficiently steeped in the marketing concept to know that the ramifications of your market are not confined to what you make, but defined by the need you serve.

All sorts of unnecessary ruses are often used to obtain your competitors' literature when all that is required in most cases is to offer him yours in exchange. If you are the one reluctant to part with publicity material in case it falls into the wrong hands you are mistaken on two counts. Firstly, you are denying your publications their name and their case for existence; secondly, any determined competitor need only use the help of a friendly customer to obtain all the material required. To a discriminate inquirer trade associations and specialized information bureaux can also provide supplementary and sometimes very interesting material.

Although the acquisition of sales and technical literature complements the intelligence task it is only one element in its exploitation for marketing purposes. The material will be received, sorted, indexed and when called for analysed by the market or marketing research function and, most importantly, arrangements will be put in hand to keep the material up-to-date.

National market intelligence

National exhibitions not open to foreign goods provide a good field for market and marketing intelligence related to a nationally defined market. A subsequent comparison with intelligence gathered at an international exhibition held in the same country supplements the first intelligence report most effectively. In export-viable countries a national exhibition also provides valuable insights into current technical and design trends, and thus into a potential third market competition.

Exhibition merit intelligence

Exhibition merit intelligence is a valuable aid to a merit rating study. In exhibition conscious organizations such intelligence is obtained as a result of definite instructions, on the basis of detailed questionnaires or in the form of memoranda or reports. It comes from many sources: from stand personnel attending exhibitions, from members of the staff and executives visiting exhibitions and also from outside sources such as press notices, trade journals, official reports, etc. On the whole, information gathered on a non-systematic basis suffers from the deficiency that it is either too general or too particular in one detail or altogether too superficial to be of real value. Often it is collected by individuals on an *ad hoc* basis and regarded by them as their own property. It is then a question of how much of it is reported back and how useful such personality-filtered information is to the organization receiving it. It is not unknown for such intelligence to be regarded as a personal asset, a means of building a reputation for being an expert in a market or territory.

Press reports vary considerably in value. Statistical data which should be clear and outstanding are often lost in the folds of a chatty text or given in a form more puzzling than revealing. Photographs of brightly lit attractive stands do credit to the stand designer but say nothing about the lack of ventilation, the smell and the accumulated rubbish which in fact made attendance an ordeal.

In the absence of independent comprehensive merit rating data about an exhibition, an examination of available exhibition intelligence may have to serve the purpose of selection. In the present state of the stock of objective information about exhibitions it seems imperative to use each opportunity to collect exhibition intelligence from as many sources as possible. Your own staff, visiting exhibitions or in their role as stand personnel, when suitably briefed should be best qualified to gather such information. It is, however, important that the task of collecting exhibition intelligence should not infringe on the main task, whatever that may be.

Comments by customers, competitors and independent observers are valuable, provided they are categorized and weighted according to their origin and possible bias. It is sometimes necessary to extract the few intelligence items significant for your particular need from a mass of details of varying quality and veracity, but on the other hand one or two cogent comments on a particular aspect of an exhibition can influence your decision to participate.

Publicity and Public Relations

Publicity, advertising and public relations are subjects so extensively written about, researched, analysed and documented that it seems superfluous to add still more to the vast amount of information available, but the context of exhibitions, particularly of exhibitions serving industrial markets, offers a valid justification.

The ubiquity and penetration of advertising has made it so widely known that almost everybody feels himself or herself to be, if not an expert, at least very well-informed. It has also been pointed out that the all-pervading nature of advertising contains an inherent self-promoting element so that in some cases the awareness and recall of an artful advertisement or its technique become more significant than the awareness and recall of the advertised product. Some exhibition stands bear witness to this promoting of the promotion syndrome and devices intended to attract attention to an exhibit manage to do so very effectively, except that they mostly attract the wrong audience and even that audience later remembers the devices very well and the exhibits not at all.

Public relations also have an excellent field in which to operate. The stand and its exhibits, visits of exalted persons, an international audience, official receptions, lectures, products of scientific significance or new to the market, executives, ministers, press conferences for both the technical and daily press, film shows, tests, demonstrations, medals, awards, news bulletins, radio and television are all their domain.

Both publicity and public relations activities are greatly assisted by the availability of modern technical facilities, such as audio-visual equipment, laser lighting and holographic presentations, multi-colour duplicators, computer-generated graphics, electronic desktop publishing. All provide means of reacting to situations created by the exhibition, by special events, by successes or by unexpected demands.

Some comments on publicity and public relations have already been made in the discussion of stand activities.

Publicity at Exhibitions

Whatever marketing virtues are attributed or denied to exhibitions, there is no doubt that they provide to publicity and public relations exceptional opportunities and means of expression. The elements of publicity can be displayed to a large, appropriate and mostly appreciative audience and distributed to well-chosen recipients. The very subjects which publicity usually publicizes on paper can be seen in body, touched, tested and heard. Audiences can be counted in thousands and by visiting exhibitions they express their wish to be informed and to receive the message which it is publicity's task to give them.

From the exhibitor's point of view the importance of publicity is that in addition to its main exhibition activity it has crucial duties to perform in the pre-exhibition and post-exhibition period. In the pre-exhibition period it is actively involved or closely connected with stand design and the preparation of all routine and special items of publicity required before, during and after the exhibition. The task of selecting and inviting prospective visitors, publicizing of participation all items in Checklists 39, 40 and 41 (pages 179–181) indicate the importance of the function and of the marketing impact it can make. In the post-exhibition period publicity participates in the follow-up actions and is concerned with publicizing special successes, orders, awards and other achievements of the exhibition effort.

From a marketing point of view we have a unique situation. The exhibition as a universal marketing tool offers opportunities for performing an impressive range of marketing tasks and is at the same time an exceptionally good medium for two of these tasks—publicity and public relations. Their mission in turn is to support all other marketing functions. It sounds almost like a classic example of synergism, defined as a condition under which two agents working co-operatively have an effect greater than the sum of the two taken independently.

The required co-operation is often missing. A few examples from a very large selection of observed shortcomings will illustrate the point.

● At an international exhibition of great marketing merit the exhibitor, a leading manufacturer of typewriters, offered a leaflet describing his range of alphabets for a great number of languages. The translation of the leaflet in German, the language of the exhibition host country, was full of grammatical and orthographic errors. One would be justified in assuming that the exhibitor's publicity department had in their files, as a matter of routine intelligence, a collection of competitors' catalogues from which the correct translation of technical terms, let alone grammar and spelling, could be easily copied.

● At another exhibition the public relations executive of a very large firm appeared on the opening day and left in the afternoon, leaving behind a number of press releases and photographs with instructions to the stand personnel to deliver them to the exhibition press office piece by piece at daily intervals. The fact that a few days later a trade mission of particular importance to that exhibitor was due to arrive carried less weight than the return home for Sunday. His attendance on Saturday was (expressed by him in appropriate publicity relations language) a sufficient sacrifice on the altar of corporate loyalty.

● A trade journal reported the following about the group effort of a Trade Association and a group stand of 18 firms participating repeatedly in an important international exhibition:

> . . . and provided a multi-lingual brochure/folder revealing vastly more information than visitors have ever enjoyed before, although through no fault of theirs only six of the 18 firms participating in the joint display had contributed to its compilation. And fewer still had thought it worth while to see that the Fair Press Office, a sumptuous suite thronged with journalists from all over the world, was suitably supplied with the promotional material it should have had.

This last example of ineffectual use of available publicity media is the more surprising as the firms concerned were in fact in the data processing, reproduction and business equipment industry; an industry, one would think, intimately concerned with effective communication.

Publicity, when dealing with industrial products, should be equipped to cope with the problems created by the producer-seller-buyer *transposition characteristics*, with problems of incorporation into other products, of the time-distance factor and of the potential loss of identity.

Industrial products can range from simple nuts and bolts and complex miniature precision components to giant earth-moving equipment, rolling mills and power station equipment. Because of this diversity of range, size and value it would be wrong to generalize about how best to equip publicity to enable it to deal with these problems effectively. However, when marketing strategies for industrial products are formulated, two attributes play an important part in that formulation—the *technological position* of the product and its *areas of applications*.

These two attributes will help publicity to identify targets and will indicate the strategy of approach. The identification of all known potential publicity targets and the selection of an optimum target range is an essential prerequisite of any publicity activity. For an exhibition effort the identification of targets assumes an even greater importance, as all publicity activities are performed in a limited space of time and there is no opportunity for corrective measures, for repeat actions or for second phase improvements. In supporting the ephemeral exhibition effort, publicity has also the task of providing visitors with information of a more permanent nature. It should assist them in remembering and recalling what they have seen. In short, at an exhibition publicity must do even better than it normally does.

Public Relations at Exhibitions

One precept for public relations is that they should create a climate in which all other marketing functions can operate to the best possible effect; another, coined by a cynical and obviously disillusioned writer, describes the task of public relations as extracting the maximum reputation from a minimum of achievement. What once, in less sophisticated marketing times, was goodwill, prestige or plain reputation has now become an image. The reputation once attached to the name of an inventor, a pioneering entrepreneur or a commercially successful enterprise has become the corporate image. The quality associated with the trade mark or brand name of a product has become the product image. The building of reputations has moved from the early flamboyant intuitive efforts of patent medicine manufacturers to contemporary image building.

Marketing psychologists and motivation researchers discovered that what they already knew about ordinary consumers, namely that they are human beings, also applies to buyers of industrial products. Being human means that when making buying decisions buyers of industrial products, apart from rational requirements of performance, technical suitability, price, delivery, etc., may also seek in a product emotional values of security, see in it sexual symbols, expect from it a boost to their ego and altogether be influenced by the image of the product, the manufacturer and the supplier. One of the difficulties in assessing the implications of these apparently qualitatively valid observations is determining the quantitative relationship of the rational, economic and technological factors to the emotional ones. Another difficulty is the complexity of the industrial products buying process, which in many cases may involve not one or two but five, six or more buying influences and decisions. To make things even more difficult, these several buying influences are vested in people with different social and technological backgrounds, placed in different strata of executive power and of course with different individual proportions of rational and emotional ego.

An interesting semantic sidelight is thrown on the subject by a manual of public relations techniques with the title *The Engineering of Consent*, and by public relations practitioners who speak of 'social engineering' and 'yes engineering'. Thus engineering assumes the meaning of persuasion, mind moulding, conditioning of reflexes and manipulation. Whether this is a compliment to engineers or an indication that engineering in the mind of public relations practitioners is linguistically more respectable than manipulation is perhaps best decided by the new discipline of psycholinguistics. There is hardly any aspect of public relations which needs a more accurate definition of individual requirements and about which it is more difficult to generalize than that of the optimum corporate and product image.

In the ideal situation the product image will be determined by the company's overall marketing strategy and by the role which the particular product or range of products plays in that strategy. New products or products resulting from a diversification programme may pose special problems and so does entry into new technological or market territories. Marketing, publicity and the establishing and maintaining of an image, whether corporate or product, is a continuous and live process which should be developed, carried out and modified in harmony with and response to the environment in which it operates. Changes in the technological state of art of the field concerned, in the social, economic or political climate, in user requirements or in methods of production can affect that strategy and require constant alertness.

Mergers, take-overs, international configurations and changes in management or financial structures, exert their own special influences on corporate and product images. Service requirements of products orphaned by mergers or of troublesome products acquired by mergers, rearrangements of distribution outlets and overseas agencies and intrusion into the family of products of erstwhile competitors with a history of claims and counter-claims are some of the factors which can upset an established marketing routine. The basic requirement is that the image building action should be planned to serve a declared purpose, to make a desired impression. Engineers can contribute to that planning by analysing the engineering factors involved in the new situation not only from a design, production or application point of view but also from a wider marketing perspective. Once more engineers should have an open attitude of mind and an understanding of the fact that all marketing functions are of importance even if the techniques used are as exotic as those used by public relations.

Public relations on their part should try to understand the difficulties of the engineer when faced with such terms as the rationalization of human emotions, concretization of abstract qualities, psychological penetration factors and others. Faced with these bewildering terms from an alien discipline engineers withdraw into their shell, from which it will be difficult to extricate useful information. Public relations must not be too quickly discouraged by such behaviour, which their resident psychologist will readily explain.

To many engineers public relations activities appear as strange phenomena which in their inner thoughts they consider even more superfluous to serious industrial endeavour than the somewhat unproductive but apparently indispensable sales activities and the definitely parasitic advertising efforts. After all, public relations are practised most prominently in the field of consumer goods and these are of no interest to true engineers, except perhaps when they act in the role of consumers. Yet while many of the products classed as consumer goods or consumer durables (cars, refrigerators, vacuum cleaners, etc.) are technically complex articles with a high engineering content, their sales are promoted predominantly on the strength of price, appearance and other non-engineering features. By virtue of their sales volume these products exert an important influence on the economic life of a country and of course affect the livelihood, salary levels and standing of all engineers directly and indirectly engaged in the industries concerned.

In quite a few engineering enterprises profits from consumer durables support less profitable 'real' engineering ventures. Once again, irrespective of justified or unjustified attitudes of approval, apathy or hostility it behoves the engineers, in their own interest, to understand what public relations can and should do in terms of benefits for industrial products, for products with engineering content and for engineers who design, make and service these products.

The public relations function assumes special importance when the motives for exhibiting include the two defensive functions of redeeming a tarnished image and counteracting prejudices, antagonisms or hostility (see Checklist 10, page 81). The closest co-operation between all concerned in the matter is essential and it is not enough for the person charged with the public relations exercise to be assured, by others, that there really is an improvement or that there are no valid grounds for prejudice. To discharge their task effectively public relations practitioners must assume the role of a critical customer or user audience and ask searching and perhaps unkind questions until they can really believe in the truth of the sermon they are asked to preach. Such probing is a difficult undertaking which at first may create a certain amount of animosity. But as tact and diplomacy can be assumed to be part of public relations' stock in trade, co-operation usually follows once the objectives are understood. If it is found that the redeeming exercise is justified, then public relations can do their job much better for being fully informed. If it is found that the exercise would be premature, it will be recognized that what might be called a negative public relations action was avoided and further loss of prestige averted.

The above remarks are prompted by many experiences which varied in the severity of after-effects, but where in all cases a first ineffective 'repair' exercise had to be redeemed in turn by an, in the circumstances, even more embarrassing second one.

Technicians and Publicity

When dealing with industrial exhibitions publicity relies to a large extent on technical information for the core substance of its efforts. This technical information comes originally from engineers of all kinds of disciplines, from designers, experimenters, researchers and also from technologists, scientists, academics and similar sources.

Let us now for the sake of simplicity use the collective term of 'technicians' for this by no means complete set of technical informants and let us examine their relation to publicity. Depending on the size and structure of the organization, the information may come directly or indirectly from technical sources but, even if it is filtered through marketing functions or more likely sales functions, the background, the basic data and the substance of the information have a predominantly technical content. In some organizations the information has to travel all the way up to the highest reaches of the executive floor before it can come down to the more modest levels of publicity. In others lack of interest or even disdain in higher quarters encourages direct lower level contacts, which then occasionally offend against policies of which they are unaware. The *filters of approval and correction* are many and varied and sometimes at odds with each other. In these organizations both exhibitions and publicity suffer from attitudes of apathy and misunderstanding of their industrial marketing mission and from amateurish do-it-yourself misuse dressed up as enlightened acceptance.

The existence or absence of attitudes is a concern of management and it would be easy to say 'let management change these attitudes, it is after all their responsibility'. In the field of industrial products the technical content of any activity makes it imperative that an atmosphere should be created in which attitudes are not only modified by influence from outside the technical side of the organization but generated from inside it as well. In other words *technicians* in the widest sense of the term should be made aware of *marketing concepts* and of the importance of exhibitions and publicity.

In the effective performance of tasks, the solution of problems or the acquisition of knowledge technicians rely on communications with their technological environment, from which they obtain information about materials, products, processes and services connected with their field of operation and about new discoveries, innovations and improvements in their spheres of interest. At the same time technicians are directly or indirectly, deliberately or unintentionally, the source of similar information for other technicians.

Some information is given and obtained in the form of apparently dry factual data, reports or specifications and some as undisguised sales literature but all such information contains at least some elements of allusive, concealed or inferential publicity, be it in the text or in the manner of presentation.

In their work technicians rely on three main channels of communication, the channel with their internal functional environment, the channel with their technological environment and the channel with their market. All communications flowing through these channels have publicity ingredients of varying degrees of importance.

When publicity is discussed with technicians it soon becomes clear that what in fact they praise, denigrate or cut down to size, is not publicity in its wider sense, but only advertising and mostly just technical press advertising. Public relations are not really regarded as publicity; exhibitions are a special case and mostly a nuisance; catalogues, leaflets and such like are stationery; instruction manuals and spares lists are the responsibility of the service department. Technicians very seldom recognize that almost all direct and indirect communications between them and the environment contain elements of publicity.

A well-conceived house style and an effective trade mark can be very good publicity and are designed for that purpose. An evasive reply to a complaint, a badly printed drawing or inadequate technical details of a specification can all be very bad publicity—although they are not intended to be any publicity at all. A speedily despatched additional instruction sheet, a clearly detailed installation drawing or a polite and explicit letter can be very good publicity actions even if not consciously executed with a publicity effect in mind. Packaging which not only contains the industrial goods despatched but also protects them from damage, eases recognition on store shelves and encourages proper treatment produces just as good publicity; in the same way that an efficient, polite and well-informed telephone operator generates good public relations. Most of these items make their direct or indirect appearance at exhibitions as well.

Quality, performance, accuracy, endurance, cheapness, ease of use, good service, even prestige by association are promised by publicity on behalf of technicians. The effectiveness of publicity depends in no small measure on technicians honouring the promises given by it. The conflicts arising from that situation are numerous. Publicity will try to see in the industrial product attributes which technicians consider as greatly exaggerated; technicians will emphasize factors which to publicity have no publicity value. They both use the term 'commercial' to criticize each other. 'Technicians reproach publicity as being too commercial, publicity throw up their hands in horror at the utter non-commercialism of technicians. The results are often very interesting. In one situation publicity, despairing of receiving an attractive, even if realistic, statement from technicians, attributes to an industrial product the meaningless virtue of being 'manufactured to the highest imaginable accuracy'. In another technicians evade metrological obligations by informing publicity, with a slight hint of derision, that products are 'finished to commercial limits'—whatever that might mean.

The ultimate success of publicity is determined by the soundness of the marketing concepts on which it is based and by the expertise with which the publicity effort is executed. But in one important aspect publicity differs from other marketing functions. In performing its allocated role, it proclaims loudly and publicly to all it can reach what it does and how it does it. At the same time, even when it assumes the most factual and authoritative form publicity is no more than a set of promises. At an exhibition the validity of many, if not all, of these promises can be tested by an examination of the exhibits, by further probing and by a demand of proof.

Engineers and Publicity Practitioners

The art or craft of publicity, according to some of its exponents aspiring to the status of science, is an expertise and the performance and execution of that expertise is best left to the specialists of the profession. In their ranks—in accordance with laws of normal distribution—there will be some who are very talented, some who are very experienced, not so many who are both and a great many whose main hallmark is mediocrity. The same law applies to engineers. Both professions will of course have their quotas of incompetence, but these need not be considered here.

To be effective industrial publicity must rely on the co-operative effort of two professions and the result of that co-operation will depend to a large extent on the quality of the partners. Good professionals in industrial publicity have by definition an appreciation of industrial products and industrial problems; they are also conditioned and trained to deal with difficult informants. Engineers on the whole are rather difficult to deal with, particularly when imbued with a self-righteous if unfounded feeling of being always factual, precise and objective.

When dealing with their problems, engineers are almost invariably involved in finding compromise solutions. Competing requirements of high accuracy and low production cost, strength and low weight, good finish and reasonable price, accessibility and compactness and many others involve engineers in the process of reconciliation of conflicting demands, of optimization of decisions, of compromise. But when it comes to dealings with other professions engineers' attitudes become stiff and unbending. They join the 'all or nothing' school, demanding absolute numerical proof supported by an impressive array of figures behind the decimal point or requiring accurate predictions of

164

behaviour and performance. Co-operation between publicity and engineering is such a natural requirement that there should be no need to emphasize it. But the experiences of long-established specialized agencies indicate what widely spread surveys confirm: that such co-operation is the exception not the rule. In some cases there is no recognition of the requirement, in some only one side or the other feels strongly about it and in others there is a marked indifference or even declared animosity. Indifference is probably the attitude most difficult to correct as it is usually well disguised by a mantle of operational respectability known as 'everybody doing their job'.

Lack of interest or negative attitudes between engineering, sales and publicity can stem from either side. When it exists it is a symptom of causes mostly traceable to deficiencies in management techniques that cannot be examined here. There is, however, no doubt that the indifference of engineers to marketing concepts is an important contributory factor. Engineers consider publicity practitioners as somewhat erratic individuals, slightly mad, given to exaggeration and listening only with half an ear to interesting stories of great technical difficulties heroically overcome and of complex problems brilliantly solved.

The slightly haughty scorn and the reluctant faint praise, mixed with an implied disparagement of any commercial activity, with which technical engineers treat sales engineers are meted out to publicity practitioners with much less reluctance and much greater gusto. After all there is always the possibility that there is at least a grain of truth in the assertion that if there were no sales engineers there would be no need for technical engineers. In their heart of hearts engineers think that it is fairer to say that if there were no technicians there would be no sales.

But surely publicity is not really necessary. Perhaps it is useful in certain circumstances but not when you have a sound industrial product, well-known to all interested users. Besides, even if it were necessary, it should be more factual, less vague and give more technical details.

Publicity practitioners consider engineers as too wrapped in detail, mostly concerned only with immediate technical problems and seldom capable of seeing their efforts as part of a larger marketing operation. When asked to approve publicity statements about the product, which may border on the superlative, they are full of reserve and fairness to competitors. But when asked whether the products are vulnerable to failure or whether user complaints are justified, they assert that the products always—well nearly always—perform as required, and that there are no—well hardly any—complaints from users.

Stand Design and Publicity

The need for close understanding between the functions of stand design and publicity is self-evident but it is not enough to accept displays of witty slogans or the conviviality of social encounters as signs that such understanding exists. Stand management should ensure that declarations of close co-operation are valid not only in the volatile areas of creative design but also in the more earthly areas of stand ergonomics and facilities for the storage, display and distribution of publicity material.

At an exhibition, stand design and publicity functions operate in a very expensive medium. A lack of co-operation, even if camouflaged by pretensions of 'shared ideas', can be very costly. Occasionally marketing, their nominal task master, leaves the two functions to their own devices and stand design and publicity become self-promoting activities in which exhibits and stand personnel are only secondary elements manipulated for the attainment of the ultimate goal—a stand design reproduced in glossy magazines and widely discussed among other stand designers and publicity practitioners.

Exhibition Organizers' Publicity

The quality and impact of publicity given to the exhibition by its organizers in the pre-exhibition period is a factor which influences the attendance of visitors and indirectly the participation of exhibitors. Effective publicity efforts initiated by the organizers can greatly assist exhibitors in attracting visitors. Many organizers supply publicity material to exhibitors for use in their own invitation activities. Exhibitions with a duration time of more than four to five days are also advertised during the exhibition period, particularly when the general public is admitted to industrial exhibitions either during the whole period or on special days.

The publicity facilities which exhibition organizers offer to exhibitors can influence the number of visitors who come to their stands and the ease with which these stands can be located. Such facilities may also assist in publicizing the exhibitor's successes, achievements, awards and prices and provide publicity support for post-exhibition follow-up actions.

In several countries, in addition to the relevant trade press, the daily press, radio and television devote a considerable amount of space and time to important exhibitions and provide opportunities for interviews and for the dissemination of news about products, interesting developments or important visitors. Sadly, quite a few exhibitors neglect these opportunities. It is the task of the exhibitor's publicity practitioner to assess the suitability of the opportunities available, to exploit them as fully as possible and to co-ordinate their own efforts with those of the exhibition organizers.

Sales and Technical Literature

A plea is made on behalf of industrial products destined for international markets. Industrial products are fortunate in that they can use an almost universally understandable ideographic language for the presentation of their shapes and functions. It is the language of sketches, technical drawings, schemes and photographs. The use of expressive drawings, diagrams and action photographs in catalogues and service manuals not only dispenses with costly and often faulty translations but also creates goodwill. The format of service manuals is also important; it should be adapted to standards existing in the country of destination and where appropriate stain-impervious paper should be used.

It is important to realize that sales literature, drawings, specifications, plans or schemes are on many occasions the first items your customer or prospective customer receives from you. They are in a way your ambassadors and you only need to check your own reaction when you receive a well-printed and well-designed letterhead or a badly reproduced, smudged and difficult-to-read drawing to appreciate the implications.

Guarantees of performance or quality may need a legal check in new territories and price lists and quotations may require an up-to-date check of the currency conversion rate. Literature or special items for public relations functions may need a last minute assessment of the economic or political situation or perhaps the inclusion of a special achievement. Direct mail will probably be used in the pre-exhibition period as one of the invitation elements and in the post-exhibition period in the follow-up action.

Modern reprographic techniques of varying degrees of sophistication up to desktop publishing should make the task easier and its execution speedier than ever before.

The marketing and other environments of your targets will indicate whether you retain your own style irrespective of the destination, in which case you need to check compatibility with local restraints (social, legal and of taste and custom). If on the other hand you decide, for good marketing reasons, to comply with the style of the destination country, you should check whether you are really adopting a genuine style or only an ineffective imitation which can give more offense than the retaining of your own style.

Translations should not only be linguistically of the highest standard but should also comply with the technical idiom used in the relevant branch of technology in the country of destination. When justified by the volume of literature required in foreign languages and by the variety of destinations, recent developments in electronic translation systems can be used.

Most publicity elements involve creative work and it is just as possible to produce excellent publicity on a moderate budget as it is to produce indifferent or even bad publicity on a very generous one.

House Journals

House journals vary so much in content, make-up and quality that their suitability for stand publicity and public relations purposes must be judged entirely on individual merits for stated objectives. If it is your objective to persuade your recipient that the organization places great importance on welfare and your house journal can bear witness to that, then it is suitable, but for that purpose only. If it features sales and export achievements with the usual emphasis on personal attainments it may be useful in some locations and not in others—again depending on its quality and on the recipient.

Technical bulletins guided by definite editorial objectives and handed to selected recipients are excellent means of informing your audience of your achievement in applications, usage or research and development, as the case may be. The literary character and quality of a house journal is of course a matter of taste and expressed preferences can only be personal ones. It is, however, advisable to study the strata of your recipients from a professional status and ethnic point of view, so as not to be tactless or facetious, because sometimes what is received with a grin and a chuckle in one place may cause bewilderment or disgust in another.

Sometimes fears are expressed that too effusive technical bulletins inform the competition of potential opportunities. The answer is that if you are not already one step ahead of the competition then it is too late anyway.

Exhibition Projects

Exhibiting, to be effective, requires a range of dedicated multi-disciplinary skills and calls for the co-ordination of information, resources and activities for which responsibility is located in different functional departments of an enterprise. The operational characteristics of an exhibition effort are:

Defined objectives
Defined human and material requirements

Strict time schedules
Defined sequences of actions required for implementation

These make the exhibition effort eminently suitable for treatment as a special activity and for the application of project and project management concepts. These are used by some companies in the normal course of their business and by others for unusual or complex activities outside their normal routine. The project management concept is not universally applicable but, depending on the organizational structure of your company and the magnitude and frequency of your exhibition efforts, it may well be worthwhile to consider its utility for your purposes.

A comprehensive treatment of project teams and project management is beyond the scope of this book but the following general observations will, it is hoped, be of interest in the context of dealing with exhibitions.

A project team can be an *ad hoc*, temporary or semi-permanent unit with responsibility for one or more specific exhibition efforts. It can consist of no more than one or two persons or it can be a large interdisciplinary or interdepartmental group of various talents and aptitudes. It is a knowledge- and experience-based body depending to a high degree on mutual support and co-operation within the team and within the organization.

The advantages of a project team are its relative autonomy and flexibility in action, ease of recruiting additional expertise if required and ease of access to top management. Project teams, if not successful, can be disbanded without undue loss of personal or departmental pride.

The tasks entrusted to a project team can be as all-embracing as the totality of preparations, stand design, actual exhibition activities, analysis and follow-up or as restricted as the review of the exhibition scene in a new market, training of the stand team and exhibition merit intelligence. A project team or perhaps only its task force can be charged with visiting an exhibition in which you participate, to supplement your stand team and to carry out all the 'away from the stand' survey and intelligence tasks. A project team, however small or large, can be entrusted with the task of surveying up-to-date display techniques and equipment accessories and relating the findings to your particular exhibition programme. The talents of the project team can be applied to any one, several or a combination of the elements shown in the chain of activities of an exhibition effort (Figure 2, page 10).

Project planning, scheduling and control techniques can vary as much as those used in other organized activities and can be, depending on the tasks, sequential Gantt type planning charts, network plans showing interrelations among critical project elements, precedence diagrams, critical path methods (CPM), programme evaluation and review techniques (PERT), graphical evaluation and review techniques (GERT) or more sophisticated computer-based techniques.

Training

It is common to read in theoretical essays on organizations that training is an essential ingredient of any complex organizational activity. In practice one is more likely to find the training function relegated to the lower strata of the organizational pyramid than to see it elevated to the status of an important management service function, which in fact it is. By the same token training is worthy of a proportionate recognition of its importance in the marketing budget.

Complaints and exhortations concerning the skill shortages and vocational training deficiencies of British industry appear with unfailing frequency in the technical and daily press. Attitudes of management who see training as an intrusion into routine business, attitudes of accounts departments treating training expenditure as cost rather than investment, comparisons with foreign competitors who spend more on training and the shortcomings of general and special education are all quoted as some of the ills which must be cured before international competitors can be successfully challenged.

There are of course exceptions and many companies operate training programmes of different kinds. Some are comprehensive, some aim mainly at compensating for specific skill shortages and some are restricted to production problems. Information technology claims most of the attention, calling for training of company personnel from the chief executive downwards.

Training programmes dealing with marketing techniques and skills may or may not include brief sessions on the subject of exhibitions. External 'one-off' courses, seminars, films and videos dealing with exhibitions serve a very useful purpose provided that the lessons learned are sustained, expanded and modified by in-house training, not least to compensate for changes in personnel, circumstances or marketing strategies, but most importantly to provide a flow of new ideas and to maintain the proficiency of the personnel involved. However, most external and internal training programmes deal mainly with what to do and what not to do once you have decided to exhibit. Very few, if any, deal with the fundamental issues of motives for exhibiting, selection and decision-making beyond advising you to select the exhibition that is 'right for your purpose'.

Long experience shows that in the practice of international marketing of industrial products the benefits of good training programmes are cumulative and that the losses suffered by not training or casual hit-or-miss training might well exceed the cost of proper training. This applies to training for exhibitions more than to training for any other marketing function, as at exhibitions considerable costs are incurred, retrieval of lost opportunities is very difficult if not impossible and all deficiencies are exposed to potential customers and competitors alike.

The scope of an exhibition's training programme should be defined by your particular training needs and these in turn are conditioned by the extent of your exhibition programme, by the qualifications and experience of your personnel and by your capacity to undertake effective training. The realistic definition of training needs is the most important aspect of a training programme. Once these needs are stated, it will become clear whether in-house training entirely with your own resources or in-house training with some outside assistance or extramural training will ensure best results.

Overtraining beyond the boundaries of reasonable need is both wasteful and a source of disappointment and discontent.

The sections of this book dealing with exhibition stand personnel visiting exhibitions and exhibition intelligence will help to define the personnel requiring training, and the sections on the marketing merits and environments of exhibitions will indicate the scope and contents of the training programme.

Checklists 30–43

VISITING EXHIBITIONS	
Visitors—independent	
Visitors—exhibitors	
Motives for visiting:	
buying interests:	
acquisition or resale of:	
components	
instruments	
complete products	
equipment	
plant	
suppliers:	
present	
new/potential	
lapsed	
customers' interests	
intelligence interests	
fringe interests	
combined visits interests	
Visiting tasks:	
active:	
pre-selected contacts	
incidental/chance contacts	
passive:	
non-personal information	
observations	
active-passive (combined)	
Visiting contacts:	
type	
technique	
time	
frequency	
Authority of visitor related to:	
supplier contacts	
customer contacts	
other	

Checklist 30   VISITING EXHIBITIONS

This checklist deals with visiting tasks, their motivation, definition of interests and personal contact techniques. The review of visiting tasks should be made with the help of the topography (Figure 1) of the particular exhibition which is visited, the exhibition time elements (Checklist 2) and if appropriate with exhibitions intelligence (Checklists 31 and 32). If the authority of a visitor requires clarification, the discussion of this subject in the text will indicate the specific areas of responsibility which need definition and checking. Case study 8 (exhibition visiting time elements) and Figures 10 and 11 provide a good background for a review of visiting tasks.

EXHIBITION INTELLIGENCE	
Personal tasks:	
interviews	
observations	
lectures	
symposia	
meetings	
Printed matter:	
sales and technical literature	
service literature	
performance data	
price lists	
publicity material, company reports	
Materials:	
samples	
products	
components	
Other tasks:	
attending and/or participating:	
test runs	
demonstrations	
trials	

Checklist 31   EXHIBITION INTELLIGENCE ACTIVITIES

This checklist sets out personal and material elements of intelligence tasks which can be conducted as a separate function, as part of stand personnel duties or as functions combined with exhibition visiting activities. When intelligence tasks are combined with other duties, it is nevertheless important to identify the intelligence elements of these combined tasks and to allocate to them merits of importance and priority.

EXHIBITION MERIT INTELLIGENCE	
Intelligence technique:	
internal personnel assignment:	
special task	
combined with other tasks	
external assignment	
non-personal collection of data	
Exhibition structure:	
quality of halls, display areas	
services, facilities, amenities	
standards of organization	
Exhibition merits:	
organizers' statistical data	
independent surveys	
previews, reports, special issues:	
press	
technical journals	
other media	
reports and comments of:	
participating stand personnel	
visiting personnel	
comments of exhibitors:	
customers	
competitors	
others	
comments of visitors:	
customers	
competitors	
others	

Checklist 32   EXHIBITION MERIT INTELLIGENCE

Exhibition merit intelligence can be a separate task of an intelligence assignment or part of it. It can also be wholly or partly executed by desk research methods. While general exhibition intelligence tasks are usually motivated by marketing objectives, exhibition merit intelligence should be exercised almost as a natural reflex action, even if not specified as a definite task. This checklist can be used to assess the extent of available information, the need for specific action and the relative importance of the elements involved.

	GENERAL AND SPECIAL EXHIBITION LITERATURE	
	Sales and technical literature:	
	general purpose design	
	special purpose design for:	
	selected markets:	
	industries	
	countries	
	exhibitions generally	
	individual exhibitions	
	Main literature elements:	
	sales dominant	
	technical dominant	
	combined sales and technical:	
	catalogues, brochures, ring binders	
	drawings, sketches, photographs	
	technical data sheets	
	Subjects described:	
	products, components, materials	
	processes, techniques, services	
	capacities, capabilities, concepts	
	range of subjects:	
	total activity range	
	individual exhibits (pamphlets, leaflets):	
	special features/modifications	
	particular market suitability	
	new products	
	Special exhibition literature:	
	stand location (map, guide)	
	invitations to visit stand	
	lists of available items of literature	
	requests forms for literature:	
	to be obtained on stand	
	to be sent later	

Checklist 33　　　　　　　EXHIBITION LITERATURE I

This checklist deals with exhibition literature designed for general and special purposes. The subjects listed can be supplemented to include specific themes which are in line with special marketing aims and targets.

	MARKETING SUPPORT LITERATURE	
	Supporting marketing elements:	
	guarantees:	
	performance	
	life	
	quality	
	compliance with standards	
	compliance with regulations	
	testimonials:	
	approval authority	
	performance	
	endurance	
	customers	
	users	
	price lists	
	quotations	
	customer requirement forms:	
	technical details	
	dimensional	
	quantity and delivery	
	Service and spares support (maps, lists):	
	location of facilities:	
	international	
	national	
	regional	
	local	
	manuals:	
	service	
	maintenance	
	operation	
	installation	
	spares:	
	lists	
	selection charts	
	price lists	

Checklist 34   EXHIBITION LITERATURE II

Depending on the dominant motives for exhibiting the marketing support literature is usually included in a selection of general and special literature. However, in the case of voluminous and expensive items, such as service manuals, discrimination in handing them out should be exercised.

PUBLIC RELATIONS AND INDIRECT PUBLICITY LITERATURE	
Literature for public relation functions:	
company reports	
company activities brochure	
house journals (internal/external)	
special exhibition issues	
press releases	
Indirect publicity literature:	
reprints:	
editorial articles	
learned/scientific papers	
reports of symposia	
independent assessments	
press reviews	
technical bulletins:	
scientific/theoretical	
research and development	
practice/applications	
popularizing	
textbooks:	
technical data pocket books:	
general purpose	
special purpose	

Checklist 35   EXHIBITION LITERATURE III

Unlike the marketing support literature (Checklist 34) the items listed in this checklist can be distributed separately when justified by special PR requirements or in connection with participation in seminars or symposia or when required for specially selected targets.

	EXHIBITION LITERATURE PRODUCTION	
	Texts:	
	exhibitor's language	
	one foreign language	
	multilingual	
	Format:	
	uniform	
	multiform:	
	international standard	
	target-market standard	
	special format	
	Make-up:	
	catalogues	
	brochures	
	pamphlets	
	sheets	
	covers	
	folders	
	wallets	
	self-binders	
	ring-binders	
	Quality:	
	average	
	superior	
	luxury	
	Packing:	
	for transport	
	for stand storage	
	dispensing from stand	
	added publicity	

Checklist 36   EXHIBITION LITERATURE IV

This checklist is concerned with the production and make-up elements of publicity literature. The design purpose and texts are governed by marketing considerations of subjects (Checklist 33); the format and make-up are mainly affected by recipients (Checklists 40 and 41) but also by destination (Checklist 42) and location (Checklist 38). The format is important for foreign destinations. Packing, when considered in time, can assist the handling of publicity material on the exhibition stand.

	PUBLICITY EQUIPMENT AND MATERIALS	
	Display purposes:	
	models:	
	static	
	mobile/animated	
	projectors:	
	transparencies	
	films	
	audio-visual media	
	lasers	
	holographs	
	Stand use	
	badges for:	
	stand personnel	
	visitors	
	gifts, souvenirs:	
	non-utility	
	utility	
	leisure	
	promotions	

Checklist 37   DISPLAY EQUIPMENT AND OTHER PUBLICITY MATERIALS

In addition to exhibition literature other means of publicity are listed as examples of items which apart from their publicity tasks are also used to attract attention to the stand and its exhibits.

	LOCATIONS FOR PUBLICITY ELEMENTS	
	Exhibition site:	
	approaches	
	entrance	
	exit	
	ground/area	
	halls	
	site fringes	
	site neighbourhood	
	Exhibition stands:	
	exhibition halls:	
	own stand	
	other stands	
	open air areas:	
	own stand	
	other stands	
	Lecture theatre/cinema:	
	own stand	
	other stands	
	exhibition site	
	outside exhibition	
	Other exhibitions:	
	competing in/with:	
	market	
	time	
	place	
	attraction to visitors	

Checklist 38   EXHIBITION AND OTHER LOCATIONS FOR PUBLICITY ELEMENTS

This checklist indicates the different locations for publicity elements which are either already available or are specially produced for a particular exhibition. If the exhibition site offers attractive locations for models or posters which are available, this checklist can be used for a cost comparison of different display locations. If another exhibition in which you don't participate competes for your visitors you may require special posters or leaflets to attract them to the exhibition in which you participate.

PUBLICITY AND PUBLIC RELATIONS FUNCTIONS	
Direct personal participation in:	
press conferences	
important visitors	
group visits/missions/delegations	
authorities	
exhibition events	
organizing	
participating	
guest	
Indirect personal participation, guidance, delegation:	
exhibition/extramural events:	
demonstrations/tests/trials	
film shows	
lectures	
congresses	
conferences	
symposia	
special visits	
receptions/dinners/parties	
cultural events	
Persons assigned:	
stand personnel	
visiting company personnel:	
executives	
lecturers	
outside assistance	

Checklist 39   DIRECT AND INDIRECT PERSONAL PUBLICITY AND PR FUNCTIONS

This activity checklist distinguishes functions in which publicity and public relations personnel take an active personal part and those in which personal participation is indirect. Indirect participation may require the briefing of a delegate to a conference or, if he is that type, not only briefing but also accompanying him and attentively listening for the sound of dropped bricks. On the other hand stand personnel may be quite capable of taking on some of the publicity or public relations functions, in which case implied or formal delegation will meet the situation.

RECIPIENTS OF PUBLICITY AT EXHIBITION	
Other exhibitors, direct interest:	
customers, users	
suppliers	
contractors, operators	
Visitors, direct interest:	
customers, users	
suppliers	
contractors, operators	
consultants	
Visitors, indirect interest:	
officials	
reporters	
exhibition surveys	
market/marketing researchers	
Exhibition organizers:	
administration	
catalogue	
publicity	
Exhibition publicity:	
official press bureaux	
news bulletins	
exhibition gazette	
reception offices	
visitors, exhibitors	
officials	
important visitors	
information facilities	
offices, kiosks	
stands	
special	

Checklist 40 DIRECT AND INDIRECT INTEREST RECIPIENTS OF PUBLICITY AT EXHIBITIONS

When the review of general and special publicity and public relations elements is made by means of Checklists 33 to 38, the items selected should be checked against this checklist so as to ensure that all potential recipients at the exhibition will be served by suitable material. This checklist may reveal the need for special items which perhaps were not required in the past for a similar exhibition.

	INDIRECT PROMOTION OF EXHIBITION EFFORT	
	Purchasing agencies—government, semi-official	
	Trade missions—official, visiting, special	
	Development authorities—regional, national	
	Financial, investment, credit and leasing services	
	Trade promotion/information/advisory services	
	Trade information bureaux	
	Trade centres—national, international	
	Press—daily, trade, technical	
	Trade directories	
	Catalogue/compendia services	
	Data supply services	
	Embassies—diplomatic and commercial posts	
	Authorities—government, regional, municipal	
	Associations—professional, trade	
	Learned societies	
	Educational establishments:	
	universities, technical colleges	
	trade schools, training centres	
	Publishing houses	
	Libraries:	
	general	
	specialized	
	Approval institutions—standards, certification	
	Test/laboratory/survey establishments	
	Special interest bodies:	
	consumers/users—protection	
	safety—industrial, public, domestic	
	environment	
	operators'/users' associations	
	Tourist offices	
	Travel agencies	
	Air lines	
	Hotels	

Checklist 41   EXHIBITION EFFORT PROMOTION—RECIPIENTS OF INDIRECT INTEREST

This checklist indicates recipients of indirect interest who should receive promotional and information material concerning your exhibition effort. This checklist will enable you to examine the suitability of the items to be sent to these destinations and to avoid the indiscriminate despatch of bundles of costly material which due to its bulk is often relegated to the waste paper basket instead of serving its promotional purpose.

181

DESTINATION COUNTRIES AND DESPATCH TIMES	
Geographic destination:	
exhibitor's home country	
recipients' home countries	
exhibition host country (EXHC)	
countries associated with EXHC:	
economically	
politically	
special relations	
geographic neighbours	
countries relevant to exhibitor's markets	
Despatch time:	
routine times	
preparation period	
pre-exhibition period	
exhibition period	
post-exhibition period	

Checklist 42 GEOGRAPHIC DESTINATION AND DESPATCH TIME ELEMENTS OF PUBLICITY

When the selection of publicity and public relations literature and other materials is completed the feasibility of producing them in time for the exhibition effort can be checked against the destination and despatch time elements of this checklist. The destination headings can be expanded, e.g. in place of the headings 'recipients' home countries', several actual countries can be inserted. The location of recipients of promotion and information can be then co-ordinated with the country and time headings of this checklist. By allocating merit ratings to, e.g. destination countries, priorities and realistic production and despatch times can be established.

	EXHIBITOR'S INTERNAL INFORMATION	
	Exhibitor's internal marketing functions:	
	internal divisions/departments	
	associated companies	
	subsidiaries	
	agents	
	distributors	
	wholesalers	
	retailers	
	Exhibitor's external marketing activities:	
	customers	
	users	
	consultants	
	suppliers	
	contractors	
	operators	

Checklist 43   RECIPIENTS OF EXHIBITION EFFORT INFORMATION OUTSIDE EXHIBITION

In addition to recipients of publicity material that are expected at the exhibition you may find it advisable as a matter of marketing policy, or of courtesy, to provide information about your exhibition effort to your own organization even if you know that the recipients are not likely to visit the exhibition.

INDEX

Page numbers in parentheses represent references to checklists,
figures or tables.
An asterisk following a word indicates a *see also* reference. For example,
under 'Exhibitors' there is a sub-entry 'exhibitor environment*';
the asterisk here indicates that the main entry 'Environment(s)'
will also be relevant.